Insurgencies: Essays in Planning Theory

Covering transactive planning, radical planning, the concept of the "good city", civil society, rethinking poverty, and the diversity of planning cultures, this collection of Friedmann's most important and influential essays tells a coherent and compelling story about how the evolution of thinking about planning over several decades has helped to shape its practice.

With each of the chapters introduced by a brief essay providing background information about its origins and the author's intentions, and followed by a series of study questions to help focus classroom discussions, as well as by a small number of suggested readings, *Insurgencies: Essays in Planning Theory* is an ideal text for the study of planning theory and history.

John Friedmann is Professor Emeritus in the School of Public Affairs at UCLA and an Honorary Professor in the School of Community and Regional Planning at the University of British Columbia. Internationally recognized for his path-breaking work on regional development and planning, he holds honorary doctorates from the University of Dortmund and the Pontifical Catholic University in Santiago, Chile. In 2006 he received the first UN-Habitat Lecture Award for lifetime achievement.

THE RTPI Library Series

Editors: Robert Upton, *Infrastructure Planning Commission in England* **and Patsy Healey,** *University of Newcastle, UK*

Published by Routledge in conjunction with The Royal Town Planning Institute, this series of leading-edge texts looks at all aspects of spatial planning theory and practice from a comparative and international perspective.

Planning in Postmodern Times
Philip Allmendinger

The Making of the European Spatial Development Perspective
Andreas Faludi and Bas Waterhout

Planning for Crime Prevention
Richard Schneider and Ted Kitchen

The Planning Polity
Mark Tewdwr-Jones

Shadows of Power
An Allegory of Prudence in Land-Use Planning
Jean Hillier

Urban Planning and Cultural Identity
William JV Neill

Place Identity, Participation and Planning
Edited by Cliff Hague and Paul Jenkins

Planning for Diversity
Dory Reeves

Planning the Good Community
New Urbanism in Theory and Practice
Jill Grant

Planning, Law and Economics
Barrie Needham

Indicators for Urban and Regional Planning
Cecilia Wong

Insurgencies:
Essays in Planning Theory

John Friedmann

Routledge
Taylor & Francis Group

LONDON AND NEW YORK

First published 2011
by Routledge
2 Park Square, Milton Park, Abingdon, Oxon, OX14 4RN

Simultaneously published in the USA and Canada
by Routledge
270 Madison Avenue, New York, NY 10016

Routledge is an imprint of the Taylor & Francis Group, an informa business

Typeset in 10.5pt on 13pt Goudy Old Style by
Saxon Graphics Ltd, Derby
Printed and bound in Great Britain by
TJ International Ltd, Padstow, Cornwall

British Library Cataloguing in Publication Data
A catalogue record for this book is available from the British Library

Library of Congress Cataloging-in-Publication Data
Friedmann, John.
Insurgencies : essays in planning theory / John Friedmann.
p. cm. -- (The RTPI library series)
Includes bibliographical references and index.
1. City planning. 2. City planning--Citizen participation. 3. Regional planning. I. Title.
HT166.F737 2011
307.1'216--dc22
2010031379

ISBN13: 978-0-415-78151-0 (hbk)
ISBN13: 978-0-415-78152-7 (pbk)
ISBN13: 978-0-203-83211-0 (ebk)

For Leonie
from whom I have learned more than I can tell

Contents

Foreword

Patsy Healey, School of Architecture, Planning and Landscape,
Newcastle University, UK

John Friedmann is perhaps the greatest planning scholar of the 20th century, and undeniably so in the field of planning theory. His work has made major contributions to debates about urban and regional development strategies and to theorising the practice of planning as a societal endeavour. For over half a century of creative thinking, Friedmann has articulated his own struggles to grasp the nature and purpose of planning activity – in papers, in books and in practice engagements, and in working with generations of doctoral students from across the world. Throughout his work, Friedmann maintains a critical concern with what it takes to move towards a 'good city' and 'good society'.

In this book, Friedmann provides a kind of intellectual autobiography of his explorations in planning theory. He does this through a collection of papers and book chapters produced between 1973 and 2010. Each is introduced with a commentary, and concludes with discussion questions for students. Few people who have studied planning can have failed to come across some of this material. I encountered his writing first through his work on development in Venezuela (Friedmann 1966), and then through his book, *Transactive Planning* (1973). Re-reading this landmark text now, I recognise how much has become so deeply embedded in my own thinking that I have failed to remember the debt I owe to him. But I also notice many things that I did not appreciate when I first read his books and papers. It is often the case when we read a new work that we really only grasp the surface, missing the underlying layers of meaning and reference – perhaps because we lack experience, or maybe we are preoccupied with developing a particular 'position' of our own. We readers are also more influenced by the intellectual climate of our times than we may like to think. This climate may screen out or actively dismiss insights and arguments which reach towards a different way of thinking. Friedmann's way of thinking about societal development and what a progressive planning agenda means would now be considered 'mainstream' in planning theory. Yet contributors to planning theory discussions today rarely acknowledge that Friedmann has been there before them. Nor is his work given a label or cited as a 'position', perhaps because he always sets his own ideas in relation to others. But in these clearly-written essays and commentaries, we encounter his scholarly mind as it engages with continual critical exploration of the idea and practice of planning. Through it, we come to see the conceptual dimension of the planning endeavour, the core of 'planning theory', as an evolving exploration of common themes.

Most readers will be struck by his well-informed historical understanding of the evolution of western societies, and his feeling for the way the past weaves forward into the future but does not determine it. This is combined with a global perspective, which not only takes in practice experiences in Latin America and East Asia, but also attempts to engage with Asian modes of philosophical writing (see Chapter 3). From this broad perspective, his focus is on action, on what it takes to make a difference, to actively promote a progressive, radical orientation. For Friedmann, the planning endeavour is about changing situations and societies, to move towards conditions more likely to promote human flourishing within environmental limits, rather than the pursuit of material benefits for political and economic elites.

There are, of course, many ways in which such an endeavour can be conceptualised. Friedmann, in his Introduction and in *Transactive Planning*, tells how his exposure to the practice of 'development planning' in Latin America made him realise that the kind of planning theory he had been taught in the Chicago school of planning in the early 1950s, and the general dominance of neo-classical economics in public policy-making in the United States, was inadequate to address the complex contexts of different Latin American cities and countries. Designing planning systems and procedures, informed by models, which led to plans and projects which could then be 'implemented' in a linear way to bring about transformative change was rather too obviously inappropriate. By the 1970s, the issue of 'implementation' and 'context' was attracting considerable attention in the planning field.

What Friedmann did, however, was to shift philosophical focus. Well ahead of the rest of us, he articulated a social ontology and a non-positivist epistemology. People, he stresses, are not just rational economic beings, seeking to maximise our material conditions. We are complex thinking and feeling creatures, imaginative and creative, living in social worlds with all kinds of others and in interaction with whom we shape our identities, our cultures and our practices. The knowledge we use and develop is very important to us, but is not just the systematised knowledge of scientists and technical experts, but the experiential knowledge we develop through the practice of living. The relation between knowledge and practice, knowledge and action, a major theme of Friedmann's work, is interactive and related to practices, not linear. In this philosophical shift, Friedmann is an often unacknowledged forerunner of both communicative planning theory, and those working now with concepts of complexity and emergence.

Compared to communicative planning theory, however, his empirical reference is to how societies and communities, cities and regions, develop and change, rather than to the micro-practices of 'doing planning work'. For Friedmann, the planning endeavour is about achieving transformative *development*, in which the key is to find ways to release and promote the possibilities for moving in progressive directions. It is not about the mechanical blueprinting of futures according to some conception imagined in the present, but about shaping emergent trajectories to encourage innovative adaptations, experiments and social learning. He combines, in this understanding, an American grounding in pragmatic philosophy with a European radical social orientation, along with his Latin American and Asian practice experiences.

In the Introduction to this book, and in the commentaries that introduce each chapter, the themes which weave through Friedmann's work in planning theory are continually recalled, developed and refreshed. I have already introduced several of them. The first is the importance of a perspective on society and development which breaks out of the narrow focus of neo-classical economics, towards a multi-dimensional and holistic view of human existence. This encompasses a collective life not just of state, economy and civil society, but also political community (see Chapter 6). Secondly, in understanding social formations, the perspective, Friedmann argues, should centre not on governments and states, but on people and households as they go about producing their lives. In Chapter 3, Friedmann underlines that the struggle for the 'good life' starts not in the worlds of elites and technocrats, but in the flow of daily life.

Thirdly, the planning endeavour should focus on transformative development which changes in the parameters of the systems and structures that limit people's opportunities to flourish and pursue their search, individually and collectively, for a 'good life'. It is about 'system change'. Friedmann warns against ideologically-driven revolutionary change or change agendas driven by dogma or narrow doctrine, since it is ordinary people and especially the poorest who may well suffer the most in such experiences. Instead, he argues that transformative change may come about through the accumulation of small changes. Incremental changes and small-scale initiatives can build up over time into transformative momentum. Fourthly, and perhaps the most well-known of Friedmann's contributions, the contribution of planning endeavour is to bring knowledge to bear on the flow of action. This relation between knowledge and action should be understood interactively, as a continual process of social learning. It is not about articulating a 'theory' and then 'applying' it to a practice situation. Here the pragmatist influences on Friedmann's thought are particularly strong. Finally, he asserts a moral orientation to planning endeavour, through a commitment to a progressive perspective centred on according everyone respect and dignity, within a recognition of global limits of environmental capacities and resource availability.

These themes – a view on social organisation, a perspective on the relation of people and states, a notion of how social change comes about, a conceptualisation of the knowledge/action relationship, and a moral orientation, generate probing questions we could ask of any contribution to planning theory but are rarely articulated as clearly and as comprehensively as in Friedmann's work. This collection of his essays is thus not just of general interest as a contribution to the history of planning thought and a biographical account of a planning theorist's intellectual journey. It also refreshes the contemporary work of those contributing to 'theorising' and 'conceptualising' the planning endeavour and suggests ways in which we should perhaps impose some discipline on ourselves. In Chapter 10, Friedmann reminds us of his view of the methodological options for planning theorists – undertaking 'reflective practice, empirical and/or critical inquiry and normative explorations' (p. 208 of Chapter 10 commentary). But he also worries about the expanding diversity of directions that are being developed as contributions to the field of planning theory. In his essay in Chapter 7, he conveys an image of planning theorists as 'riding off on different horses, each galloping into the sunset in a different direction' (Chapter 7, p. 132). Implicitly, he demands that we curve back to the core concerns of the planning field, refreshing it with our discoveries before galloping off again. This book offers his own reflections as an adventurous and creative 'explorer' within the planning field, continually bringing his own discoveries back to re-work and re-imagine our understanding of the planning endeavour.

Bibliography

Friedmann, J. (1966) *Regional Development Policy: A case study of Venezuela*, Cambridge, MA, MIT Press.

Friedmann, J. (1973) *Retracking America: A theory of transactive planning*, New York, Anchor Press.

Acknowledgements

The essays collected in this volume extend over a period of 37 years. At various points in time, I received comments from colleagues and students that helped to shape the texts you are now reading. They may remember having read this or that draft, but their names are not linked in my mind to any specific piece. I want to remember them collectively now, and hope they will forgive me for this lapse. The one person whom I do want to name and to whose critical eye I owe 'more than I can tell' is the dedicatee of this volume: Leonie Sandercock, my partner in life and work over the past quarter century.

Listed below are the original places of publication for all of the chapters reprinted here, along with the permissions of the present copyright holders.

Chapter 1. "The transactive style of planning", *Retracking America: A theory of transactive planning*, Garden City, NY: Anchor/Doubleday, 1973, pp. 171–85. © John Friedmann.

Chapter 2. "The epistemology of social practice: a critique of objective knowledge", *Theory and Society*, 6, 1978, pp. 75–92. © Springer Verlag. Reprinted by permission.

Chapter 3. "Preface", *The Good Society*, Cambridge, MA: MIT Press, 1979, pp. xi–xvi. © MIT Press. Reprinted by permission.

Chapter 4. "The mediations of radical planning", *Planning in the Public Domain: From knowledge to action*, Princeton, NJ: Princeton University Press, 1987, pp. 389–412. © Princeton University Press. Reprinted by permission.

Chapter 5. "Rethinking poverty: the (dis)empowerment model", *Empowerment: The politics of alternative development*, Cambridge, MA: Blackwell, 1992, pp. 55–71. © John Friedmann.

Chapter 6. "The new political economy of planning: the rise of civil society", in M. Douglass and J. Friedmann (eds) *Cities for Citizens: Planning and the rise of civil society in a global age*, New York: Wiley & Sons, 1998, pp. 19–29. © John Wiley & Sons. Reprinted by permission.

Chapter 7. "Planning theory revisited", *European Planning Studies*, 6 (3), 1998, pp. 245–53. © Routledge, Taylor and Francis Group. Reprinted by permission.

Chapter 8. "The good city: in defense of utopian thinking", *International Journal of Urban and Regional Research*, 24 (2), 2000, pp. 460–72. © Wiley-Blackwell. Reprinted by permission.

Chapter 9. "Globalization and the emerging culture of planning", *Progress in Planning*, 64, 2005, pp. 183–212. © Elsevier. Reprinted by permission.

Chapter 10. "The uses of planning theory: a bibliographic essay", *Journal of Planning Education and Research*, 28, 2008, pp. 247–57. © Sage Publications. Reprinted by permission.

Finally, I wish to thank Sheng Zhong for her invaluable research assistance in preparing this volume.

Introduction

It is nearly carnival time in Brazil. Turn on the radio, and you can abandon yourself to the seductive samba rhythms of 1956. I am in Belém do Pará, the crumbling state capital at the mouth of the vast Amazon delta where equatorial rains arrive on the dot every afternoon, descending with such torrential force that even the ubiquitous *urubú*, the large black vultures, seek shelter underneath the eaves of the hotel. The city rests until 4 o'clock, when the rain stops, and with the steam still rising from the pavement, it's time to get back to work.

I am on my first overseas assignment, teaching regional planning to a group of 36 students pre-selected to work for the newly created Amazon Development Authority (SPVEA). Because I don't speak Portuguese, I communicate through my interpreter, Mario, a young Brazilian poet. As the culmination of our course, we have decided to make a study tour of the Amazon upstream to Manaus, with stop-overs in Macapá, Santarém, and Belterra, fragile outposts on the edge of the rain forest. The boat on which we are traveling is SPVEA's latest acquisition for the promotion of tourism and has been put at our exclusive disposal.

Twelve days on the Amazon, that immense *rio-mar* (river ocean) of legend! And yet, as we steam up-river at what seems a snail's pace, an experience new to most of us, we spend two cloistered hours each morning in a seminar on planning theory, a topic on which I got hooked in graduate school. Planning, especially in its version linked to development, and with the two distinctive terms often conflated, was the watchword of the post-war era, lately imported to Brazil. Earlier in the course, students had heard lectures from an array of speakers on esoteric topics such as planning psychology, post-war planning in France, planning in French Equatorial Africa, political aspects of planning, techniques of planning, agricultural planning, urban planning, planning implementation, planning and climate, budgetary planning, and so forth. It was time, I thought, to put some of my own, still incoherent thoughts together about what planning might mean, beginning with the question that puzzled many of us: *What is this new-fangled soft technology called planning?* It was a bizarre experience, to say the least. Young and inexperienced, profoundly ignorant of the country where I was teaching, I nevertheless held forth with great assurance about how the Amazon might be "developed" through this imported, all-purpose and largely unanalyzed term. My students were good-natured and put up with me. Later that year, while awaiting reassignment in Rio de Janeiro, I actually wrote my first book on the subject, a book that, I am happy to say, was never published in English and, at this late date, is best forgotten as juvenilia.[1]

And yet, the question with which we started and to which we always returned, never left me: What is planning? Or rather, how should we productively, and critically, think about planning? What you are now reading is the record of my quest for an answer, beginning with a chapter from a book on transactive planning in 1973 and ending with an essay published 35 years later on "The Uses of Planning Theory". I remained in Brazil for nearly three years, with all the missionary zeal of someone who was conscious of participating in an historical experiment in which countries whose economies were said to be "underdeveloped" would, by embracing rational, comprehensive planning, achieve higher levels of material well-being for their populations. With America's Marshall Plan helping to rebuild Europe's ravaged economies, their speedy recovery pointed the way. Donor countries, with the United States in the lead, were now insisting on the submission of development plans as a condition for their loans. Although primarily the work of economists, other experts such as myself, who had enlisted in the cause, attempted to link abstract targets geared to boost the national GDP (Gross Domestic Product) to specific regional and local projects based on what we understood to be the spatial dynamics of economic growth. The worldwide enthusiasm for development through state-led planning is reflected in a special section I edited of UNESCO's *International Social Science Journal* on "The Study and Practice of Planning" including contributions from such luminaries as Robert Dahl, Jan Tinbergen, and Ruth Glass (Friedmann 1959). Disillusionment would inevitably follow, but not for another 20 years.

Work on a theory of planning, however, was not the common practice of econometricians such as Nobel Prize winners Jan Tinbergen and Wassily Leontief, who were chiefly preoccupied with technical issues of national economic planning. Instead, the leading theorist in our fledgling field was Herbert Simon, a brilliant social scientist whose early work on decision-making dominated the field (Simon 1945, 1957, 1969).[2] Simon was a rationalist, but when it came to decision-making, he was pragmatic as well. His "synoptic" decision model was based on the idea of "satisficing" (as opposed to optimizing, let alone maximizing choices), and continued to hold sway, even though "satisficing" could hardly be considered an operational criterion.[3] Closer to urban planning itself, a signal contribution was made early on by Martin Meyerson and Edward Banfield in their study of public housing in Chicago (1955). Their perspective was political and, like Machiavelli in 15th century Florence, the authors despaired of rationality applied to human affairs. A third contribution, equally skeptical of holistic planning, was by Charles

Lindblom, a professor of labor economics at Yale, whose "The Science of Muddling Through" is one of the most widely quoted articles on planning ever written (1959).[4]

Academic skeptics, however, had little influence on development planning where I worked. Boosted by the World Bank, the Alliance for Progress, the Swedish Nobel Prize committee, and other institutions, planning flourished at all pertinent scales – city, regional, and national. As understood at the time, it was a technocratic utopia that allowed governments to announce their intentions in a cascade of long-, middle-, and short-range plans that for all their normative character often by-passed political realities. But stating intentions of this sort was relatively cheap. In Brazil, for instance, the most powerful position in government was held by the Minister of Finance, not because he had a plan – he didn't – but because budgetary resources were released to operating units only on a political basis that required direct, personal contact with the Minister himself. In the end, Brazil did produce a national development plan, the first of which was drafted single-handedly by the distinguished economist Celso Furtado on loan from the United Nations Commission for Latin America (ECLA). Once approved by Washington, this plan would open the spigot of international aid.[5] Within the country, however, it lacked executive force. The myth of synoptic, coordinative planning effectively screened the actual improvisational character of decision-making that was the daily bread of politics in Brazil, beginning with the federal Minister, all the way down to the lowliest unit in the furthest reaches of the country.[6]

A new planning paradigm

To learn this was part of my ongoing education even as I continued to practice and teach development and planning theory. My international work continued with a two-year stint with the American Operations Mission to the Republic of Korea in the reconstruction period after the war, a professorship at MIT during which I did extensive research on regional development in Venezuela, and four years with the Ford Foundation in Santiago, Chile, where I served as advisor to the national government. It was in Chile, from 1964 to 1969, that I had my *eureka* experience that proved to be decisive for my pursuit of the social meaning and significance of planning. The rational decision-making model that had caused me (and others) so much grief continued to be invoked despite mounting evidence that the actual historical dynamics produced outcomes that could not be foretold with any claim to certainty.[7] Here, then, was a classic instance of a Kuhnian paradigm shift in our own field.[8] The insight that had come to me in a flash one morning was that an altogether different way of thinking about planning was as the art of *linking knowledge to action in a recursive process of social learning*. To flesh out the ramifications of my new understanding would take years to work out, but its first glimmerings were already apparent in an essay, "Notes on Societal Action" (Friedmann 1969), with a fuller statement coming four years later in *Retracking America: A theory of transactive planning* (Friedmann 1973) (see Chapter 1, this volume). My "discovery" of the knowledge/action link did more, in fact, than provide a new conceptual framework for planning; it laid out an entire research program on epistemology and social practice.[9] When *Retracking* was published, I was still enamored of state-centric planning. After returning to the United States in 1969 to teach full-time as head of the UCLA planning program, I would eventually shift to the more "radical" planning by agents of civil society (Friedmann 1987).

A few years later, during a fruitful sabbatical year in London, I decided to take on social learning as one of the more difficult epistemological issues raised by the new paradigm. I did so in the context of the philosophy of science, because the old planning with its rational pretensions had claimed to be based on science; it was conceived as a form of social engineering. Beginning with a critique of Sir Karl Popper's falsification theorem (the idea that one black swan would undermine the universalistic hypothesis that all swans are white), I argued that in the case of what I called a transformative planning – that is, by initiating moral actions in the public realm, as Aristotle had enjoined us to do – we are not interested in falsification or even the verification of hypotheses but in working towards the creation of something new (Arendt 1958). Transformative planning was by its very nature a one-off experiment, whose actual course would constantly be subject to correction through a reflective process of social learning (see Chapter 2, this volume).

An epistemological break

The 1970s proved to be a turning point in world history. How to describe in a few sentences what happened? Some observers called it the re-capitalization of capital. What is clear is that the decade ushered in what we now refer to as globalization, a process in which national boundaries were receding in importance, as they yielded to urban-centered global networks – economic, cultural, political, and social. A handful of "world cities" (Friedmann and Wolff 1982; Friedmann 1985) began competing fiercely for in-bound foreign capital. Under the banner of neo-liberalism, the national state, which had been dominant throughout the post-war era, gradually retreated from its steering functions. With the state's regulatory powers drastically reduced, private capital was free to do much as it pleased, especially in the financial sector, while many of the state's former responsibilities for social welfare were transferred, albeit without central funding, to local communities. Aging factories in the industrial heartlands of America, Great Britain, and Germany were shutting down, re-opening production in so-called NICs – newly industrializing countries – where labor costs were only a fraction of what they had been in the heavily unionized West. China's east coast was one of these. Mao Zedong had died in 1976, and after a brief transition struggle between the Old Guard (the "Gang of Four") and the powerful reform movement under Deng Xiaoping, Communist China opened its borders to join the globalizing economy, with India following a couple of decades later. With the dawn of this neo-liberal age, as it was called, the world's love affair with state planning was drawing to a close. In the frenzy of global restructuring, few people gave more than cursory attention to the first glimmerings of what would soon loom as a worldwide environmental crisis, including climate change and an unsustainable ecological footprint. In the early 1970s, *The Limits to Growth: A Report for the Club of Rome's Project on the Predicament of Mankind* created something of a stir, but with re-capitalization in full swing, the whole idea that the economy was about to exceed the resource capacity of the globe was quickly dismissed on both scientific and ideological grounds (Meadows *et al* 1972; Cole *et al* 1973).

It took some time for theorists to grasp the implications of these global changes for planning. By the mid-1970s, and on a Guggenheim fellowship in London's Centre for Environmental Studies, I took time off for a philosophical exploration of the moral foundations of a good society (Friedmann 1979; see Chapter 3, this volume). I was aiming not for a static utopia outside of history, as so many classical utopias had done, but for a way of transforming American society through a process of self-development driven by small action-oriented groups – ephemeral good societies – bonded through dialogue and non-hierarchical relations, defending and enlarging the spaces for their own reproduction in the larger society. Underlying this idea was an anarchist conception of changing the existing power structures of state and capital through the soft power of non-violent action from below. For all their turbulence, the 1960s had shown how this might be done through the concerted struggles of progressive social movements.

Meanwhile, however, the global project of re-capitalization was proceeding apace. The new ethos was pointedly expressed by Aurelio Peccei, President of the Club of Rome:

It is the task of our press, techno-structure, academia, and also political class – a few new leaders, after all, are enough – to keep public opinion informed of the reality of one world, and of the repercussions its macro-problems have on every country, and indeed, every family. If this is done, I am sure that our peoples will prove mature enough to support with their vote, and if necessary with their own sacrifice, not only this new thinking and this new approach, but also the strategy and policy decisions they will require. (Peccei 1969: 245)

To Peccei it seemed a simple matter: "a few new leaders, after all, are enough". The ultimate corporate manager, Peccei made no attempt to make the future planners of the world accountable to anyone other than themselves. His transnational dream of a benevolent world dictatorship – imagined as the corporate model with which he was familiar – was geared to perpetual capital accumulation. All it required was "mature people" who would vote their support of this project in a sort of global plebiscite. And because national sovereignty would stand in the way of this grand project, it would have to be restrained – always, of course, in the name of high-sounding ideals, such as Tinbergen's "common heritage of mankind" principle (Tinbergen 1976: 83–4).

I devoted the first half of the next decade to the writing of *Planning in the Public Domain*. By then it had become clear that Peccei's dream was well on the way to being realized. For the most part, critical voices had been silenced, and global re-capitalization was in full swing. In Anglo-America, urban planners were left out of these happenings or did what was expected of them, but some of us focused on the social outcomes of globalization, which were mostly negative and local. This was the context that led me to what one might call an epistemological break in telling the history of planning ideas. From its beginnings at the turn of the 18th century, with the industrial revolution under way, planning had been viewed exclusively from the perspective of the state. This was especially true of the Saint-Simonian *politechniciens* in Paris who, having discovered "society" now wanted nothing else but to remake it according to rational (engineering) principles.[10] I was fascinated by their story, but in doing so, had overlooked an entire dimension of intellectual and political history. It took a colleague of mine, Rebecca Morales, to remind me of it. After I had given a lecture on the Social Reform tradition of planning, she asked a provocative question: where was the kind of progressive community planning for which our school at UCLA had become noted? The answer hit me like a bolt of lightning. Having been fixated on the state, I had completely neglected the multiple counter-narratives on the Left of the political spectrum, beginning with the early utopianism of Robert Owen, Charles Fourier, and Pierre Joseph Proudhon, followed by Marx and Engels' historical materialism and so on down through the 19th and 20th centuries to our own near-contemporaries such as Henri Lefebvre, Jürgen Habermas, Ivan Illich, Dolores Hayden, and many others who had valiantly swum against the mainstream, advocating different visions of society – communist, socialist, anarchist, feminist, ecologist. Without them, the story of planning was woefully incomplete. Collectively, I called their contributions the social mobilization tradition of planning, because it originated with and found its supporters from among people, most of whom were leading quite ordinary lives, and whose power to change the conditions and circumstances of their lives came only when they joined up with social movements and political parties. This was the "radical planning" that our activist faculty at UCLA had missed from my account, and which I hastened to rectify (see Chapter 4, this volume).

My next book was *Empowerment: The politics of alternative development* (Friedmann 1992). Here I returned to my first preoccupation of development planning in poor countries, only this time with a new understanding. Poverty, I argued, was not simply to be income-poor; it could also and more potently be described as a lack of access to a number of identifiable bases of social power – housing, time available to households after subsistence needs had been met, social networks and organizations, knowledge and skills, information, tools of production, and financial resources (see Chapter 5, this volume). At the center of this array of "bases," however, was not the atomistic individual, as most economists would have it, but the complex social construct of the household economy together with its multiple social relations. An important aspect of this "alternative politics" was the recognition of use values – a typically neglected aspect of development policies – as vitally important for the production of life and livelihood (Polanyi 1977). Use values refer to all things produced for which there is no market, such as social reproduction in households, the love, care, and nurturing of children, volunteer work in the community, political practices, playing music for pleasure, etc. Without the inclusion of use values, social solidarity would be difficult to imagine and the logic of exchange values would reign supreme. Introducing use values as equally necessary for the production of life and livelihood was to acknowledge social solidarity as an important element in the struggle to escape both poverty and dis/empowerment.[11] Other chapters in *Empowerment* dealt with rural development, gender issues, ecological sustainability, and other topics, but my theoretical contributions were the ones mentioned above. In dealing with development, I wanted to extricate my thinking from the straightjacket of neo-classical economics, fully aware that mainstream development theory was fatally linked to economists' way of thinking.[12]

A genuine alternative would have to shift away from state-centric planning to a different starting point. The concluding chapter of *Empowerment* therefore addressed the question of non-governmental organizations – the so-called third sector, or more broadly, civil society.[13] Along with others, I entertained a guarded hope that an alternative politics might be possible through the voluntary actions of civil society, both indigenous and international. It was a move in the right direction. But the global reach of neo-liberal policies at the time left little space for a genuine alternative.[14]

A follow-up book came out a year later, in a collaboration with some of my students (Friedmann and Rangan 1993). Prompted by them, I was beginning to embrace an environmental perspective, and *In Defense of Livelihood* covered a wide range of environmental topics from Africa, Latin America, and South Asia, such as resource management in Northern Senegal, a resistance movement to the construction of a large dam in southern Brazil, popular environmental action in the Garhwali Himalayas; seven case studies in all. I continued to work along this line by organizing an international conference, papers from which were eventually included in *Emergences: Women's struggle for livelihood in Latin America* (Friedmann, Abers and Autler 1996).

The year of its publication was also the year of my retirement from UCLA. We celebrated this with yet another international conference, this one taking on the topic of civil society in its relation to planning (Douglass and Friedmann 1998). My keynote contribution (see Chapter 6, this volume) was to describe what I saw as a new political economy of planning that engaged organized civil society directly in ways of which the more traditional "community" planning approach was incapable. The theoretical debates at the conference erupted into conflict among some participants, as advocates of Habermasian communicative action clashed with political "realists" who advocated Machiavellian strategies. Nevertheless, civil society was beginning to enter the vocabulary of planning, and the theme was subsequently taken up by Mike Douglass, co-editor of this volume, in his work on urbanization in Pacific Asia (Douglass *et al* 2002, 2007; Ho and Douglass 2008).[15]

Post-retirement

My "post-retirement" years led to four publications on planning theory that are included in the present volume (Chapters 7–10). Chapter 7, an invited lecture at the University of Nijmegen in the Netherlands, is a state-of-the-art stock-taking of planning theory towards the end of the millennium. It tries to answer the puzzling question why, after four decades of active theorizing, it had not been possible to come up with a common definition or even a broad and undisputed understanding of planning theory.

With Chapter 8, "The good city: in defense of utopian thinking", I return to my earlier preoccupation with values in planning. Its central claim is this:

> Every human being has the right, by nature, to the full development of their innate intellectual, physical and spiritual potentials in the context of wider communities.

I believed then, as I do now, that this foundational value for planning is cross-culturally valid, although I realize that this claim may be disputed in some parts of the world, particularly in its application to women. I attempted to ground what I call "human flourishing" in natural law even as I acknowledged the moral constraints under which we have to make our lives as members of larger communities.[16] The statement assumes that all of us have unrealized capacities for growth, and that it is our right (as well as moral obligation) to realize them. I put this idea forward as a normative foundation for planning, always with the understanding that some social constraints may have to yield if "human flourishing" is to become a guiding beacon for our work. The latter proviso, which is insufficiently articulated in this chapter, is part of the ongoing social struggles to remove the constraints of chronic dis/empowerment, gender-bias, and racism that have become the object of specific social movements around the world.

Chapter 9 introduces the concept of planning culture and presents case studies as well as an argument for the multiplicity of ways that planning is understood and performed in an increasingly globalized world. Although there are now multinational and even world congresses of planners, like those of other major professions, it's uncertain how much of the talk at these conferences is fully understood even by those present. Each presenter, frequently speaking in a language that is not his or her own, and from experiences that stem from a national planning culture that is probably unfamiliar to most of the audience, is likely to be misunderstood. My essay wanted to raise awareness of how institutionalized planning and its performance differs from country to country and even city to city, and how we need to make an effort to learn about these differences if we are to move forward as our discourse on planning becomes increasingly global in its reach.

The final essay in this volume (Chapter 10) is a long retrospective survey organized around the theme of the uses of planning theory and its relevance for education and practice. It suggests three ways that theorizing can contribute to our field. The first is by evolving a deeply considered humanist philosophy and tracing its implications for planning practice. The second is by adapting planning practices to their real-world constraints with regard to scale, complexity, and time. And the third is by translating knowledge and ideas generated in academic fields other than planning into our own necessarily restricted but always expanding domain. The essay concludes that planning theory needs to be understood as a transdisciplinary endeavor involving a global community of scholars, and that their contributions are vital to our profession.

In an Epilogue, I take a forward look, sketching out what I had always wanted to achieve, the elements of a public philosophy for the 21st century. This is no longer Reason operating in History, but a call for social activists whom I call citizen-planners to strive towards a sustainable and just world order and, within the Inferno that we know – as the great Italian writer Italo Calvino admonished us – to find that which is not Inferno and give it space.

Some personal reflections

In 1966, I published "Planning as a vocation" (Friedmann 1966). This two-part essay was patterned after Max Weber's famous "Politics as a vocation" (Weber 1946 [1921]), where vocation stands for both a profession and a personal calling. Written five years before its actual publication, this essay was my first comprehensive attempt to bring together the relevant social science literature that had emerged in the policy sciences in the decade and a half following World War II around the theme of planning. Weber had become the central figure in American sociology during this period, and his concepts of instrumental and normative rationality were by and large taken as axiomatic. By now, having served the US government for many years, I was quite aware of some of the dysfunctional aspects of public bureaucracy. Nevertheless, I was still struggling to hold on to the idea of Reason in History, the Hegelian "flea in the ear" that would continue to irritate me. I was indeed desperate to discover some larger meaning in history – the history I had lived through and in which I was now participating as an adult – as opposed to the proverbial "tale told by an idiot".

Having been born in 1926 in the aftermath of World War I, I had experienced political struggles between democracy and fascism during the 1930s, had seen my father persecuted because of his Jewish ancestry in 1938, and two years later, had arrived in the United States on the last boat from Europe as a refugee. I was thus acutely conscious of living through an extraordinary historical period. In the aftermath of the war, Jean Paul Sartre had announced to the assembled journalists of the world's media who had come to hear the famous French philosopher, that "God is dead".[17] Others told us that we were living in an Age of Anxiety, where the old gods had fallen, and the most horrific acts of humans against other human beings had been committed with bureaucratic punctiliousness, from the Holocaust to the nuclear annihilation of entire cities. Hannah Arendt had found the right words for this when she called it the "banality of evil". Existentialists proclaimed that "everything was now permitted". More optimistically, some Americans, such as Henry Luce, the publisher of *Time* and *Life*, envisioned an American century in which the American Way would triumph worldwide. But was that anything other than a positive gloss on a new imperialism? In 1961, given this state of the world, I was hoping to find some transcendent meaning in the workings of Reason in History, as it manifested itself, so I thought, in post-war development planning. But what I concluded in the end was nothing like that at all. As evident from this introduction and the 10 essays in this volume, I eventually abandoned my search for meaning in universal history for a greatly scaled-down agenda. There was no way for planning ever to be part of a Hegelian apotheosis of the state. No Reason in History with capital letters then, but planning as a vocation nonetheless. What would that look like?

I have talked here about a paradigm shift in the latter part of the 1960s, when planning began to abandon its concentration on organizational decision-making in favor of an attempt to link up knowledge and action. And then, roughly a decade later, I talked about an epistemological break that would allow for a radical planning agenda to be centered no longer in the (Hegelian) state but in a mobilized civil society, sometimes in the small spaces of the city in the form of urban social movements and resistance (Castells 1983; Friedmann 2002), at other times and more decisively, in transnational social movements and large-scale civic organizations with global capabilities. Here was a case for the self-articulation of society through planning and action. It is a less heroic image of planning than the superseded Hegelian model, but it is all the reason in history we are likely to get.

In closing, then, allow me tell you, the reader, why the idea of planning as a vocation still appeals to me, and why despite many setbacks, errors, and disenchantments, I nevertheless believe that planning as a field of professional study and practice is as valid a vocation as any other on the horizon. For some young people this claim may be sufficient reason to stumble into our field with an ardent desire to "do good competently" or to "change the world". But here is my personal list of reasons why the idea of planning should not be abandoned:

- planning deals with important public issues;
- it is oriented to obtaining results in the "real world" whose realization requires political strategies;
- it is transactive, communicative, collaborative;
- it seeks dynamic balances between the part and the whole, the technical and normative, the empirical and theoretical, the pragmatic and utopian, the near present and the distant future, exchange values and use values;
- it allows us to be visionary with an emphasis on values that include social justice, ecological sustainability, civic empowerment, social solidarity, and human flourishing;
- it is transdisciplinary and can be made operational at multiple scales, from local neighborhoods to transnational and global spaces and the political forces they generate; and finally,
- it is engaged in continuous social learning.

That, I would argue, is enough for one's life to be lived, a tall agenda with which to engage the world through one's work and be fulfilled.

Notes

1. Some years later, a Portuguese version was published by the Getúlio Vargas Foundation in Rio de Janeiro.
2. The decision-making approach continues to this day as a sub-discipline of planning and takes various forms, such as risk analysis, systems analysis, and operations research, among others.
3. In Simon's language, to "satisfice" meant that in a hierarchical organizational structure a responsible decision maker would regard a particular proposed course of action as satisfactory or "good enough" for the purposes at hand.
4. The question of planning vs market rationality had been fiercely debated on ideological grounds in Great Britain in the immediate post-war era. See Hayek 1944, 1955; Wootton 1945; and Mannheim 1951. In practical politics, however, the balance of power at the time clearly favored the pro-planning position.
5. The authority for the review and approval of national development plans was set up under the Alliance for Progress (1961–1973), an arrangement that operated under the auspices of the Organization of American States. For a short while, Furtado became Brazil's Minister of Planning in 1961.
6. In a study of national planning in Venezuela (Friedmann 1965), I identified five latent political objectives of development planning in that country: strengthening the Presidency; improving the political process; creating a development society; reducing social conflict; and mobilizing additional resources (pp. 49ff).
7. I had earlier made a valiant effort to reconcile the Hegelian idea of Reason in History with contemporary politics as I understood it in a two-part essay that was published five years after having written it (Friedmann 1966). The difficulty I had in getting it into print was largely due to its excessive length.
8. Reference is to Thomas S. Kuhn whose book, *The Structure of Scientific Revolutions* (1961), showed how theoretical paradigms in science were established and maintained despite growing empirical evidence that challenged accepted theories or called for new explanations. At certain points in the history of a science, according to Kuhn, paradigm shifts lead to the rapid abandonment of mainstream theories, which are then replaced by new, more fruitful models of explanation. As an inherently social activity, science is not an autonomous realm (Latour 1993).
9. Planning epistemology includes such questions as: whose knowledge is pertinent for planning; what sort of knowledge can planners claim to have; how do planners deal with risk and uncertainty; what is the reliability of planning models and forecasts; and how should planning be organized to provide the best possible knowledge base. The question of social action or practice raises issues such as the role of planners and planning; the relationship between planning and implementation; the value bases of planned action; social learning; and the politics of planning, to mention a few.
10. Planning schools in Japan retain a faint echo of Saint Simon and his disciples. Administratively located in faculties of engineering, the programs are called "social engineering".
11. For more on use values, see the Epilogue.
12. For a devastating account of what mainstream techno-politics looks like in practice, see Timothy Mitchell's critical dissection of its role in Egypt (Mitchell 2002).
13. The other sectors were the state and the corporate economy.
14. For balanced views of non-governmental organizations and their role in combating mass poverty, see Bennett (1995), Ndegwa (1995) and Edwards and Hulme (1996).

15. An important precursor to this focus on civil society in the making of cities and communities was Castells' *magnum opus*, *The City and the Grassroots* (1983). In this volume, which summarizes a decade's empirical work on urban social movements, Castells had laid the foundation for seeing civil society as an actor in the co-production of urban space.
16. Natural law or the law of nature (*lex naturalis*) posits the existence of a law whose content is set by nature and that therefore has validity everywhere. The constraint posed by our membership in larger communities, and therefore the affirmation of sociality as an essential part of our being-in-the-world, is one of many such limits which we must learn to respect in constructing the good society.
17. Sartre was actually quoting the 19th century German philosopher Nietzsche.

Bibliography

Arendt, H. (1958) *The Human Condition*, Chicago: University of Chicago Press.

Bennett, J. (1995) *Meeting Needs: NGO coordination in practice*, London: Earthscan.

Castells, M. (1983) *The City and the Grassroots: A cross-cultural theory of urban social movements*, Berkeley: University of California Press.

Cole, H.S.D. *et al* (1973) *Models of Doom: a critique of the limits of growth*, New York: Universe Books.

Douglass, M. and Friedmann, J. (eds) (1998) *Cities for Citizens: Planning and the rise of civil society*, New York: John Wiley & Sons.

Douglass, M. *et al* (eds) (2002) 'Globalization and civic space in Pacific Asia', special issue of *Third World Planning Review*, 24:3.

Douglass, M. *et al* (eds) (2007) *Globalization, the City and the Rise of Civil Society: The social production of civic spaces in Pacific Asia*, London: Routledge.

Edwards, M. and Hulm, D. (eds) (1996) *Beyond the Magic Bullet: NGO performance and accountability in the post-cold-war world*, West Hartford, CT: Kumarian Press.

Friedmann, J. (ed.) (1959) 'The study and practice of planning', special section of *International Social Science Journal*, 11(3): 327–409.

——(1965) *Venezuela: from doctrine to dialogue*, with an introduction by B. Gross, Syracuse, NY: Syracuse University Press.

——(1966) 'Planning as a vocation', *Plan Canada*: Part I 6(3): 99–132, Part II 7 (1): 8-2-6.

——(1969) 'Notes on societal action', *Journal of the American Institute of Planners*, 35(5): 311–8.

——(1973) *Retracking America: A theory of transactive planning*, Garden City, NY: Doubleday/Anchor.

——(1979) *The Good Society*, Cambridge, MA: MIT Press.

——(1985) 'The world city hypothesis', *Development and Change*, 16(1): 69–84.

——(1987) *Planning in the Public Domain: From knowledge to action*, Princeton: Princeton University Press.

——(1992) *Empowerment: The politics of alternative development*, Cambridge, MA: Blackwell.

——(1998) 'The new political economy of planning: the rise of civil society', in M. Douglass and J. Friedmann (eds) *Cities for Citizens*, New York: John Wiley & Sons, 19–38.

——(2002) *The Prospect of Cities*, Minneapolis: Minnesota University Press, ch. 5.

Friedmann, J. and Rangan, H. (eds) (1993) *In Defense of Livelihood: comparative studies on environmental action*, West Hartford, CN: Kumarian Press, for the United Nations Research Centre for Social Development (UNRISD).

Friedmann, J. and Wolff, G. (1982) 'World city formation: an agenda for research and action', *International Journal of Urban and Regional Research*, 6(3): 309–44.

Friedmann, J., Abers, R. and Autler, L. (eds) (1996) *Emergences: Women's struggles for livelihood in Latin America*, University of California at Los Angeles, Latin American Center Publications.

Hayek, F.A. (1944) *The Road to Serfdom*, London: George Routledge & Sons.

——(1955) *The Counter-revolution of Science: Studies on the abuse of reason*, New York: Free Press.

Ho, K.C. and Douglass, M. (eds) (2008) 'Place-making and livability in Pacific Asian cities', special issue, *International Development Planning Review*, 30: 3.

Kuhn, T. S. (1961) *The Structure of Scientific Revolutions*, Chicago: University of Chicago Press.

Latour, B. (1993) *We Have Never Been Modern*, Cambridge, MA: Harvard University Press.

Lindblom, C. (1959) 'The science of muddling through', *Public Administration Review*, 19(20): 79–99.

Mannheim, K. (1951) *Freedom, Power and Democratic Planning*, London: Routledge & Kegan Paul.

Meadows, D.H. *et al* (1972) *The Limits to Growth: A report for the Club of Rome's project on the predicament of mankind*, New York: Universal Books.

Meyerson, M. and Banfield, E.C. (1955) *Politics, Planning, and the Public Interest: The case of public housing in Chicago*, New York: The Free Press.

Mitchell, T. (2002) *Rule of Experts: Egypt, techno-politics, modernity*, Berkeley: University of California Press.

Ndegwa, S.N. (1995) *The Two Faces of Civil Society: NGOs and politics in Africa*, West Hartford, CT: Kumarian Press.

Peccei, A. (1969) *The Chasm Ahead*, London: Collier & Macmillan.

Polanyi, K. (1977) *The Livelihood of Man*, (ed.) H.W. Pearson, New York: The Academic Press.

Simon, H. (1945) *Administrative Behavior*, New York: The Free Press.

——(1957) *Models of Man: Social and rational*, New York: John Wiley & Sons.

——(1969) *The Sciences of the Artificial*, Cambridge, MA: MIT Press.

Tinbergen, J., coordinator (1976) *RIO: Reshaping the International Order: a report to the Club of Rome*, New York: E. P. Dutton.

Weber, M. (1946) 'Politics as a vocation', in H.H. Gerth and C.W. Mills (eds) *Max Weber: Essays in sociology*, New York: Oxford University Press (Orig.1921).

Wootton, B. (1945) *Freedom under Planning*, Chapel Hill: University of North Carolina Press.

1

The transactive style of planning

The book from which this chapter is taken was written at the end of one of the most turbulent periods in American history, a decade marked by the Vietnam war, the civil rights struggle, burning cities, political assassinations, and the first intimations of the "limits to growth" that for many people was to become a central issue by the end of the millennium. Its larger argument was that the kind of planning we were teaching and practicing at the time was based on an out-dated worldview that needed to be rethought from the ground up.

The old view of planning was of a relatively static world in which planners were objective analysts who had access to pertinent knowledge about the future and could effectively communicate what they knew to political decision-makers through written documents, such as policy drafts or a plan. The articulation of values implicit in this view was not the planners' responsibility but politicians'. Planning was understood to be essentially a technical, value-free activity in the public realm.

The new "transactive" model I proposed was based on a different epistemology (see Chapter 2). Its starting point was that the future can neither be known nor designed, that the world is a slippery place (as the pre-Columbian Aztec poet tells us), that risk is inherent in action, and that to be effective, planners must get as close as possible to the action itself. (Later I changed this to acknowledge planners not merely as advisors but as actors in their own right; see Chapters 4 and 6.) Still missing from this early version of a transactive style of planning is a critical understanding of rationality in relation to action and of the ways inevitable value conflicts must be acknowledged and dealt with in planning practice (see Chapter 10).

Planning in this chapter is treated broadly as the linking of knowledge to action, with the proviso that action feeds back into knowledge as recursive social learning. But what sort of knowledge is pertinent to action? In this first formulation, I distinguish between the planner and an unspecified client-actor, arguing that whereas the former is in possession of certain kinds of "processed" knowledge – abstract, formal, and often quantitative – the latter has usually unarticulated knowledge based on personal experience. In problem-solving, I argue, the power of knowledge is significantly raised when processed knowledge is joined to experiential knowledge in the course of the action itself. Further, the most effective way to join or rather meld these two ways of knowing is through a chain of interpersonal transactions or, more succinctly, through dialogue (see Chapter 3).

From this perspective, the central issue in planning is authentic communication between planner and client-actor. This calls for each to reach out to the other, to attend carefully to what is being said as well as the reasons behind it, and then to respond, in a series of ongoing, open-ended conversations about the problem at hand. This is the essential message of transactive planning and, if carried out in good faith, transforms what we used to understand by "planning" into a collaborative effort that bridges the communications gap between planner and client-actor.

In formulating this model I drew upon my extensive experiences as an advisor to governments, both national and foreign, at the executive level. Twenty years later, the transactive model reappeared in a new form as communicative action, influenced by the German sociologist Jürgen Habermas, but was applied chiefly in local community settings (Forester 1989, 1999; Fischer 2009).

Finally, a note on language. The following text was written at a time when using the male form of the personal pronoun to stand for humanity in general was still the normal way of writing. I hope the reader will bear this in mind and not accuse the author of unintended gender bias. Essays written a decade later already reflect the new gender awareness which was then coming into widespread use. But in the early 70s when the present chapter was written, this was not yet the case.

Bibliography

Fischer, F. (2009) "Discursive planning: social justice as discourse", in P. Marcuse *et al* (eds) *In Search of the Just City*, London; New York: Routledge.

Forester, J. (1989) *Planning in the Face of Power*, Berkeley, Los Angeles: University of California Press.

——(1999) *The Deliberative Practitioner: Encouraging participatory planning processes*, Cambridge, MA: MIT Press.

From *Retracking America*

Originally published in 1973

Bridging the communication gap

Transactive planning changes knowledge into action through an unbroken sequence of interpersonal relations. As a particular style of planning, it can be applied to both allocation and innovation. This chapter states the principal conditions for transactive planning and explores its major implications.

Transactive planning is a response to the widening gulf in communication between technical planners and their clients. To simplify the discussion, let us assume that planners as well as clients are individual persons rather than institutions, and that clients generate streams of action on which they wish to be advised.

This assumption is not altogether unrealistic. Institutions do not relate to each other as wholes, but through a complex series of exchanges among individuals. Although these individuals behave primarily according to their formal role prescriptions, each role masks a singular personality. Roles are defined by a set of abstract behavior patterns, but the person assuming a particular role may be straightforward or devious, disposed to be tranquil or angry, approachable or remote, eager for power or reluctant to assume responsibility. The planner steeped in the practice of the transactive style will try to reach out to the person who stands behind the formal role.

Planners and clients may experience difficulties communicating valid meanings to each other. The barriers to effective communication between those who have access primarily to processed knowledge and those whose knowledge rests chiefly on personal experience are rising. We have seen that this problem is not unique to America; it is found to some extent in all societies that seek the help of technical experts. Messages may be exchanged, but the relevant meanings are not effectively communicated. As a result, the linkage of knowledge with action is often weak or nonexistent. This is true even where planning forms part of the client system itself; even there, actions tend to proceed largely on the basis of acquired routines and the personal knowledge of the decision makers. Planners talk primarily to other planners, and their counsel falls on unresponsive ears. As we shall see, however, the establishment of a more satisfactory form of communication is not simply a matter of translating the abstract and highly symbolic language of the planner into the simpler and more experience-related vocabulary of the client. The real solution involves a restructuring of the basic relationship between planner and client.

Each has a different method of knowing: the planner works chiefly with processed knowledge abstracted from the world and manipulated according to certain postulates of theory and scientific method; his client works primarily from the personal knowledge he draws directly from experience. Although personal knowledge is much richer in content and in its ability to differentiate among the minutiae of daily life, it is less systematized and orderly than processed knowledge. It is also less capable of being generalized and, therefore, is applicable only to situations where the environment has not been subject to substantial change. The "rule of thumb" by which practical people orient their actions is useful only so long as the context of action remains the same. Processed knowledge, on the other hand, implies a theory about some aspect of the world. Limited in scope, it offers a general explanation for the behavior of a small number of variables operating under a specified set of constraints.

The difficulties of relating these two methods of knowing to each other reside not only in their different foci of attention and degrees of practical relevance (processed knowledge suppresses the operational detail that may be of critical importance to clients), but also in language. The planner's language is conceptual and mathematical, consciously drained of the lifeblood of human intercourse in its striving for scientific objectivity. It is intended to present the results of his research in ways that will enable others, chiefly other planners, to verify each statement in terms of its logic, consistency with empirical observation, and theoretical coherence. Most planners prefer communicating their ideas in documents complete with charts, tables, graphs, and maps, as well as long appendices containing complex mathematical derivations and statistical analyses. The concepts, models, and theories to which these documents refer are often unfamiliar to the clients to whom they are supposedly addressed.

The language of clients lacks the formal restrictions that hedge in planning documents. It, too, employs a jargon to speed communications, but the jargon will be experience- rather than concept-related. Client language is less precise than the language of planners, and it may encompass congeries of facts and events that, even though they form a meaningful whole in terms of practice, are unrelated at the level of theory. Planners may therefore seize upon a favorite term from their client's specialized vocabulary and subject it to such rigorous analysis that what originally might have been a meaningful expression to the client is given back to him as a series of different but theoretically related concepts that reflect a processed reality.

Housing administrators, for example, have long been accustomed to derive quantitative program targets from what they call the housing deficit, which is calculated on the basis of new household formations, a physical index of housing quality, and an estimated rate of housing obsolescence. Planners have recently replaced this concept with what they believe to be a theoretically more valid model for establishing the housing needs of a population. They postulate an *effective housing demand* that arises in the context of particular submarkets organized according to major income levels and locality. Each submarket has unique characteristics with respect to the type of housing offered, the credit available, and the degree to which it is able to satisfy the social – as distinct from the economic – demand of each population group. Aggregate housing demand, therefore, is seen to evolve not only in accord with the differential growth rates of the affected population groups but also in relation to changes in the growth and distribution of personal income and in the structural characteristics of each submarket.

I do not know how housing administrators will react to this conceptually more satisfying model for calculating housing requirements, but I suspect that they will not be overly pleased. They may even accuse the planner of purposefully misconstruing the "real" (i.e. experiential) meaning contained in the traditional and administratively more convenient term of housing deficit.

The language of clients – so difficult to incorporate into the formalized vocabulary of the planner – is tied to specific operational contexts. Its meanings shift with changes in the context, and its manner of expression is frequently as important as the actual words employed. This is probably the reason why planners prefer written to verbal communications, and why the latter tend to be in the form of highly stylized presentations. Tone of voice, emphasis, subtle changes in grammatical structure and word sequence, so important in the face-to-face communications of action-oriented persons, are consistently de-emphasized by planners. Whereas planners' formal communications could be translated by a computer into a foreign language without substantial loss of meaning, a tape-recorded conversation among clients could not.

Planners relate primarily to other members of their profession and to the university departments responsible for the transmission and advancement of professional knowledge. Clients, on the other hand, relate chiefly to organizations of their own kind. The reference group of each acts as a cultural matrix that helps to confirm and strengthen differences of approach and behavior.

Reference groups are powerful institutions for molding behavior. This is especially true for the planner, whose situation tends to be less secure than that of his clients. His professional association not only keeps him continuously informed through newsletters, specialized journals, and conferences, but also confers on him the dignity and status of formal membership in a profession. The association reassures him when his competence is being challenged by outsiders and provides support when it is needed. In order to receive these benefits, the planner must conform to the norms of professional conduct. There are countless planning documents whose content is not primarily addressed to clients but to other planning professionals. For a planner's reputation is made more by impressing his fellow practitioners than by successfully serving his clients.

The reference systems of clients work in similar ways to enhance (or destroy) individual reputations. To the extent that clients also become professionalized – a trend that is very strong in American society – differences between planners and clients diminish, but the impediments to effective communication remain.

The mutual dependence of planner and client, coupled with a relative inability to exchange meaningful messages, leads to ambiguous and stereotyped attitudes that do little to resolve the basic problem. Speaking among themselves, planners say: "Ours is clearly a superior form of knowledge that enables us to gain incisive insights into conditions of structured complexity. As members of a professional elite, we are able to achieve a greater rationality than our clients. Effective problem-solving lies in the widespread use of processed knowledge." But they also admire the practical successes of their clients and secretly deplore their own inability to score in the same game.

The clients, on the other hand, in the sheltering environment of their own groups, counter the planners' claims: "Experience clearly counts most. Ours is a superior kind of knowledge, tested under fire. Planners are impractical dreamers who know more and more about less and less. Nothing of what they know can be applied. Problems get solved because we are in charge." But they also admire the planners' knowledge of things that are not visible to the unaided eye and so transcend the possibilities of knowledge grounded in experience.

What can be done to overcome these barriers to effective communication between planners and clients? The traditional means, an exchange of formal documents, has not proved spectacularly successful in the past. Strangely enough, most planners are probably still unaware of this.

A few years ago, I served as an advisor to the government of Chile on questions of urban and regional development. Several foreign experts working with me were connected with a number of central institutions, such as the National Planning Office and the Ministry of Housing. My own office, however, was independent and not formally associated with any agency of the government.

After a few months of initial reconnaissance, I thought that I had obtained a sufficient grasp of the situation to make a series of far-reaching recommendations. I set forth these recommendations very carefully in a lengthy memorandum, which, translated into Spanish, was carried by messenger to a number of leading government figures. A covering letter explained the general purpose of my effort. After letting two weeks go by, I arranged for an interview with each person who had received a copy. During the interviews, formal courtesies were exchanged, and some noncommittal references were made to the memorandum on which I had labored for several months. Afterwards I returned to my office to wait for a formal reply, but none ever came.

What had gone wrong? A good part of the answer can be found in my failure to establish, long before I ever set to work on the memorandum, a transactive relationship with the people whose encouragement I wanted. There was, indeed, no compelling reason why the government of Chile should have adopted any part of my recommendations. Who was I, after all, except an expert with a vague professional reputation abroad? Was it not presumptuous, not to say arrogant, for me, a foreigner who had spent only a few months in Chile, to suggest a whole series of sweeping reforms to responsible people who had been working for a good part of their political lives on problems of which I myself had only recently become aware?[1]

All these questions converge upon a single answer. If the communication gap between planner and client is to be closed, a continuing series of personal and primarily verbal transactions between them is needed, through which processed knowledge is fused with personal knowledge and both are fused with action.

Transactive planning as the life of dialogue

In transactive planning, two levels of communication have to be distinguished. The first is the level of person-centered communication. It presumes a relationship that is applicable to all forms of human intercourse. This I shall call the life of dialogue. The second is the level of subject-matter-related communication, which is sustained by the primary relation of dialogue and cannot be understood independently of it. Both levels are indispensable to planning. Where they become dissociated, thought is reduced to theorems and action to pure energy.

The life of dialogue always occurs as a relationship between two persons, a You and an I. Its characteristic features may be briefly stated:

1. *Dialogue presumes a relationship that is grounded in the authenticity of the person and accepts his "otherness" as a basis for meaningful communication.* In the life of dialogue, each person seeks to address the other directly. To be authentic means to discover yourself through dialogue with many others. And therefore we can say: The life of dialogue engenders a process of mutual self-discovery. At each stage in the process, you attempt to integrate discoveries about yourself into the already existing structure of your personality, thereby changing and expanding it. To do this well, you must have found an inner security based on a consciousness of what you have become and are yet capable of becoming; a basic confidence in your ability to integrate new learning; and, finally, a willingness to open yourself to others.

Opening yourself to another implies an acceptance of the other in his radical difference from yourself. The life of dialogue is not possible between two persons who hide behind their many masks and are therefore incapable of growing and extending their knowledge about themselves. It requires an openness that confirms the other in all the differences of his being. It is precisely this that makes changes in self possible. Through dialogue, you accept the freedom of the other to choose himself.

2. Dialogue presumes a relation in which thinking, moral judgment, feeling, and empathy are fused in authentic acts of being. The authentic person is an indivisible whole. Nevertheless, four states of his being can be distinguished. The permanent dissociation of these may lead to a warping and even to the destruction of the person. Intellect alone is barren; moral judgment alone is self-righteous; feeling alone is destructive; and empathy alone is unresponsive. These four states of being must be held in mutual tension so that each may regulate the others. The point of intersection among them may be called the center of the fully integrated person, whose thought is tempered by moral judgment, whose judgment is tempered by feeling, and whose feeling is tempered by empathy.

Where these four states are brought into conjunction, speech becomes simply an extension of being, and the meanings of speech are backed up by the person as a whole: they can be taken on good faith. This does not always make them right, however. The learning person in the life of dialogue can make mistakes, he may be torn by inner doubts and conflicts, and he may be incapable of expressing himself integrally, leaving his meanings ambiguous and only partially articulated. Nevertheless, the standards of his speech are based not upon the extremes of truth, morality, feeling, and empathy taken each alone, but on the values that result from the conjunction of these states.

3. Dialogue presumes a relation in which conflict is accepted. The acceptance of the other in the plenitude of his being as a person different from yourself implies that the relationship cannot always be harmonious. Conflict arises out of your different ways of looking at the world, your different feelings about the world, and your different ways of judging the world. It may also arise from a failure to make your meanings clear within the context of the other's perceptions and feelings. But conflict can be overcome by a mutual desire to continue in the life of dialogue. This is the basis for resolving conflict at the level of interpersonal relations.

4. Dialogue presumes a relationship of total communication in which gestures and other modes of expression are as vital to meaning as the substance of what is being said. Everything you say and everything you do – or fail to do – carries a message to the perceptive other. Dialogue is a web of meanings from which not a single strand can be separated. Where gesture and speech convey contradictory meanings, the authenticity of dialogue is put in doubt. Such contradictory behavior is, by itself, no proof of lack of authenticity, but it gives rise to a suspicion of bad faith.

5. *Dialogue presumes a relation of shared interests and commitments.* The life of dialogue cannot be sustained unless there is a sense of partaking in the interests of the other. Mutual participation in a matter of common concern is not a precondition of authentic dialogue; it may evolve through dialogue. Where it fails to evolve, the dialogue is interrupted.

We sometimes use one another to advance different interests. To the extent that this occurs, dialogue becomes an instrument to subordinate the other to your will. Presenting yourself to the other according to the demands of the situation is an inescapable part of dialogue, but "using" the other for interests that are not shared destroys any possibility of sustaining it. The life of dialogue is a relation of equality between two persons. It must not be perverted into an instrumental relationship.

6. *Dialogue presumes a relationship of reciprocity and mutual obligation.* Though dialogue is possible only between two persons who are free to choose themselves, this freedom is by no means unlimited. Dialogue is a contractual relationship. In accepting the other in his radical difference, you also assume responsibility for the consequences of this relationship. The act of "accepting" implies an act of "giving." The other "gives" or "entrusts" himself to you as a person, as you entrust yourself in turn. This exchange need not be balanced equally: no records are or can be kept. Nevertheless, a one-sided giving cannot continue for long. To the extent that you are willing to "accept" the other, your obligations to him will increase, and you must be willing to give at least a part of yourself in return.

7. *Dialogue presumes a relationship that unfolds in real time.* Dialogue takes place in the "here and now" even as it relates what has gone before to what is yet to come. It is therefore a time-binding relationship capable of infinite evolution. Nevertheless, it cannot escape the constraints of a given situation and must ultimately become relevant to the particular conditions of each participant's life. Storytelling is not dialogue; dreams are not dialogue. You cannot crawl out of time; dialogue is not a route of escape. Dialogue brings you back into time and into the conditions of your being here.

As described, the life of dialogue suggests an intimacy that most people associate with the relationship between husband and wife, parents and children, and close friends. In the circle of this extended family, non-utilitarian, person-centered relationships predominate. Outside its magic circle, relationships are expected to rest on a working, professional basis, to be centered on specific roles rather than persons – a form of behavior that carefully isolates intellectual and technical contributions from their matrix of moral judgments and feelings and presumes purely utilitarian transactions, in which no sharing need occur.

But this conception is basically wrong. The world of planning need not be qualitatively set apart from the world of non-utilitarian relationships. On the contrary, the impersonal, professional style of communication has been notoriously unsuccessful in joining knowledge to action.

It is true, of course, that one cannot maintain deep personal relationships with everyone one meets. But a person-centered relationship can be sustained at varying degrees of intensity and over periods of time that extend from only a few minutes to an entire life. Looking back at the requirements of dialogue, we see that the conditions are applicable to any relationship. We can be open and alert to the other, whoever he may be. We can accept him as a person different from ourselves without being threatening or feeling threatened in turn. We can try to hold our intellectual, moral, affective, and empathetic states of being in mutual tension. We can accept conflict as an inevitable part of dialogue and not its termination. We can look for the patterns of shared interests. And we can concentrate the life of dialogue on the here and now.

An attitude favorable to dialogue tends to call forth on the part of the other a desire to engage in it. Some persons are more difficult to reach than others, but in most cases, the response to an attempted dialogue is dialogue.

Transactive planning is carried on the ground swell of dialogue. When I prepared the memorandum for the Chilean Government, the basis for dialogue had not yet been established. Later, all this changed. In recruiting the advisory staff, emphasis was given to the personal qualities of each advisor – his ability to be a person (not a role-playing professional alone), to establish direct relations with others that would not be perceived as threatening, to be sensitive to the needs of others, and to learn quickly from complex, novel situations. Technical qualifications were also considered important, but they carried less weight.

At the start, the newly recruited advisor spent from six months to a year learning about the multi-faceted situation in which he had been placed and establishing relations of dialogue with a few key persons in the offices to which he was assigned. Although his formal role was not eliminated, it was so loosely structured that the advisor was able to emerge as a person. And once a relationship of this kind had been established, transactive planning could begin in earnest.

The process of mutual learning

Planners are forever coming up against new situations, but they confront them with knowledge that is little more than an aid to rapid and effective learning. Their theories, hypotheses, conceptual schemes, and analytical methods are useful only for converting the raw data of observation into general statements about reality. The validity of these statements is limited to a set of specified conditions. But the problems on which planners work – whether the design for a new town, a program for harnessing the waters of a river, or a policy for the development of scientific capabilities–must be studied in the fullness of historical circumstances. The number of variables that must be considered is substantially greater than those included in the analytical models of scientific work.

The planner's special skill, therefore, lies in his ability to be a rapid learner. His is an intelligence that is trained in the uses of processed knowledge for the purpose of acquiring new knowledge about reality. He comes equipped to bring order into a seemingly chaotic universe of data and sense impressions, to reduce this to a structure of relative simplicity, to isolate the processes responsible for the emergence and maintenance of the structure, to probe its propensities for change, and to locate the points of potentially effective intervention. Regardless of his specific procedure, the planner makes substantial use of analytical techniques in his work. The greater his virtuosity in this regard, the greater his pride in the results obtained. As I have said, his interests as a professional often get the better of his interest in serving his client. The following story serves to illustrate the point.

Some time ago, the US Department of Transportation sought the advice of a major research corporation on a proposal to decentralize its services. The corporation contracted with a group of professors at a number of different universities to prepare scholarly papers on the subject. The professors dug into their files, prepared the papers on schedule, and collected their fees. The papers were subsequently edited, and the completed set was forwarded to Washington, together with a summary of findings and recommendations. But neither the corporation nor the professors knew the exact reasons for the original request; nor were they aware of what factions pulled in what directions, what arguments had been already made, who were the figures in the unfolding drama of departmental politics. How could work done in ignorance of these things have been relevant to their client except by chance?

In this as in so many other situations, planning was carried out with no regard for the processes of goal clarification and policy formation. The research corporation and the professors conceived of their task exclusively in technical terms. They had no stake in the results of their studies. They failed to take their client on a learning trip.

What might have been done? Assuming that the original request for technical assistance was a serious one, an office might have been established in Washington for as long as necessary. Personal contacts might have been established with the originators of the request in the department, flesh-and-blood people with passions of their own. A review of the department's activities might have been jointly undertaken to see which might be decentralized and why. In problems such as these, the outside technical expert can be of greatest help by structuring the questions in a useful way and supplying concepts to help clarify the basic issues involved. The experts in this case might have served a catalytic role in organizing such a study, mediating among the different factions, proposing hypotheses, and summarizing the current state of theoretical knowledge. In doing all these things, they would have had to be in daily contact with the client staff. Personal relationships would gradually have developed. And in the end, the solution would have appeared as a discovery of the client himself.

In mutual learning, planner and client each learn from the other – the planner from the client's personal knowledge, the client from the planner's technical expertise. In this process, the knowledge of both undergoes a major change. A common image of the situation evolves through dialogue; a new understanding of the possibilities for change is discovered. And in accord with this new knowledge, the client will be predisposed to act.[2]

Notes

1. The language in which the memorandum was written was reasonably straightforward and non-technical, so that the failure to understand the quantitative manipulations and conceptual refinements contained in many planning reports was not a point at issue here.
2. There are problems so technical that the authority of experts will be accepted at face value. These problems are usually close to the operational level, such as the design specifications of a bridge. Mutual learning is not applicable to these cases. It is useful only where the personal knowledge of the client is an important component of any solution that may be offered.

Study questions

This extract from a chapter written in the early 1970s sets out the principal elements of a new model of planning and its practices, which I called transactive. Its purpose is to address an urgent question that I identify as a problem of communication. There appears to be a widening gulf of meaning and understanding between those who advise and those who act in the world, even though the difference between them is not always as clear as theory would have it. The central argument here is that this gulf can be narrowed and bridged through communicative practices, which I define here as dialogue.

Planning can be understood as the linkage between knowledge and action in particular settings or contexts. But there are many other ways that planning can be thought of. What are some other possible definitions? What is *your* conception of planning? And how is planning used and understood in ordinary speech? What difference does it make for practice which definition you use?

I found the knowledge/action paradigm useful for thinking about planning. It introduces two major questions. First, what is meant by knowledge? This is a question in the epistemology of planning (see Chapter 2). And second, what is meant by action? These questions lead us to an actor-centered theory of planning for desirable social change.

Discuss the two forms of knowledge introduced in this chapter: scientific/ technical or what I call here "processed" and experiential knowledge. Distinguish between these two forms and think of some examples to illustrate each.

I argue that these two forms of knowledge need to be joined or "fused" through a process of "mutual learning," and that the gaping gulf that prevents planning knowledge from being translated into action can be closed or at least narrowed in this way. Think of some example from your own experience that would seem to substantiate this theory of learning. Ask practicing planners about their experiences and what they have learned in the course of their practice, and whether they have ever experienced what I call here "mutual learning".

Central to the concept of transactive planning is the practice of dialogue. What I mean by dialogue is set out in a series of seven propositions. This of course is an ideal model that is rarely present under "real world" conditions. It is nonetheless useful to consider these seven aspects of dialogue as well as the power of the spoken word that addresses the other in their full being as a person rather than as someone who plays a distinctive social role. By talking to a senior planner in your community, ask her or him how they spend their working days and how much of their time is spent in direct, face-to-face speech with others who are not planners. You may find that most of what they actually do is, precisely, to engage others in various ways through what the German philosopher Jürgen Habermas has called speech acts, that is, attempts to reach a mutual understanding. Further, ask them whether to be effective in transactions with others, it is necessary, first, to establish a relation of mutual trust. If this hypothesis turns out to be the case, then what they engage in is here called dialogue.

Planning can accordingly be understood as a process that unfolds in "real time" and consists of a series of face-to-face transactions between planners and clients. In this way, the planner moves ever closer to the action itself. In addition, those whom I identify here as clients are enlisted in the planning process itself, becoming what I call the Epilogue to this book citizen planners.

Contemporary planning practice has moved increasingly in the direction of participatory processes, showing that the gap between knowledge and action is closing, especially in North America. The term "transactive" is no longer in common use. Instead, planning theorists today speak of communicative action, a concept developed by John Forester and others that in many respects is similar to transactive planning. Compare Forester's theoretical formulation (see below under additional readings) with the one employed in this chapter. The debate of course continues, as such debates will, but at this point we will set them aside to further explore the central concepts of transactive planning.

Selected additional readings

Planning epistemology
Sandercock, L. (1998) *Towards Cosmopolis: Planning for multicultural cities*, New York: John Wiley.

Communicative action
Forester, J. (1989) *Planning in the Face of Power*, Berkeley: University of California Press.

Participatory planning
Forester, J. (1999) *The Deliberative Practitioner: Encouraging participatory planning processes*, Cambridge, MA: MIT Press.

Collaborative planning
Innes, J.E. and Booher, D.E. (2010) Planning with Complexity: An introduction to collaborative rationality for public policy. London: Routledge.

Healey, P. (2007) *Urban Complexity and Spatial Strategies: Towards a relational planning for our times*, London: Routledge.

Actor-network theory
Latour, B. (2005) *Reassembling the Social: An introduction to actor-network theory*, Oxford: Oxford University Press.

2

The epistemology of social practice

I spent the academic year 1975/76 as a Guggenheim scholar at the Centre for Environmental Studies in London. It was there I came across Paul Feyerabend's polemical study in the philosophy of science, *Against Method,* which had just been published (Feyerabend 1975). This book gave me the idea to explore more deeply the epistemological assumptions of transactive planning (see Chapter 1). A former student of Sir Karl Popper, doyen of philosophers of science, Feyerabend argued against the monistic theories of his teacher under the provocative slogan "anything goes". There was to be no single scientific method, no single truth revealed by bona fide scientists who had meticulously sifted through experimental results, systematically eliminating all challenges to a formally stated hypothesis, but an open-ended pursuit of knowledge claims and counter-claims. Feyerabend's was a radical manifesto, creating a philosophical space for multiple knowledges, a concept which, nearly a quarter century later, Leonie Sandercock incorporated into her path-breaking book, *Towards Cosmopolis* (1998).

I took Popper's writings on science to be a defense of a scientific elite that based its privileged status on claims of exclusive access to objective and therefore trustworthy knowledge about the physical world. Although ostensibly writing about experimental physics, Popper claimed domain over the human sciences as well. It seemed to me then, as it does now, that he provided a philosophical foundation for the technocratic approach to planning that had been forcefully advocated by one of my teachers at the University of Chicago in the 1950s, Rexford G. Tugwell, who had been a prominent New Dealer under the Roosevelt administration. In *Retracking America,* I had made the case for a different sort of planning in which knowledge was to be joined to action. The question therefore became what sort of knowledge – what epistemology – would be appropriate for this task. A great deal was at stake in these debates. In transformative planning, was there only one truth or a plurality of truths? Was gaining objective knowledge possible at all? Was planning a science-based profession as many planning academics claimed? And indeed, were we still talking about "planning" at all or about something altogether different, such as "social practice," or as Aristotle might have defined it, "moral action in the public realm"? And if this was the case, who were the actors?

According to Popper, science – a pursuit he regarded as inherently enlightened and progressive – had as its aim the construction of robust theories that could then be turned into bridges, airplanes, satellites, lasers and other useful applications. Abstract theories became robust through repeated efforts to falsify them. In social practice, on the other hand, where experiments cannot be carried out under rigorously controlled conditions, one has to proceed by inserting theories into the flow of life, as Patsy Healey has so eloquently put it, and only then, on the basis of observing actual results, revise both theories and the actions based on them. Social practice is here conceived as an ongoing process of problem-solving through social learning. Popper's model of three separate worlds – the world of objective ideas, subjective experience, and physical/historical states – was a Platonic conception of a science "without a knowing subject". Transformative planning, on the other hand, came out of America's pragmatist traditions and more specifically John Dewey's many writings, in which human experience was the principal source of cognition (Healey 2009). It was Dewey who encouraged us to learn by attempting to change the world.

Bibliography

Feyerabend, P. (1975) *Against Method: An outline of an anarchistic theory of knowledge*, London: New Left Books.

Sandercock, L. (1998) *Towards Cosmopolis: Multicultural planning for cities*, New York: John Wiley.

Healey, P. (2009) 'The pragmatic tradition in planning thought', *Journal of Planning Education and Research*, 28 (3): 1–16.

The Epistemology of Social Practice

Originally published 1978

Relying upon a faith that our universe is not a chaos, but an ordered cosmos, I believe that through sincere and courageous effort man can learn what is true. I believe that inherent in what is true is that which will serve creation in its highest form, which is humanity. I believe that truth shall make man free – free from its ills of the flesh and the spirit. I rely upon an unfolding knowledge of the truth to provide a solution for the problems and conflicts that vex humanity. I therefore dedicate myself to the task of seeking the truth.

(Arthur H. Compton, cited in Garret *et al* 1966)

Knowledge … is not a series of self-consistent theories that converges towards an ideal view; it is not a gradual approach to truth. It is rather an ever-increasing ocean of mutually incompatible (and perhaps incommensurable) alternatives, each single theory, each fairy tale, each myth that is part of the collection forcing the others into greater articulation and all of them contributing, via this process of competition, to the development of consciousness. Nothing is ever settled, no view can ever be omitted from a comprehensive account.

(Paul K. Feyerabend 1975: 30)

If you want knowledge, you must take part in the practice of changing reality.

(Mao Tse-Tung 1966: 8)

The legitimizing claims of technocracy, or rule by know-how, rest on two arguments: practical success and epistemology. The first is nearly always convincing. We trust the successful eye surgeon to operate, and we allow the experienced pilot to fly us from one airport to another. But if things go wrong, as they generally will in social construction, technocracy falls back on a second line of defense that is more elaborate, more subtle, and is designed by philosophical specialists. Its gist is this: ultimate reality is singular and integral, and its varied manifestations are capable of being known objectively. It follows that assertions can be made about the world that are objectively true or at least reveal a truth that is continuously unfolding. But the ability to make such assertions differs among people according to their training and vocation. Those whose mastery of the techniques for acquiring objective knowledge is superior, or who have superior access to such knowledge, are also justified in making decisions and committing resources for those whose knowledge is restricted and inferior. To validate this conclusion requires only an agreement that it is always better to act on a basis of "true" knowledge than from ignorance or error.

My immediate intention is to criticize this position and to propose an alternative epistemology for use in social construction. But in the longer view, my aim is to subvert technocracy and to reveal its third and last line of defense. With its pretensions to scientific authority stripped away, technocracy will show its ultimate obscenity: each PhD is backed up by a gun.

Karl Popper is the leading exponent of the view that the only reliable knowledge about the world – reliable, because it has systematically sifted through error – is objective knowledge. And knowledge is objective, according to Popper, when it exists independently of an observer, when it is "knowledge without a knowing subject" (Popper 1972). To remove all taints of subjectivity, Popper equates objective knowledge with the logical contents of the propositions that comprise a theory. Logic stands presumably outside human volition; it is, as it were, part of our genetic code (Popper 1972: 73). Propositions, of course, may have an empirical referent as well, but it is primarily their logical contents which make formal propositions capable of relentless, critical examination. Those propositions that have successfully withstood examination constitute the currently best available knowledge and may therefore be regarded as the most reliable guides to action. But theories that have been found in error must be ruthlessly discarded (Feyerabend 1975: 172).[1] And so it happens that whereas the theories that have not yet been falsified are merely *posits*, the only thing we know for sure is theories that have been proven wrong (Reichenbach 1951: 240).[2]

To arrive at this conclusion, Popper (1972) posits the existence (in the ontological sense) of three "worlds": the world of physical states or historical events (W I); the world of subjective experience (W II); and the world of objective ideas, consisting of theories, logical relations, and problem situations "in themselves" (W III). The relationship between Worlds I and III is mediated by W II. This is especially true when objective knowledge from W III is to be used as a basis for intervention in W I. It is the technocrat residing in W II who must transpose the abstract propositions of W III into the practical reason of W I (Figure 2.1). However, and this is central to Popper's doctrine, W III as such, existing for itself alone, *does not require the mediation of W II*. Even though it is a world of sentences, models, and equations, and therefore made by man, its constructs exist *independently of any knowing subject*. If all the scientists now living were to die, W III would still remain, a cipher wrapped in silent mysteries.

Having thus divided the world, Popper proceeds to outline a paradigm of scientific method for its study. He calls it the method of *conjecture and refutation* (Figure 2.2).

In this formulation, P stands for problem, TT for tentative theory, and EE for the crucial moment of error elimination. The initial problem (P1) is given, *but all subsequent problems arise entirely within W III*; they are discovered there,

Relate to subject–object dualism

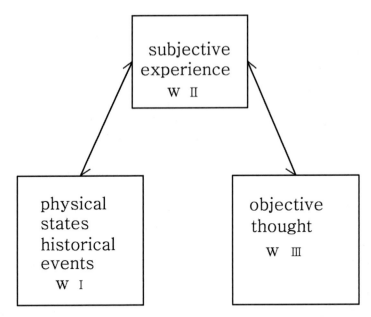

Figure 2.1: Relations among Popper's three worlds

$$P_1 \longrightarrow TT \longrightarrow EE \longrightarrow P_2 \longrightarrow \cdots P_n$$

Figure 2.2: Popper's paradigm of the scientific method

i.e. they are objectively present. If we regard this model, as Popper wishes us to do, as a virtually infinite series of steps $(P2 - \ldots P_n)$, *the entire process of obtaining knowledge will be seen to occur in W III*. Except for occasional forays into the world of material phenomena for the collection of data, it needs no external referent at all. "The activity of understanding consists essentially in operating with third-world objects" (Popper 1972: 164).

At the same time, error elimination would seem to presume the existence of an objective world "out there" that allows one to assert that a given "tentative theory" corresponds *more closely* to the truth than any other known theory. In a famous formulation, Popper summarizes this view as follows:

> IDEAS ... that is ... STATEMENTS OR PROPOSITIONS OR THEORIES ... may be formulated in ... ASSERTIONS ... which may be TRUE ... and their TRUTH ... may be reduced, by way of DERIVATIONS ... to that of ... PRIMITIVE PROPOSITIONS. The attempt to establish (rather than reduce) by these means their TRUTH leads to an infinite regress. (Ibid: 124)

To follow Popper's precept (i.e. to reduce ideas to ever more primitive propositions), tentative theories must be formulated in ways that will permit their testing for error; *they must be rendered vulnerable to criticism*. This criterion automatically excludes all potential statements about the world that cannot be so formulated. To put it more dramatically, *it excludes most sentences that can be thought*[3] (Popper 1976).

Making tentative theories "vulnerable" means they must be stated in operational and measurable form. This requirement does not merely reduce assertions to "primitive propositions" but radically simplifies the world through a process of abstraction. Events must be factored into a small and finite number of critical variables whose behavior may be studied, one by one, based on the assumption that all other variables are maintained at constant values. The moment this assumption is relaxed, and the model approximates once more the real world, nothing of scientific significance may be derived from it. It is in this sense that Popper's tentative theories may be regarded as poor in information. Their virtue resides in the universal meanings which may be abstracted from the complex of particular situations.[4]

This conclusion leads to yet another: once a tentative theory has been purified through the rigorous elimination of error, it may be inserted as a posit – a sort of building block – into the vast and growing edifice of knowledge. But these posits are merely the best that are available; they are statements that have not yet been falsified. In the end, when they, too, are proved to be in error, they must be wrenched from their position in the structure of knowledge and discarded. And if the structure should collapse, so be it! Another will be put up in its place (Kuhn 1971).

From the standpoint of social construction, objective knowledge has a number of other characteristics that are significant.

1. It is invariably about observations of phenomena that occurred in the past. This is of little consequence in the physical (experimental) sciences where the environment for observation is rigorously controlled. But it matters greatly in the human sciences where history – the varied succession of events – is of the essence.[5] Given an historically specific context for action that can be understood only with categories taken from the world of subjective experience (individual and social biography), World III-type knowledge elaborated from data collected in the past may or may not be suitable as a guide to action. In advance of the action itself, we simply do not know which it will be.

2. It is universally valid, a-historical knowledge. The truth value of any proposition is, of course, conditioned by the particular circumstances surrounding the determination of the data points on which the proposition rests. By controlling for these circumstances either experimentally or, as in neo-classical economics, by formal modeling ("homo oeconomicus"), the proposition stakes out a claim to validity that is independent of both time and place. It is the tentative truth *abstracted* from historical experience.

3. *It is expressed in language that is codified, abstract, and often mathematical.* Tentative theories do not exist outside this special language; they are expressed in it and must assume its form. Two consequences flow from this condition. First, in order to gain access to objective knowledge, the special language in which it is expressed has to be learned. Acquiring this language requires many years of arduous training, with the result that access to objective knowledge comes to be restricted to a scientific-technocratic elite.[6] Second, once a person has been trained in a W III language, it is easy and, indeed, seductive to read its abstract formulations as though they were the sensuous objects of W I they merely symbolize. Language determines how we perceive the world. One of the most common errors in the human sciences is consequently to confuse the map with the terrain.

4. *It is both cumulative and progressive.* It posits a finite universe that is intelligible precisely because it is closed.[7] Thus we find Popper resorting to a structural metaphor of knowledge: "We are workers," he writes, "who are adding to the growth of objective knowledge as masons work on a cathedral. Our work is fallible like all human work. We constantly make mistakes, and there are objective standards of which we may fall short – standards of truth, content, validity, and others" (Popper 1972: 121). And, at another point, he quotes approvingly from Einstein's famous letter to Nils Bohr: "You believe in the dice-playing God, and I in the perfect rule of law within a world of some objective reality which I try to catch in a wildly speculative way" (ibid: 184). From this, one may deduce that Popper's universe, like Einstein's, is one in which rational order prevails *intrinsically*. It is an order in which causal relations of the form A → B may be discovered and in which all relations obey a single principle.[8]

Having gained a critical understanding of objective knowledge, we must now press forward to consider its applicability to problems of social construction. Research in W III is ultimately justified not by the greater understanding it may yield, *but by its usefulness in controlling events in WI.*[9] How is this to be done? In Popper's view of things, how may knowledge obtained in W III be rendered useful in W I? What *organizational forms* are required so that objective, a-historical, and abstract knowledge may be employed in controlling historical events? Two such related forms may be identified:

1. The *technical division of labor* into thinkers and doers.[10] Beyond this simple division, labor may be further divided along professional lines, each profession developing an esoteric terminology, enabling it to stake out a monopoly over a restricted area of knowledge.
2. *The social division of labor*: thinkers are elevated above doers and have the power of command. Monopoly control is transformed into social power.

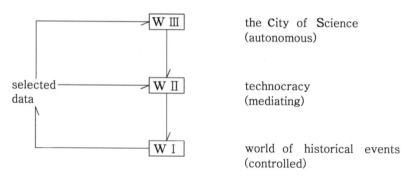

Figure 2.3: Objective knowledge and the hierarchy of power

This organizational form suggests the following arrangement of Popper's three worlds and their respective agents (Figure 2.3).

And so it comes about that the claims of objective knowledge are *totalized*, demanding the subservience of W I to the commands passed down from the technocracy that draws its license from the canons of objective knowledge. Any threatened interference by those who have not been properly initiated into their language games (Wittgenstein) is peremptorily dismissed as ignorant. Within its own sphere, science is autonomous and free, while mediating technocracy is free by reason of its association with World III. The duty of World I is to obey.[11]

It can be shown, I think, that this doctrine of objective knowledge – which, incidentally, is not explicitly Popper's but which may be derived from it – is broadly compatible with and, indeed, is reinforced by the metaphor of an *organic* social order whose evolution is directed from a central position. According to this metaphor, society is like the body of a complex animal that has a central nervous system and brain that manage the whole body disposing over the behavior of its limbs in ways that will be of collective benefit. The "purpose" of the limbs in this philosophy is to follow the instructions of the brain.

This position has been stated with particular force by Rexford G. Tugwell who, during the early New Deal, was one of Franklin Roosevelt's most trusted advisers and was subsequently Governor of Puerto Rico. In a 1948 invited address to the Michigan Academy of Arts and. Sciences, he said:

> As populations increase throughout the world and as technologies are perfected, an increased cohesion and firmness in the groupings of human beings make it more and more reasonable to think of them in organic terms. *This is not to affirm that society is an organism in the biological sense; it is to suggest, however, that useful comparisons between individuals and societies are feasible.* It is not intended here to explore these analogies and their uses; it

is merely to indicate that the rationale of planning rests on the recognition that well-outlined, distinct, and autonomous colonies of men exist and that they move in coherent ways toward defined objectives, constantly searching for redefinitions of direction and for better means of movement. That direction does exist, and that ways of reaching objectives are constantly sought, is another way of saying that planning is done; it may be done well or badly, but it is done. It is another way of saying, also, that human colonies thus far resemble biological organisms: *that specialization has taken place; and that one of the specialized organs is an agency for defining direction of movement and devising means for guidance in the defined direction. This is the Planning Agency.* (Tugwell 1948: 34; reprinted in Padilla 1975, emphasis added.)

According to Tugwell, the planner-technocrats devise the Plan, but the Plan must represent not only expert analysis and synthesis, "but something like a community judgment that the synthesis is acceptable. It must be a device which, when put into effect, will not involve such substantial dissent as will hamper its operations by non-conformance. *It is the responsibility of the collective mind, in other words, to represent the conscience, the good intention, the disinterested moral judgment, of the social organism as well as its detached and objective designation of the emerging Gestalt"*[12] (ibid: 38–9, emphasis added).

Tugwell's is the rhetoric of the corporate state in which all parts are to be harmoniously joined. It is a state ruled by experts whose decisions are intended to prevail.[13] In this respect, the corporate state is structurally no different from the state in centrally planned economies, where we find a similar emphasis on planning as a "scientific endeavor", a similar distrust of citizen involvement.[14]

In the final analysis, the doctrine of objective knowledge insists upon its own inherent superiority over the claims of every other kind of knowing. Expert knowledge may not be perfect knowledge, *but it is the best there is!* It is this unwarranted assumption which underwrites the technocratic construction of society.[15]

I suggested earlier that the totalitarian implications of this doctrine would appear to stand in contradiction to Popper's own political convictions. Popper seems able to circumvent this contradiction by remaining firmly locked into World III. His three realms, but especially Worlds I and III, are treated as virtually autonomous, and so as subject to "internal" laws which work best when they are left alone. In engineering, for example, Nature's laws (discovered in W III) are applied directly in W I, a world that is partly subject to these laws. Engineering is therefore not an act of "un-natural" interference with the workings of W I but a fruitful harnessing of Nature's laws to human purposes. Social planning, on the other hand, would clearly alter the "internal" laws of the market economy which operates "spontaneously" in W I.[16] As a result, the delicate balance established among the three Popperian worlds would be

Power *

disturbed. It is such wobbly reasoning as this which seems to underlie his own notorious preference for *laissez-faire*. But Popper's doctrine succeeds not only in masking the true relations of power in capitalist society. It also justifies and helps sustain central command planning, an outcome he did not foresee.

A critique of the doctrine of objective knowledge could, of course, rest its case here. But unmasking its ideological function would not in the least affect its epistemological claims. The following points, many of them suggested by a reading of Paul Feyerabend (1975), are intended as a prolegomenon to a more thorough-going epistemological critique. My perspective will be that of social construction, of *how knowledge comes to be linked to social action.*

1. I shall begin with a metaphysical assumption: whereas objective knowledge assumes a potentially finite (and therefore potentially knowable) world of n phenomena, I shall argue that the world is open to the future and remains forever an unfinished world (a world of $n + 1$ phenomena). Therefore, what is known with confidence at any given moment with respect to what is not yet known, stands in a relation of 1 to infinity. What we can know about the world is infinitesimally small and will always remain so.[17]

2. Only living knowledge can be used for the construction of the world. But the edifice of objective knowledge is built upon the boneyard of theories that have been falsified. What remains are theories, conjectures, and guesses that, for one reason or another, have successfully withstood such criticism in the past. These theories are not themselves secure. Scientists are morally bound to expose even their best posits to ruthlessly critical examination.[18] To use objective knowledge in any other way would be to mislead oneself and others by invoking the authority of Science to validate what is inherently incapable of being validated.[19]

3. As I have tried to show, the tentative theories of science are information-poor, even though their explanatory power may be strong. (They are information-poor in the sense that they do not help us to predict happenings in the real world with reasonable accuracy respecting the location of the specific event in a comprehensive time-space continuum.) On the other hand, what is needed for social construction are theories that are *rich* in information and, for that very reason, not falsifiable at all by the approved method of science *but falsifiable only in practice.* The closest thing to such theories are simulation models. But simulation models are not theories in Popper's sense.[20]

4. Social construction requires knowledge that is specific and concrete; but objective knowledge is general, abstract, and a-historical. It tells us about how things are (or would seem to be) if the relevant environment could be controlled. But the real world within which social construction occurs (and scientific work is carried on), is not a test tube environment. And so,

the very logic of objective knowledge and the obligation to convert this knowledge into usable propositions about the historical world (W I) must perform certain intellectual operations that bear no relation to the methodology of objective science and are therefore not controlled, not verifiable, nor even subject to public inspection.

5. The future is extremely unlikely to repeat the identical sequence of events which constitute the past. Yet it is commonly agreed, that social construction must be oriented towards the future. Objective knowledge, which is inherently about the past, is thus in large measure irrelevant as a basis for statements about possible future events. Strictly speaking, knowledge about the future cannot have an objective character. It follows that there are also no experts on the future. Whatever may be their basis, assertions about what has not occurred as yet express merely subjective hopes and expectations.[21]

6. The construction of knowledge is part of a process of social construction. Any substantial challenge of the established paradigms of science, therefore, involves political struggle and requires access to social power (Symington 1976: 194–405). Technocrats who would deny this are using an ideological argument to justify their arbitrary use of power.

7. To orient ourselves in the world, and to engage in social construction, requires comprehensive theories. But being rich in information, comprehensive theories are difficult to test. All actions, therefore, come to be embedded in a kind of myth that stands in place of validated knowledge. Because scientific endeavor is also an action, it is itself involved in more comprehensive myths in which it appears as merely a moment.[22]

If we take these objections seriously, the very idea of an "objective" knowledge evaporates.[23] What remains is an attempt by scientists to construct knowledge by their own peculiar methods (whatever they may be, for they need not at all conform to the methodological doctrine Karl Popper wishes to impose on them) *and in competition with other, non-scientific forms of knowing.* To quote Paul Feyerabend again, "The whole history of a subject is utilized in the attempt to improve its most recent and most 'advanced' stage. The separation between the history of a science, its philosophy, and the science itself dissolves into thin air, and so does the separation between science and non-science" (1975: 47–8).

With objective knowledge "dissolved into thin air," the moral claim to [& power] authority advanced by technocrats vanishes as well. We are left, then, with the question of how knowledge from whatever source is to be joined to organized action in the construction of social reality.[24]

In reply, I should like to propose an epistemological model of social practice. In line with a tradition that may be traced to Aristotle, social practice refers to

moral action in the public realm (Arendt 1958: chapter 2; Bernstein 1971).[25]
It is action that is guided by certain norms of how we ought to live with one
another, *and it is always directed toward objects beyond oneself or one's immediate
group.*

To develop an epistemology of social practice, we shall have to do away
with the Popperian division of the world into three, and return to the single
world we know, the sensuous world of human experience. Like Popper's, our
model also begins with a problem. It is a problem, however, that arises from
social relations in the real world and not "autonomously" from within World
III.

This beginning is crucial. All theories of rational action start with goals and
objectives that must be formulated in advance of the action (Parsons and Shils
1951). This is done to ensure the fitness of the means. But goals which are
formulated *without simultaneously considering the means of their realization* remain
pious dreams. Social practice, on the other hand, begins with a problem of
human (social) existence that matters to someone and engages his attention.
Two things follow from this beginning: first, social practice can arise anywhere
within a given social formation, that is to say, *it can arise at multiple locations
simultaneously*; second, social practice is directed at specific problems that arise
from the dominant system of social relations: *it is by nature a conflictive process*
(Simmie 1974).

Adopting an explicit anti-Popperian stance, I propose to abandon the
sequence of TT → EE and, with it, the whole theory of knowledge as
falsification, and substitute for it a dynamic, living theory of knowledge *that
requires us to set new facts into the world.* The process by which this is
accomplished is social practice and is, in turn, divided into four sub-processes:
social values (SV), theory of reality (TR), political strategy (PS), and social
action (SA). So construed, *social practice may also be regarded, in its complementary
aspect, as a model of social learning* (Figure 2.4).[26]

A closer look at the four crucial terms of social practice would seem to be
in order. This can be done by providing a precise definition for each.
Accordingly:

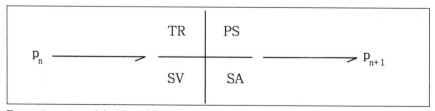

Figure 2.4: A model of Social Practice and social learning

Note: Problem P_n is the result of prior social learning; it is not objectively given.

social values are images in terms of which a given problem situation is to be transformed;

theory of reality is an image or model of the problem situation as well as an account of why it is as it appears to be and of its internal tendencies of change;

political strategy is a more or less detailed plan of action to transform the given situation in accord with social values and the appropriate image of reality;

social action involves the mobilization and use of resources guided by the strategy of action. It seeks to transmute social values into historical reality. The actor in the situation may be an individual, a small group, or an organized social movement.

In this model, cognition is linked to the world of events via social action (SA) and the results of that action. The adequacy of the theory of reality (TR) and/ or the political strategy (PS) is therefore dependent on the results of action (SA) *and the extent to which these results satisfy the given social values (SV)*. Such knowledge is useful in solving social problems, but it is *not* formally cumulative knowledge. Indeed, much of the knowledge obtained may leave no visible traces of itself; it is experiential or tacit knowledge (Polanyi 1967, see also Polanyi 1958).[27]

In social practice, the equivalent of Popper's process of error elimination (EE) is the *critical evaluation and successive revision* of components of the model as things "go wrong," i.e. as consequence are produced that fail to correspond to actors' hopes and expectations:

Table 2.1

Change	Hold Constant	Adjust
1. Political strategy	Theory of reality Social values	Social action
2. Theory of reality	Social values	Political strategy Social action
3. Social values	——	Theory of reality Political strategy Social action

These levels of change are arranged in rising order of difficulty. Because it involves a rupture with all previous experience, changing social values is also the most difficult step to accomplish.[28]

This model of social practice has a number of tangible advantages for social construction which are not found with alternate epistemologies:

1. In social practice, acting and knowing are united in a single process of learning. Because the social division of labor (and therefore also the hierarchy of power) between knower and doer disappears, social practice may be conceived as a profoundly democratic process. This characteristic is reinforced by the fact alluded to earlier, that social practice can simultaneously arise at multiple "locations" within a social system. It is, therefore, not restricted to an elite of initiates; it is not totalitarian, in principle.

2. Knowledge obtained in the course of social practice is generated from a conflictive process which, inevitably, has a political dimension. This is even true for the formation of the appropriate theories of reality (TR) because, as shown in Figure 2.5, the model of social practice can as well be applied to theory formation.[29]

3. The model overcomes the difficulties that are posed by Popper's three-part division of the world; specifically, it does away with the hermetism of science and undermines the claimed superiority of technocracy. Anyone who wishes may engage in social practice; *it is no one's monopoly* (see 1 above).

4. The dubious distinction between objective and subjective knowledge likewise disappears. Abstract (science-based) and concrete (experience-based) knowledge combine, *on equal terms*, in a single act of learning and practice.

5. Normative assertions are explicitly introduced into the learning process (instead of being smuggled in) and are thus made vulnerable to criticism.

6. The generation of new knowledge or, more properly, new learning, is always related to concrete problem situations. However, what is learned in one situation may be abstracted and put to work in another situation. It can, for instance, become the basis for constructing an appropriate theory of reality.

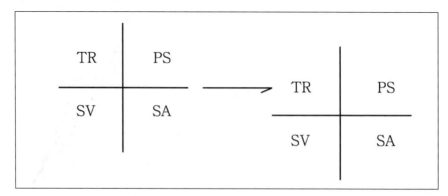

Figure 2.5: A model of theory formation

Although as an epistemology for social construction, it is clearly superior to objective knowledge, social practice is far from replacing rule by know-how. Despite wavering self-confidence and its *conspicuous lack of success*, technocracy remains as firmly entrenched as it has ever been. Much remains to be done as we try to answer the question insistently posed by Barclay Hudson (1975, 1976): What will it take to make the epistemology of social practice possible in the context of social construction? Surely, this is one of the most challenging tasks we face today.

Notes

1. "The content of a theory consists in the sum total of those basic statements which contradict it; it is the class of its potential falsifiers. Increased content means increased vulnerability, hence theories of large content are to be preferred to theories of small content. Increase of content is welcome, decrease of content is to be avoided. A theory that contradicts an accepted basic statement must be given up. *Ad hoc* hypotheses are forbidden." (Feyerabend 1975: 172).
2. "A posit is a statement which we treat as true even although we do not know whether it is so." (Reichenbach 1951: 240).
3. In this sense, it would be correct to call Popper a logical positivist. Popper objects to this label, but the difference between his own position and that espoused by logical positivists would seem to reduce to a question of style. See Popper (1976), Chapter 17.
4. For instance, Tolstoy's *War and Peace* may be true in human terms, but the logical contents of the novel cannot in any way be tested scientifically. A scientific proposition would be the following: "Among workers and businessmen, residence in a small town is associated with greater political conservatism." When measured against *War and Peace*, this "tentative theory" is poor in information content. It tells us hardly anything – for example, under what circumstances this proposition would *not* hold, or the strength of the asserted "association," or even what is meant by political conservatism. As a result, it is practically worthless.
5. According to Popper, the method of conjecture and refutation is equally applicable to the physical and human sciences. See Popper (1972: 185ff).
6. The problem of language specialization raises additional questions about the validity of W III knowledge as a guide to the territory of W I, but discussion of this point would take us too far afield. Suffice it to say that the issue concerns the question of synthesis of knowledge that is the respective property of specialists.
7. As we have seen, the falsification criterion precludes the possibility that objective knowledge of the world will ever be complete. But we can gain increasingly firm posits about the world, and the probability of "scientific revolutions" will presumably decline as we reduce tentative theories to ever more "primitive" propositions. See also note 17.
8. This conclusion suggests a monistic philosophy although Popper himself is explicit about his own "tentative" pluralist position (see ibid: 294, and Chapter 8, "A Realist View of Logic, Physics, and History"). But this is curious, because "tentative" denial of monism must be understood as a logical contradiction in the theory of objective knowledge. For if "truth" is contingent on more than a single criterion of validity, *even in the last instance*, then there can be no objective knowledge; then, indeed, as Feyerabend says, "anything goes."
9. This is clear as soon as we recall the enormous public resources that go to support scientific research, representing an investment in the future.

10. Marx and Engels considered this division of labor as a root evil of human existence. They write: "Division of labour only becomes truly such from the moment when a division of material and mental labour appears. (The first form of ideologists, *priests*, is concurrent.) From this moment onwards, consciousness *can* really flatter itself that it is something other than consciousness of existing practice, that is *really* represents something without representing something real; from now on consciousness is in a position to emancipate itself from the world and to proceed to the formation of 'pure' theory, theology, philosophy, ethics, etc." (Arthur 1970: 51–2).

11. Popperian doctrine is completely abstracted from the matrix of social relationships in production. Because my concern here is primarily with Popper, I have followed his basic schema without calling attention to its lack of social relatedness. As if science were not being done by flesh and blood scientists, within specific social institutions, and with resources made available to them through definite social channels! Because it bypasses these questions, Popper's doctrine mystifies the real relationships of power that determine social outcomes, *including those of science and technology*. Moving questions of power into the center would clearly reveal the severe restrictions which hedge in the autonomy of both.

12. By "collective mind" is meant the planning agency.

13. On strengthening the powers of central planning, see Tugwell (1939, 1940: 32–49); both papers have been reprinted in Padilla (1975). According to Jack Winkler, "corporatism is an economic system in which the state directs and controls predominately privately-owned business according to four principles: unity, order, nationalism, and success" (Centre for Environmental Studies 1976: 3). And he goes on to say: "Corporatism is a mobilization system. It operates from the belief that goals are better achieved through the purposive organisation of collective effort than through spontaneous individual responses to perceived opportunities" (*ibid*: 11). The evident danger that an "organic" view of society, resting on biological analogy, may underwrite a totalitarian state was clearly perceived by Haskins (1951: chapter 14).

14. On central (command) planning, see Wiles (1962). Although by now somewhat outdated, Wiles' probably remains the best, and certainly the most provocative, study of the subject. I cannot help but include here an elusive quotation from Prime Minister Kosygin, head of the Soviet State, delivered in a speech to the State Planning Committee on March 19, 1965: "Discussion of scientific forecasts should precede the drawing up of plans for the various branches of the economy … in order to clear the way for the advanced and progressive in good time, *to know in which direction the plan should be elaborated*" (Saifulin 1973: 338). In the same volume from which this quotation is taken, forecasts are defined as "an immanent function of any science dealing – each in its own field – with the problems of the past, the present, and the future" (p.341).The case of China is widely believed to constitute an exception to this characterization of socialist planning. More intimate knowledge of its actual operations, however, is likely to dispel these ideologically tinged beliefs. China's central planning system was modeled after the Soviets' and at least in the non-agricultural sectors, would appear to be as bureaucratic and expert-ridden as any (Lardy 1975: 94–115).

15. If, when applied to social problems, "objective knowledge" were to yield consistently satisfactory results, there would be little argument. The issue lies rather in the *ideological* character of its claimed superiority. I would argue that there are not only other ways of knowing, but that some of them may yield more satisfactory outcomes than objective knowledge.

16. It is, of course, sheer mystification to suggest that the market economy is a kind of natural order which may be harnessed to human purposes but must never be changed. It does not take a great deal of "sociological imagination" to see that the market (and its so-called laws) is an institution made by human hands.

17. Popper himself appears to hold an open world-view (e.g. Popper 1972: 266) but not one in which there exists the possibility of infinite regress, in which all theories will eventually be discarded as false. And if a residue of "true theories" or theories of "high verisimilitude" should remain (*ibid:* 143), then the world must for all practical purposes be regarded as a closed and rationally constructed universe.

18. "Rational discussion consists in the attempt to criticize, and not in the attempt to prove or to make probable. Every step that makes it more vulnerable is welcome. In addition, it is recommended to abandon ideas which have been found wanting and it is forbidden to retain them in the face of strong and successful criticism unless one can present suitable counter-arguments. Develop your ideas so that they can be criticized; attack them relentlessly; do not try to protect them, but exhibit their weak spots; eliminate them as soon as such weak spots have become manifest – these are some of the rules put forth by our critical rationalists" (Feyerabend 1975: 172).

19. Even though a posit may be the best available, the confidence it inspires – based on the degree of refinement that it has undergone through the process of error elimination – may not be very great. Yet, in the construction of the world, such knowledge, because of its objective character, tends to be used with confidence, as though it were *true* knowledge. Users of knowledge would rather not hear of "posits"; they prefer facts.

20. Anyone who has ever been involved in real-time decision-making will be able to attest to the enormous demands made for information about the world and its interpretation which far exceed the ability of scientists, technocrats, and other "experts." Those who nevertheless claim to know with certainty and know, *because of their professional expertise*, are simply lying.

21. Two quotations from Antonio Gramsci (1957) put the matter clearly. In the first, Gramsci argues that future projections, based on statistical "laws," appear to assume a completely *passive* population, i.e. a population that has submitted totally to the "laws" which govern its behavior. In the second, his argument becomes more general and straightforward. How can one know what is non-existent? Foreknowledge is mythological knowledge. *The future is to be made, not predicted!* "[T]he statistical law can only be employed in political science and practice insofar as the great mass of the population remains essentially passive – with respect to the questions which interest the historian and politician – or supposedly remains passive. On the other hand, the extension of statistical laws to the science and practice of politics can have very serious consequences insofar as one assumes them in drawing up perspectives and programmes of actions ... it can result in real catastrophes whose damage can never be cleared up. Indeed, in politics the assumption of a statistical law as an essential, fatally operating law is not only a scientific error, but becomes a practical error in action; in addition it encourages mental laziness and programmatic superficiality. It should be observed that political action aims precisely at raising the multitudes out of their passivity, that is, *at destroying the laws of the greatest numbers*; how then can this be held to be a sociological law? If you think about it, the achievement of a planned or directed economy is itself destined to shatter statistical laws in the mechanical sense ...; and although such an economy will have to be based on statistics, it does not, however, mean the same thing: the reality, human knowledge is substituted for naturalistic 'spontaneity'." (p. 95) "How could foresight be an act of knowledge? One knows what has been and what

is, not what will be, what is 'non-existent', and so unknowable by definition. Foresight is therefore only a practical act which, insofar as it is not futile or a waste of time, can have no other explanation than that stated above. The problem of the foreseeability of historical events needs to be posed correctly, so that an exhaustive criticism can be made of mechanical causation, in order to deprive it of all scientific prestige and reduce it to a mere myth which was perhaps useful in the past in a backward period of development of certain subordinate groups." (p. 101)

22.	This is not to deny that science does not yield knowledge that is useful, as indeed it does. The mythological character of science relates only to its claims to render the only "true" account of the world. Feyerabend says: "Thus science is much closer to myth than a scientific philosophy is prepared to admit. It is one of the many forms of thought that have been developed by man, and not necessarily the best. It is conspicuous, noisy, and impudent, but it is inherently superior only for those who have already decided in favor of a certain ideology, or who have accepted it without ever having examined its advantages and its limits." (1975: 295)

23.	The reference is only to Popper's use of "objective" as meaning "without a knowing subject." However, the attack on objective knowledge can be carried beyond empiricism. Louis Althusser, for example, also propounds a doctrine of objective knowledge, as when he refers to history as a process "without a subject" (1971: 90). But this extension of the struggle involves another line of argument and cannot be treated here.

24.	Several of my critics have read the foregoing paragraphs as an unwarranted attack on science. To declare the scientific enterprise as worthless is certainly not my intention. Rather, my critique is directed, as I take it that Feyerabend's is as well, at the *totalitarian claims* of science, particularly at its preposterous pretension to have cornered the market on what is true. The question of objectivity in knowledge revolves not around the indisputable fact that we are real and tangible beings to each other who are capable of action and reaction, but around the meanings that you and I have for each other in the context of situations that define our respective roles. See Laing (1969). We are accustomed to use "knowledge" and "cognition" apart from such terms as "understanding" and "interpretation." And yet, there can be no cognition without concepts and theories (i.e. without frameworks for understanding), and these conceptions are not objectively given but correspond to man-made structures that allow us to apprehend reality in ways that are, directly or indirectly, useful to the knower or his sponsor.

25.	Paul Piccone calls praxis "that creative activity which reconstitutes the past in order to forge the political tools in the present to bring about a qualitatively different future" (1976: 493).

26.	This model is further explained in several recent writings of mine, most completely in Friedmann (1976). See also, Friedmann and Abonyi (1976) and Friedmann (1978).

27.	A splendid example are the writings of Mao Tse-Tung which, for the most part, were occasional pieces – speeches, lectures – drafted in the heat of political and military struggle. Yet these same pieces, summing up the learning gleaned from revolutionary practice, have instructed the entire Chinese people for more than two decades!

28.	This rupture is akin to T.S. Kuhn's famous "paradigm shift" (1962) and Althusser's "epistemological break" (1969).

29.	By applying the model to the generation of an adequate theory of reality, it is at once apparent that science is not a de-politicized process for the discovery of "objective" facts. The expertise of technocrats rests in part on a presumptively superior ability to formulate a correct theory of reality. But if this theory is itself made subject to the process of social practice, involving values, strategies, and action, no less than *antecedent* theories of reality, the expertise is claimed on false pretenses. There is no objective process for ascertaining objective knowledge because, in the end, *objective knowledge does not exist.* See also Symington (1976) and Diamond (1976).

Bibliography

Althusser, L. (1969) *For Marx,* trans. B. Brewster, New York: Panthedn.

——(1971) *Lenin and Philosophy and Other Essays,* trans. B. Brewster, London: New Left Books.

Arendt, H. (1958) *The Human Condition,* Chicago: University of Chicago Press.

Arthur, C. J. (ed.) (1970) *The German Ideology,* New York: International Publishers.

Bernstein, R.J. (1971) *Praxis and Action: Contemporary philosophies of human activity,* Philadelphia: University of Pennsylvania Press.

Diamond, N. (1976) 'Generating rebellions in science', *Theory and Society,* 3 (4): 583–99.

Feyerabend, P. (1975) *Against Method: An outline of an anarchistic theory of knowledge,* London: New Left Books.

Friedmann, J. (1976) 'The good society: a primer of its social practice', School of Architecture and Urban Planning, UCLA, Los Angeles.

——(1978) 'Innovation, flexible response, and social learning: a problem in the theory of meta-planning', in R.W. Burchell and G. Sternlieb (eds) *Planning Theory in the 1980s: A search for future directions,* New Brunswick, NJ: Transaction Books.

Friedmann, J, and G. Abonyi (1976) 'Social learning: a problem in the theory of meta-planning', *Planning and Environment* A, 8: 927–40.

Garret, A.B., Richardson, J.S. and Montague, E.J. (1966) *Chemistry: A first course in modern chemistry,* rev. edn, Boston: Ginn and Co.

Gramsci, A. (1957) *The Modern Prince and Other Writings,* New York: International Publishers.

Haskins, C.P. (1951) *Of Societies and Men,* New York: Norton.

Hudson, B.M. (1975) 'Social learning through self-help development: activist education in America and China', School of Architecture and Urban Planning, UCLA, Los Angeles

——(1976) 'University outreach to poor majorities', School of Architecture and Urban Planning, UCLA, Los Angeles.

Kuhn, T.S. (1962) *The Structure of Scientific Revolution,* Chicago: University of Chicago Press.

——(1971) *The Structure of Scientific Revolutions,* 2nd edn, Chicago: University of Chicago Press.

Laing, R.D. (1969) *Self and Others,* 2nd edn, London: Tavistock Publications.

Lardy, N.R. (1975) 'Economic planning in the People's Republic of China: central-provincial fiscal relations', in *China: A reassessment of the economy. A compendium of papers,* Joint Economic Committee, Congress of the United States, Washington DC.

Mao, T.-T. (1966) *Four Essays on Philosophy,* Peking: Foreign Language Press.

Padilla, S.M. (ed.) (1975) *Tugwell's Thoughts on Planning,* Puerto Rico: University of Puerto Rico Press.

Parsons, T. and Shils, E. (eds) (1951) *Toward a General Theory of Action,* Cambridge, Mass.: Harvard University Press.

Piccone, P. (1976) 'Gramsci's Marxism: beyond Lenin and Togliatti', *Theory and Society,* 3 (4): 485–512.

Polanyi, M. (1958) *Personal Knowledge: Towards a post-critical philosophy*, Chicago: University of Chicago Press.

——(1967) *The Tacit Dimension*, Garden City, NY: Doubleday.

Popper, K.R. (1972) *Objective Knowledge: An evolutionary approach*, Oxford: Clarendon Press.

– (1976) *Unended Quest: An intellectual autobiography*, London: Fontana.

Reichenbach, H. (1951) *The Rise of Scientific Philosophy*, Berkeley; Los Angeles: University of California Press.

Saifulin, M. (ed.) (1973) *The Future of Society; A critique of modern bourgeois philosophical and socio-political conceptions*, Moscow: Progress Publishers.

Simmie, J.M. (1974) *Citizens in Conflict: the sociology of town planning*, London: Hutchinson.

Symington, J.W. (1976) 'Science in a political context: one view by a politician', *Science*, 194: 194–205.

Tugwell, R.G. (1939) 'The fourth power', *Planning and Civic Comment* Part II (April–June), pp. 1–31.

——(1940) 'Implementing the general interest', *Public Administration Review*, 1(1): 32–49.

——(1948) 'The study of planning as a scientific endeavor', *Fiftieth Annual Report of the Michigan Academy of Science, Art, and Letters*, pp. 34–48.

Wiles, P.J.D. (1962) *The Political Economy of Communism*, Cambridge, MA: Harvard University Press.

Winkler, J. (1976) 'The type of planned economy that Britain is moving towards', discussion paper No. 2, Seminar Series on Major Social and Economic Problems of the United Kingdom in the Light of East European Experience, Centre for Environmental Studies, London.

Study questions

In the knowledge/action paradigm of planning, knowledge (or epistemology) is the central issue. The question is, what sort of knowledge has a legitimate role in planning, when planning is conceived of as an actor-centered process? Traditionally, the knowledge claims of planners have been, and in many places continue to be, scientific and technical, thus marginalizing other forms of knowing. This chapter is an attempt to discredit these claims, which are used primarily to shore up planners' authority, and to replace them with an epistemology of social (mutual) learning. In this chapter I have avoided the term "planning", using the phrase "social practice" instead. My strategy in this chapter was to deconstruct the argument of what constitutes objective knowledge by one of the leading philosophers of science, Sir Karl Popper. The scientific method, wrote Popper, proceeds through what he called error elimination, that is, the ruthless testing of a theory for its validity under stated conditions, thereby strengthening it. But in the world of social practice, this methodology is neither practicable nor useful. The aim of social practice is to set new facts into the world, and the knowledge in question is a hybrid of formal or "textbook" knowledge and the language of experience. Furthermore, the knowledge of science is tested in what Popper calls World III, which is the world of theory, whereas the knowledge of social practice is put into practice in his World I, which is the everyday sensual world in which we live.

Relate to Midgley

1. Compare the closed-world model of Popper with the open-ended world model of social practice.
2. The ancient Greek philosopher Heraclitus compared knowledge to a flowing river when he said that we can never step twice into the same river. The river is in continual flux, just as the flow of events is in the world we inhabit. Do you agree with Heraclitus? What are the implications for knowledge if we embrace his view?
3. In what sense are Popper's scientific theories information-poor? In contrast, when we act in the everyday world of experience, we try to act on the basis of information-rich analyses. It is for this reason that planners increasingly rely on qualitative analyses rather than formal modeling. Please comment.
4. The four components of the heuristic model of social learning are social action, political strategy, a theory of reality, and social values. Social action is listed first because it drives social practice. Discuss the relationships among these four components.
5. An important category of knowledge is tacit knowing. You might say that this is a knowledge you have but cannot say, as when a ballet master demonstrates a particular movement because he cannot articulate it in words. What sort of things do you know that you cannot say? How do you

communicate this knowledge to someone else? And how important is what you know but cannot say both for yourself and others? If there are many things that we know but cannot say, and if these things are important to us, how can we allow for a greater role of tacit knowing in social practice?

6. The master language of science is mathematics. What is the language of social practice? If social practice is inevitably collaborative, how do we best communicate what we know so as to be clearly understood by others?

Selected additional readings

Healey, P. (2008) 'The pragmatic tradition in planning thought', *Journal of Planning Education and Research*, 28(3): 1–16.

Latour, B. (1987) *Science in Action: How to follow scientists and engineers through society*, Cambridge: Harvard University Press.

——(1999) 'Circulating reference: sampling the soil in the Amazon forest', chapter 2 in *Pandora's Box: essays on the realities of science studies*, Cambridge: Harvard University Press.

3

Preface to *The Good Society*

The latter part of the 1970s witnessed the beginnings of a shift from the post-war Fordist to the newly globalizing, neo-liberal economic order. The re-capitalization of capital was under way. A big stirring was also happening in the humanities that would soon manifest itself as the post-modernist movement in its several guises. For citizens as well as planners, new social facts stared us *v.timely* in the face that clearly called for different responses to the ones we had been taught. Returning to the verities of the past was impossible; the only way was to move forward. But how, and what would this entail? The state was shrinking – some called it a hollowing-out of the state – and corporate ideologies emphasizing market competition reigned supreme. Political leaders were elected who saw no alternative to the new corporate order, and could not be relied upon to re-establish more equitable social relations.

On reflection, positive social change was still possible, but its source would be the social movements that carried on their struggles for emancipation from various forms of oppression. The most theoretically grounded and in many ways successful movement of the time was the women's movement, which relied for its strength and purpose on small groups of women meeting in each others' homes, and by reaching ever outward, was forming networks and political coalitions that carried their many-sided struggle for gender equality into the world. I saw these local, inevitably temporary sodalities as "good societies," small in the number of its members, bonding through inter-personal relations of dialogue, non-hierarchical in structure, and oriented towards struggles in the street, the law courts, academia, and democratic elections.

The Good Society in which I explored these struggles of the powerless for a different way of being in the world was subtitled "A personal account of its struggle with the world of social planning and a dialectical inquiry into the roots of radical practice." By social planning I meant the coercive planning powers of the state, which we could also call the Reason of the state. But what was the meaning of "dialectical" in the title? Here was one of the difficulties I had in communicating what I had in mind. In my book on transactive planning (see Chapter 1), I had already adopted the classical Chinese dialectics of yin and yang, or the unity of opposites, which I saw as a superior social logic to the dialectics of historical materialism of Marx and Engels in which thesis and antithesis would clash, with the antithesis inevitably emerging victorious, raising up from the old order what was salvageable to a new and higher historical stage. A unity of opposites, on the other hand, was in a state of continuing fluctuating tension between the two terms of opposition from which there was no release, only a temporal shifting in position and power. In a Chinese perspective, the idea of inevitable historical progress was absent.

Moreover, I had decided not to use the linear form of exposition customary in academic writing, choosing instead an aphoristic style of fragmented exposition that drew heavily on humanist literary and philosophical sources rather than the researches of social scientists. There were precedents for this, from Nietzsche to Theodor Adorno and Walter Benjamin, but many readers found it strange and had difficulty assimilating the message.

A third difficulty with the text was the idea of the Good Society itself as a perennial but temporary social phenomenon in permanent struggle with the hierarchical powers of the state. The struggle, I argued, was for opening up new spaces for dialogical relations and therefore for what I called a communalist social order that could never be totalized. The conceptual leap from Good Society to social movements was not demonstrated, however, but was tacitly assumed, and it remained unclear just how the world would change in the preferred direction. With the Quakers, I spoke about the moral powers of dialogue as an instrument of social change, but few readers were convinced. If the Good Society was of necessity small – I argued for a practical norm of from 5 to 12 members – how could it accomplish large-scale, fundamental change? My answer was via the "four-fold path" of social learning at the intersection of knowledge/action and dialogue/dialectics, but this sounded mystical and was unconvincing. I nevertheless consider the years I spent working on the Good Society as an important step in the evolution of my thinking. The operative ideas from this period reappear, now in the more familiar language of the human sciences, as "The mediations of radical planning" (see Chapter 4).

From *The Good Society*

Originally published 1979

The Good Society is a perennial concern. How ought we to build a life in common with each other? In the western world, Plato was the first philosopher to raise this question. The answer he devised in *The Republic*, often labeled a *utopia*, might be more accurately called a normative theory. Not an idle invention comprised of dreams, desires, and vague intentions, it is instead a work of fierce discipline and of commitment to the transcendent possibilities of being human.

…

Normative theory: a vision of how social relations ought to be arranged, and how we should proceed to structure them.

What leads us then to ask about the Good Society?
Our being open to the world, what Arnold Gehlen called *welt-offen*. Our ability to represent the world to ourselves through symbols. Mediated through symbols, the future rises up in our mind as a transcendent possibility, a challenge, and a hope.

Humanistic P.O.V.

Is it constrained, this Good Society, *like* The Republic, *by an explicit theory of values? How shall we know it is a good society?*
By its being rooted in a particular conception of humanity. But to keep this argument from becoming circular, the meaning of being human must be independently conceived.

Humanity out of the void? A purely arbitrary conception?
No, but grounded in that most basic of human activities, in symbol-forming speech, the faculty we have for entering into a dialogue with one another, each one a questioner and a responder alike.

?

Then we are "dyadic" beings, incomplete except as we are linked to others in a chain of dialogic encounters?
Yes. And the Good Society is that ordering of human relations that allows us to live more fully in the life of dialogue. But such a society is small in scale and must exist within a social medium that is constructed according to a different principle, the principle of hierarchy and power.

The world of social planning and the state?
That is how it is generally known. The Good Society is arrayed in opposition to this world, asserting itself in struggle to open up new territories for itself. It is a struggle that must continue without letup; it is a permanent struggle.

The Good Society then seeks to eliminate the state?

Neither to eliminate nor to replace it. The Good Society refuses hegemonic power; it does not wish to totalize itself. In attempting to do so, it would cease to be the Good Society and would transform itself according to the principle of hierarchy which is opposed to it.

So the Good Society and social planning form a "unity of opposites" in which each part is necessary to the other, and yet, at the same time, there is a fundamental contradiction holding them in conflict and apart.

Precisely. Without necessity there is no choice, and without choice no freedom. Contradictions and the struggle they imply are lodged at the very center of the Good Society: there is no final victory.

But then, what is the object of the Good Society? Does it search for anything beyond itself? What is the nature of the struggle?

Its object is to be itself, to extend itself in dialogue, creating conditions within the world of social planning that are conducive to a life in dialogue and to becoming human. That struggle is its practice. Because it seeks the transformation of the world, it may be called a radical practice.

contradiction?

Must the Good Society then be defined by its practice? Does it only exist, so to speak, in its practice, and can it not be conceived apart from it?

It is defined but also constrained by its practice. Because it lives entirely in dialogue, it cannot exceed the limits of this dialogue even *in its struggle with the powers of planning.*

Then dialogue is a method of struggle …

No. Not a method so much as a relation within which struggle occurs. Dialogue and dialectical movement form yet another unity of opposites, a unity that cannot be divided, as each of its terms is both defined and limited by the other.

A nonviolent struggle … recognize scale as a challenge/limitation to uphold said values

For a world that is made smaller, more comprehensible, in which we can reclaim our rights as autonomous, dyadic beings, in the relations of women and men, and in the worlds of work, education, and governance. In short, a struggle for a more dialogic world.

Beyond itself, or internal to itself? Is it a place, a magical, bounded space that defines it? If I wanted to find the Good Society, where would I go?

To those who fail to be involved, it does not usually disclose itself. You will find it only in practice … now here, now there, wherever you are and whenever you are prepared to join in its work. It makes its appearance in the street, the factory, the neighborhood, the school ... These are its physical settings. But they do not define nor limit the Good Society.

Meaning the Good Society exists in time ...
In time only, and its space is the space of social relations.

And can we find it also at home, within the family? Or is the family excluded from it,
a separate realm?   How is this defined?
Strictly speaking, the family is neither excluded nor included. The bourgeois family is typically withdrawn from the world; it is explicitly a private realm. As such it cannot be the Good Society. But as a household economy, it is essential to the Good Society. We also have to eat. And the family – the household – must once again engage itself as a producing unit ... producing its own life ... not merely to consume commodities and services produced by others. But to serve the Good Society and serve it well, the family must cease to make a total claim on the women, men, and children who compose it. It must become deprivatized ....   ?

And so destroy the very essence of the family?
I mean it must extend itself into the world, it must break down the barriers between the private and the public realms, it must cease to be a place for the accumulation of possessions, for the practice of exclusiveness, for the mere reproduction of social relations. It must instead become a place for the transforming practice of dialogue among its members, each of whom is a dyadic being, free and independent, accepted as an equal and in his difference, or hers, from every other member and by each. In this way the household can be changed into the staging area of the Good Society, the rallying point of its practice, a base of support.

Are not dialogic relations the typical relations within the family as we now know it?
I don't believe so. To engage in dialogue, we must be able first to see the other person as estranged. Only then can we set him or her into a new relation to ourselves. Being human implies a capacity for estrangement. But the family, with its close intimacies, is precisely the place where this seldom occurs. The space is too tight; we need more room!

To be less exclusive, more generous in the claims that it makes and more supportive
both is a difficult task ...
Difficult, yes, but not impossible. For the first time in history we may be witness to a fundamental change: the transformation of the family into a ground for dialogic encounter. There should be no break between the household and the Good Society, we should be able to pass from one to the other, scarcely aware

of the transition. Our need for each other must first become less when the dialogue can be recovered.

…

These are some of the themes in this book. It is a book of many rooms, and only some of them have been explored. My outline of the Good Society is therefore incomplete, and the reader is invited to elaborate the sketch, or to construct another theory. To do so, three conditions must be met: a foundation in specific values must be made explicit; in the light of these values, a critical theory of reality must be devised; and a consistent set of action principles to bring about a changed reality has to be stated.

…

I like to think of the philosophical method followed here as dialectical humanism. The humanist label stems from the central role assigned to dialogue as the absolute measure to judge the fitness of actions, concepts, and institutions. The dialectical part will be found in the numerous oppositions that form the substance of the argument: the unity of dialogue and dialectics, of the Good Society and the world of social planning, of the power of the Tao and the coercive power of the state, of radical practice and social learning, of self and the other, of individual and collectivity. The social transformations from within to generate conditions for the Good Society and for the life of dialogue take place in the tensions between these contradictory moments.

…

The way we communicate thoughts forms an integral part of the thought itself. Informed by this premise, I searched for a style that would accommodate the largest number of possible meanings, dramatically expanding the spectrum of communicable thought *within a given framework*. In writing about the Good Society and its practice, therefore, I decided on a format that will strike the reader as uncommon.

The basic elements of the· argument are self-contained paragraphs. Of varying length, ranging from a single sentence to several pages, they are interspersed, at appropriate places, with poems, aphorisms, short selections from philosophical writings, and other "delights" that are intended to illustrate, contradict, confirm, and illuminate the paragraphs in their immediate vicinity, adding depth and concrete imagery to the more abstract portions of the text.

As in a musical composition the paragraphs are arranged thematically. The major movements are the parts which, in turn, are divided into sections. Here the reader will find preludia, statements of major and secondary themes, variations, repetitions, interludes, recapitulations, and codas. Key concepts, such as dialogue, are first introduced in a specific context, given a formal definition in another place, and are reserved for more elaborate, systematic treatment in yet a third. Occasionally, sentences are repeated for emphasis, either verbatim or in a slightly modified form, but always in a context that is different. In this way the reader may be led to discern new meanings or clarify an older meaning that has already become familiar.

According to custom the method of scholarly argumentation is to take a major theme and proceed to break it down into its components, each part serving to sustain the whole. The implicit idea in this procedure is to persuade the skeptical reader of the author's point of view. Thinking is conceived as being linear. Here I have used a different procedure. Beginning with the elementary paragraphs, I composed them into complex patterns of meaning that were not, except in roughest outline, preconceived. Thinking *as it actually happens* is nonlinear. Therefore I also have no interest in persuading you, the reader. Instead I should like you to think from the trampoline of each paragraph into a pattern of your own.

Study questions

The foregoing selection from the preface of *The Good Society* is written in the form of a Socratic dialogue. It is the beginning of a spiritual and moral inquiry addressed to those who, by acting in the world, endeavor to find new pathways to our collective future. Central to the notion of the good society is the practice *def.* of dialogue where relations of power and hierarchy, present in virtually all human relations, are held at bay. The project of the good society is to open up and expand the spaces for dialogue in a society that is subject to the hegemonic powers of large corporations and the state. The creation of such spaces and their defense against continuing attempts to erase them is what I mean by the perennial struggle against the powers of social planning.[1] For this reason, the good society does not seek power for itself. Rather, it is a temporary social formation which, lacking a territorial base of its own, exists exclusively in its actual practices. Its space is the space of social relations.

To see what this might look like, try going on the web and Google "Transition Towns" (http://www.transitiontowns.org/). Transition Towns is an incipient social movement that is trying to extend itself into the world to prepare for climate change, peak oil, and other prospects for our world that will require new forms of living consistent with broad principles of sustainability. Starting in the UK, it has begun to spread to small communities throughout North America. The website clearly shows the role of small groups of individuals determined to bring about these changes. The web pages of this organization do not mention the good society; there is no reason why they should. And yet the small groups, which they propose to carry the word out into the world, are precisely what I have in mind by a good society. Can you think of other examples? In replicating itself, does the Transition Town movement create new spaces in which non-hierarchical relations will continue to flourish? Could we also call them spaces of democracy or, as some have said, deliberative democracy?

In the text, I claim that the good society does not seek power for itself. This implies that it does not wish to replace the state; in this sense, it is not a utopia. Another way to say this is that the good society does not wish to totalize itself. The good society and the state therefore stand in dialectical opposition to one another, but an opposition that constitutes a "unity of opposites," or force field that is inevitably in dynamic tension. The good society prevents the powers of the state from totalizing itself while the inverse of this proposition is true as well. Think of other such opposites that we encounter in everyday life and that can be symbolized by the Chinese yin and yang diagram and its endless permutations, one of the oldest (and profoundest) of philosophical concepts.

Here is another challenge. Is the family household, commonly held to be the primordial space of social reproduction, also a dialogic space and therefore a potential nucleus of the good society? And if it is not, what would it take to transform the household so that it becomes one? Can we think of it as a miniature political community whose essence is a form of deliberative democracy?

Note

1. Today I would no longer use the term "social planning" in this context, which now stands for planning by, with and for local communities. Instead, we might want to speak of *societal planning* by the state and other large and powerful interests, which shape our bodies and our minds individually as well as collectively. Resisting this power to shape our lives is also a form of radical practice.

Selected additional readings

Aristotle (1976) *The Nicomachean Ethic*, trans. J.A.K. Thomson, Harmondsworth: Penguin.
Biehl, J. (1997) *The Murray Bookchin Reader*, London: Cassel.
Flyvbjerg, B. (2001) *Making Social Science Matter*, Cambridge: Cambridge University Press.
Freire, P. (1973) *Education for Critical Consciousness*, New York: Seabury Press.
Illich, I. (1975) *Tools for Conviviality*, London: Fontana/Collins.
Rittel, H.W.J. and Webber, M.M. (1973) 'Dilemmas in a general theory of planning', *Policy Science*, 4: 155–69.

4

The mediations of radical planning

At the beginning of the 80s, I started a research project into the genealogy of the idea of planning. Just as I had done in *Retracking*, I defined planning as the recursive linking of knowledge with action or, more simply, as science-based advice in the making of public policies, rather than as any specific application of practical reasoning, such as in city planning (Chapter 1). I traced the history of this idea back to the late 18th and early 19th century, showing how the modern idea of planning was an outgrowth of the Enlightenment, and how this idea evolved over the next two centuries across a broad spectrum of academic disciplines in both Western Europe and North America.

Initially, I had identified only three intellectual traditions of planning – social reform, policy analysis, and social learning. But this panorama of planning ideas was incomplete. Missing was the great counter-tradition to state-centric planning that had accompanied the evolution of industrial capitalism from the beginning and had emerged from within civil society, geared not towards societal guidance from a central command post but social transformation from myriad points of resistance and innovative practice. Because of its origins, I called this amalgam of ideas and social movements, inspired by visions of a more just, democratic, ecologically sustainable, and emancipated society, the social mobilization tradition of planning.

From a planning standpoint, I decided to treat this "left wing" of the political spectrum – utopians, Marxists, anarchists, syndicalists, and homegrown American radicals – as a single intellectual tradition despite the many ideological differences that divided them in practice. Above and beyond their differences, I argued, they shared a critique of social oppression and a yearning for a more emancipated, egalitarian, and self-directed society.

Within this format, the final chapter of *Planning in the Public Domain*, reprinted here, can be read as a primer of radical planning for social transformation, focused on its "mediations" between transformative theory and radical practice. In this role, the planner becomes an actor herself, and the medium is dialogue or, in today's terms, communicative action (Chapter 1). The broad aim is the collective self-production of life, and the knowledge we bring to its realization, one step at a time, is obtained through mutual learning. Perhaps it is appropriate here to repeat a short excerpt from the chapter:

The theory of social transformation must never be allowed to harden into dogma and must remain open to even fundamental questioning and re-conceptualization. The organizational counterpart to this epistemological commitment is a structure of radical practice that consists of a large number of autonomous (or quasi-autonomous) centers of decision and action whose coordination remains loose and informal. Such a structure encourages a better fit with local environments, a great deal of local experimentation, a maximum of social mobilization, a self-reliant practice, and a non-dogmatic view of the problem. It is the very opposite of planning by the state … (p. 66).

This understanding of radical planning as performed largely at the political base of social movements in local communities, involving relatively small numbers of participants but with a view beyond their local sphere of action to the larger structural changes that must be accomplished on a wider scale, was the result of my work on the Good Society a decade earlier (see Chapter 3). By those unfamiliar with the earlier work, this connection was not perceived, however. In the present internet age of social mobilization, where the distinction between local and global is erased, it is simply taken for granted.

At the point where theory intersects with practice, I saw radical planners as essentially engaged in three tasks: shaping transformative theory to the requirements of an oppositional practice in specific local settings, creating opportunities for the critical appropriation of such a theory by diverse groups organized for action, and reworking this theory in ways that reflect first-hand experience gathered in the course of practice itself. I envisioned radical practice addressing bread and butter issues at the local level such as housing and jobs, while others might reach beyond localities to engage with vital questions in the larger world, such as racism, nuclear power, poverty, globalization, the ecological crisis, and war. Fundamentally, the practice of radical planning is dedicated to changing existing relations of power, whether exercised by the state or global corporations.

I saw action groups emerging spontaneously from within civil society in their concern, protest, and resistance to power. This understanding of radical practice led me to identify several processes I believed to be necessary for good practice, among them social learning (see Chapter 2), self-empowerment (see Chapter 5), networking and coalition-building, strategic action, and face-to-face dialogue (see Chapter 1). A final requirement for good practice was learning to live with contradictions and thus always to hold in tension two opposing concepts without dismissing either: theory and practice, empirical analysis and normative vision, critique and affirmation, explanation and action, and future vision and present realities. As in life generally, there is no escape from honoring both. In *Retracking America*, I had called this unity of opposites "the Tao of planning."

From *Planning in the Public Domain*

Originally published in 1987

Radical practice [in planning] must be informed and guided by appropriate theory. It must be "saturated" with theory. Without a theory of structural transformation, radical practice has no staying power: it becomes visceral, opportunistic, and reactive. When faced with an intransigent resistance that knows very well what it has to defend and has "theory" to spare, short-term tactics are headed for failure.

What do we mean by a *transformative* theory (as I shall henceforth call it)? It is a set of complexly related statements about the world that:

1. Focuses on the structural problems of capitalist society viewed in a global context – problems such as racism, patriarchy, class domination, resource degradation, impoverishment, exploitation, and alienation;
2. Provides a critical interpretation of existing reality, emphasizing those relations that, from period to period, reproduce the dark underside of the system;
3. Charts, in a historical, forward-looking perspective, the probable future course of the problem, assuming the absence of countervailing, transformative struggles;
4. Elaborates images of a preferred outcome based on an emancipatory practice; and
5. Suggests the choice of a "best" strategy for overcoming the resistance of the established powers in the realization of desired outcomes.

Such a theory cannot be arbitrarily invented. It must grow out from and be informed by long periods of sustained oppositional practice. Based on experience, it combines an amalgam of analysis, social vision, and hard strategic thinking with the intent to shape ongoing political practice, even as it continuously absorbs new learning.[1]

The starting point is always a concrete problem. A recent example is the work on deindustrialization and plant closings. This has become a major political issue in the older industrialized regions of the world, from Britain (Massey and Meegan 1982), to the United States (Bluestone and Harrison 1982), to Australia (Sandercock and Melser 1985). The problem has been laid at the door of "capital restructuring," which is seen as a response to declining rates of profit in key industrial sectors, growing international competition, and advances in production technology that have hastened the obsolescence of industrial processes which until only a short while ago were thought to be state of the art.

No less well-documented is the political practice that has focused on this question (Metzgar 1980; Luria and Russell 1981; Haas 1985; Morales and Wolff 1985). There were struggles at specific sites, such as Youngstown, Ohio, where workers had hoped to buy up the steel plant that was threatening to shut down and finally did; militant video documentaries carried the basic message to large numbers of people who had previously been unaware of what was happening around them; church-related groups worked shoulder to shoulder with labor unions and local communities to save the plants, devise alternatives, and even protect entire neighborhoods, such as Poletown in Detroit, from being razed to the ground to make way for a "restructured" industry while thousands of working-class homes were being sacrificed to the bulldozer.

These and other forms of radical practice did not accomplish their immediate purpose, which was, first, to prevent the calamity from happening; second, to devise alternatives that would provide jobs and income for the displaced working population; and third, to pass legislation that would prevent or at least mitigate similar occurrences in the future. The tactical failure of these struggles does not mean that the effort was wasted. Resistance is never wasted. The "fight back" struggle against plant closings raised people's consciousness; built a sense of human solidarity in the teeth of corporate profits; tested certain proposed solutions (such as worker buy-outs); and built new, collaborative networks within civil society, such as the links that were made spontaneously between major churches, organized labor (especially at the local level), and university-based groups of radical students and faculty. The time may not be ripe for such a coalition to score political victories in the United States; in Latin America, they have been the only significant source of resistance to the rapacious military regimes of Argentina, Brazil, Uruguay, and Chile and, in the first three of these countries, were instrumental in overturning existing dictatorships. *Q: How it is/was practiced, or how it should be?*

The necessary unity of theory and practice is one of the deep insights of the social mobilization tradition of planning. But dialectical unity is not the same as an identity, and transformative theory has its own distinctive character:

1. Expressed in language capable of reaching ordinary people.
2. Consistent in the relation of its several parts to each other.
3. Comprehensive with respect to the main variables relevant for system-wide transformation.
4. Formulated in ways that allow for the ready adaptation of general theory to unique, specific settings.

A theory having these characteristics must not be allowed to harden into doctrine. Because its usefulness is ultimately determined in practice, critical reflection on practice forms the basis of its continued renewal (Ulrich 1983).

These criteria for an appropriate theory of social transformation also provide us with a clue for identifying the central task of radical planning, which is the *mediation of theory and practice in social transformation*.

On mediation

The meaning of mediation with respect to radical planning is not immediately apparent. As a start, it is easier, perhaps, to say what, in the present context, mediation is not.

In mediating theory and practice, radical planners are not neutral agents arbitrating between two disputing parties. Neither do they present themselves as experts on theory and, therefore, on the political guidance of radical practice. Nor must they become absorbed into the everyday struggles of radical practice. In short, as mediators, they can stand neither apart from, nor above, nor within such a practice.

Instead, mediation suggests a role for radical planners that is Janus-faced: to shape transformative theory to the requirements of an oppositional practice in specific local settings, to create opportunities for the critical appropriation of transformative theory by groups organized for action, and to rework this theory in ways that will reflect firsthand experience gathered in the course of radical practice itself. In terms of social space, radical planners occupy a position tangential to radical practice at precisely the point where practice intersects theory.

The practice to which their work relates is focused on the familiar problems of people's livelihood – jobs, housing, and self-provisioning. It may be concerned with organizing alternative services for specific sectors of the population, such as children, adolescents, old people, shut-ins, immigrants, and the physically and mentally disabled, for whose needs neither the state nor the corporate economy makes adequate provision. It may also work to protect or restore the built environment – the places people call home – and shield it from the voracious mania that seeks only the highest return on investments. Or it may address more general issues such as war and peace, nuclear power, and the preservation of the natural environment for future generations. In one form or another, these are all emancipatory practices that seek to create a space for the collective self-production of life that lies beyond bureaucracy, the profit motive, or the national obsession with military overkill, unlimited growth, corporate gigantism, and the communist menace.[2]

Given the complex nature of transformative theory – its structural character, its critical reading of existing reality and the near future, its imaging of what is desired, and its broad considerations of strategy – with its double burden of responsibility toward practice and theory, the mediations of radical planning are not easily accomplished. And yet, for all of its apparent weightiness, the planner's role in radical practice is severely restricted. For in social transformation, theory and practice become everyone's concern; responsibilities for both are multiple and overlapping. Terms such as *mediation, mediator,* and *role* suggest a technical division of labor. But in radical practice, the set of mediating role is not clearly defined and, in the language of mathematics, remains a "fuzzy" set.

Before we proceed to a more detailed illustration of the principal mediations of radical planning, it is necessary to consider what sorts of knowledge planners bring to their assignment.   *"Radical planner" still as outsider inserting himself into social mvmts.*

On thinking and knowing

The tasks of mediation call for the skills of analysis, synthesis, communication, and managing group processes. Yet mediation is more than a craft.[3] In addition to possessing skills which, when found in combination, are exceedingly rare, radical planners must be able to draw on substantive knowledge. No less than other planners, they must command a ready fund of data, information, and theoretical insight pertaining to a given problem such as the environment, housing, or community economic development. Some of this knowledge will have been acquired from systematic reading, some from personal experience and observation. But all of it remains passive knowledge until the moment it is used in the process of thinking.

Most thinking is discursive and involves what Jürgen Habermas calls "communicative acts," which is everyday speech in the context of action.[4] It is only when we proceed to talk or write about a given problem that knowledge is actualized. In talking and writing, we address an audience, sometimes visible and sometimes not, from whom, sooner or later, we expect a response that will either refute or validate what we say, or else expand on it, refine it, and ultimately redirect the conversation to produce a new perception of the problem and new modes of practice.

This conversation, intermingled with practice based on theory and close observation of the results, is continuous and does not come to a halt even with a shift in problem focus. As both the oral and written records of this conversation accumulate, a "body of knowledge" is produced which aspiring planners acquire in the course of their studies. But sometimes this record of past conversations is thin, and major disputes remain unresolved. As Jerome Ravetz points out, this situation is common of emerging technical fields in which established facts are few, the problems addressed are urgent, and passions run high (Ravetz 1971: ch.14). He warns us that there are dangers inherent in the use of such knowledge, particularly in its premature application and the unwarranted expectations it arouses. But on reflection, it would seem wiser to bring even fragile and disputed knowledge to bear on practice (in full awareness of its limitations), and thus to enlarge and deepen the record, than to refrain from speaking out.

It is through communicative acts that knowledge for radical practice comes to be provisionally established. I say provisionally because the knowledge used in planning is inherently ephemeral, and nowhere more so than in the process of social transformation. Therefore, it is preferable to substitute the more dynamic concept of social learning, which is the way we critically appropriate experience for action, for the more solid "knowledge" that suggests a fixed stock of accumulated learning.

This switch to an epistemology of social learning is also indicated, because knowledge in radical planning appears as something distinct from what it is in the sciences, especially the natural sciences. Ravetz speaks of scientific knowledge as "objective and impersonal" (compare note 4, above). But in radical planning, the relevant knowledge, embedded as it is in a transformative theory, is always and necessarily contextual: it points to action, considers strategy, endeavors to reach a critical understanding of the present and near future, and is informed by specific social values. This contextualizing of knowledge is a profoundly social process in which those who stand in the front line of action – households, local communities, social movements – make a decisive contribution. It is these users of knowledge-in-practice who are the final arbiters of knowledge-in-theory. It is they who must critically appropriate theory and adapt it to their needs. [It is activists engaged in daily social struggle who must take part in dialogue with planners and so become immersed in mediated processes of social learning.] *why must they?*

The provisional nature of knowledge in planning tells us that the theory of social transformation must never be allowed to harden into dogma but must remain open to even fundamental questioning and reconceptualization. The organizational counterpart to this epistemological commitment is a structure for radical practice that consists of a large number of autonomous (or quasi-autonomous) centers of decision and action whose coordination remains loose and informal. Such a structure encourages a better fit with local environments, a great deal of local experimentation, a maximum of social mobilization, a self-reliant practice, and a non-dogmatic view of the problem. It is the very opposite of planning by the state, with its single-track vision, its remoteness from people's everyday concerns, its tendency to gloss over differences in local conditions, and its hierarchical ladders. The essential openness of transformative planning not only imposes on planners certain responsibilities in mediation, not the least of which is careful listening (Forester 1980), but also obliges them to give serious attention to polemical critiques from the front lines of practice, which in this way become integrated with the process of theory formation.[5]

if it's so removed from the state, why do activists need planners?

What radical planners do

We are now ready to return to more practical matters. I have argued that the central role of radical planning consists in mediating transformative theory with radical practice, and that in so doing, planners must draw on the tradition of social learning. Mediation was seen to involve specific skills used to confront formal knowledge with knowledge drawn from struggle and experience. As a result, the distribution of roles in radical planning is not clearly defined.

I should now like to illustrate the meaning of this "mediation" by giving some examples that will show how radical planning may contribute to the emergence of a more self-reliant, politically active community. The following discussion will be organized according to the vocabulary used by those who are engaged in struggle for the recovery of such a community.

Before proceeding, however, I should like to reiterate a point that has been made repeatedly and that we must continue to keep in view. The relevant actors in this struggle for a new society are individual households that have opted for the alternative; organized social groups based in the local community; and larger, more inclusive movements, not bounded by territorial limits. Even transformative social movements, however, whose contact networks may circle the entire globe, have their true strength in the practice of local action groups – the base, as they are sometimes called – where ordinary people are directly involved in struggles close to their everyday lives. Although these struggles must eventually be carried beyond the confines of local communities into the world, the strength and vitality of the movement as a whole are drawn from its myriad struggles at the base. Given this context, what are the concrete tasks facing the radical planner?

Selective de-linking, collective self-empowerment, and self-reliance

These three terms are complementary facets of a single strategy. If you de-link and do nothing else, the gesture remains meaningless. It is equally meaningless to talk about self-reliant development without, at the same time, considering the need for collective self-empowerment, by which I mean a continuing and permanent struggle for the equalization of access to the bases of social power. The relative access of a single-household economy may be visualized as shown in Figure 4.1.

In practical terms and for the household shown in the center of the diagram, self-empowerment means a decision to invest its resources of *time*, *energy*, and *skill* along one or more of the axes shown in the diagram, for instance, to secure more space, or a more adequately serviced space, under the cooperative control of households. In this instance, space that would facilitate the functioning of the household economy translates into land and housing, and the effort would

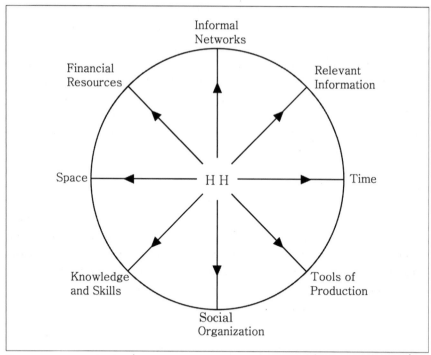

Figure 4.1: Household access to the bases of social power ≃ self-empowerment

involve advancing along *all* of the axes of self-empowerment (Hartman *et al* 1981).

As this example suggests, getting more adequate housing involves, for poor people at least, a collaborative effort.[6] Attempted self-empowerment by households, acting on their own behalf, would lead to suboptimal results for all. Indeed the bases of social power displayed in Figure 4.1 presume the existence of other households with whom one links up in a bootstrapping operation. This is plainly evident in terms such as "social organization" and "informal networks"; it is least obvious in the case of "space" and "time." But even here, the terms imply what, in the language of game theorists, is called a positive-sum game. Space must be shared with others, and rescheduling one's own activities involves their priorities as well, all of which must be harmonized.

From our discussion of the process of collective self-empowerment as a whole, the following conclusions may be drawn:

1. Self-empowerment is a mediated process.
2. It necessarily takes place around points of struggle, such as housing.
3. Its effects are synergistic, so that, by linking up with other households in struggle, more power is generated for the full realization of the objective than would be the case if each household had to "go it alone."

Radical planners mediate theory and practice at each of the relevant bases of social power. Through workshops and other means, they impart relevant knowledge and skills in collective housing struggles; they assist households in organizing themselves as a cooperative or tenant union; they assist them as well with the establishment of community orchards and gardens, workshops for the self-production of home furnishings, or community-operated nurseries, kitchens, and laundries; they help to channel appropriate information, such as impending legislative struggles, to the emerging political community; they help to network local housing struggles to related efforts elsewhere; they offer their grantsmanship skills to obtain outside funding; and they assist households in better organizing their available time for tasks that need attention (for example, through computerized skill banks).

Throughout this effort, radical planners must work to expand people's *horizon of possibilities* by relating pertinent experiences from other parts of the world and discovering ways to broaden collective efforts once the basic objectives of the group have been achieved. In this way, the momentum of radical practice is maintained, as social space is progressively liberated from control by the state and corporate capital.

Thinking without frontiers

Radical practice, we insisted, must be guided by appropriate theory, but theory itself must come from practice. Divorced from practice, it ceases to be meaningful. The mediations involved here are accomplished through communicative acts in which takes place an exchange of ideas about the proper direction of practice and its wider meaning. In this exchange, radical planners, whose job is partly to shape theory to the requirements of practice, can play a major role.

The kind of thinking involved in this mediation must not acquiesce in artificial boundaries that might constrain the free flow of ideas. What are these boundaries? Four boundaries are frequently encountered:

1. Hierarchy: Social rank, such as university degrees or institutional affiliations, may be used to draw a boundary between "valid" and "invalid" knowledge: only high social rank (it is claimed) possesses "valid" knowledge.
2. Academic disciplines: Knowledge is bounded by self-governing academic disciplines that claim to be the keepers of the most reliable knowledge in their respective subject areas.
3. Parochialism: What is accepted as true in one set of circumstances is held to be universally true: the local sets the boundaries of "valid" knowledge.
4. Theory/Practice: Formal knowledge embodied in theoretical statements is bounded from practice and is declared to be superior to practice, that is,

more perfect than the "real" world. Conversely, informal knowledge drawn from practice is bounded from theory and is declared to be superior to theory.

These and other constraints on thinking can be transcended in dialogue. One of the obligations of radical planners is to ensure that thinking about transformative practice breaks through the traditional boundaries of hierarchy, academic discipline, parochial viewpoint, and the theory/practice dichotomy, as they weave together a single cloth of theory *and* practice that is continuously tested for its fitness and durability in use.

Meaning, purpose, practical vision (recovery of wholeness)

As passive consumers, our lives are badly fragmented. We lack a reliable criterion that would enable us to pull together the many fragments of our daily experience into a coherent whole. The more fragmented experience appears to us, the less it holds the promise of meaning, the more alienated we become. Yet human life is based on the assumption that meaning is possible, that life can make sense even under adverse conditions, that striving for particular goals and objectives is more than an exercise in self-deception. People do, indeed, seek meaning, though too often they seek it in otherworldly contexts that merely reinforce their inclination to quiescence.

It is different for those who, for whatever reason, have decided to shed their passive and compliant attitudes and to become actors on the stage of historical events. For when you set out purposes and try to achieve them, you suddenly discover a firm criterion that helps you to interpret the world: the definition of a problem, the search for an appropriate strategy, and a clear grasp of the values to be realized in practice. Action simplifies by excising irrelevant information. At the same time, it unifies thought by bringing disparate information and experience into relation.

Applying these general considerations to the tasks of radical planning, we can say that households, community-based groups, and social movements can be helped in formulating realistic understandings for their practice in the context of the larger framework of transformative theory. This involves a series of mediations, including the need to bring potential actors to a critical understanding of their own situation and to identify correctly efficient levers for change in terms of which a realistic vision can be stated.

I hesitate to call this participatory planning, though it has a certain affinity to this well-known practice from societal guidance (Oakley and Marsden 1984). The main difference is that, in radical practice, the elaboration of a realistic vision concerns a future for which mobilized groups are themselves responsible. Their vision, then, is more than a wish list; *it is a commitment to its realization through practice.* And so the role of the planner changes as well. The traditional advocate planner mediates between the state and the people of a given community, shuttling information back and forth. Whatever people may contribute to the process of decision-making, the final word is spoken by the state. The radical planner, by contrast, must elicit from a potential actor, such as a community-based action group, a commitment to engage in a transformative practice of its own. The essential planning mediation is between theory and practice, where both, ultimately, belong to the people.

Cross-linking, networking, building coalitions

The discussion so far will have made clear my own belief that the small action group plays a decisive role in social transformation. This conviction was the major thesis of an earlier book, *The Good Society* (Friedmann 1979). What needs to be stressed in the present context is the importance of linking these groups to each other in informal networks and political coalitions. For the problem is not merely to make room for an alternative practice within the interstices of the state and corporate economy – those leftover, marginal areas where social practice is inconsequential, because it poses no threat to the basic configurations of power. At issue is the creation of an alternative social order, which necessarily involves a restructuring of basic relations of power. Social barriers that constrain a self-reliant practice at other than very local and even private levels of experience must be removed. This requires political action and a concerting of wills across a wide spectrum of alternative actions. Groups of often disparate backgrounds and experience, with different "realistic visions" of what is attainable, must be brought together for specific struggles in order to hasten the arrival of the new order.

The first and most immediate level at which coalitions can help to establish politically responsive institutions that will facilitate a self-reliant development is the metropolis. Tentative steps toward creating oppositional movements of this sort have already been taken. Examples include California's Campaign for Economic Democracy (chiefly active in Los Angeles); the Coalition Against Plant Shut-Downs (which is statewide in California but operates primarily in the metropolitan labor markets of Los Angeles and the Bay Area); Barry Commoner's Citizen Party (now active primarily at state and local levels); the National Organization of Women (again with a strong metropolitan accent); the anti-nuclear Alliance for Survival (California); and the grass-roots coalition Jobs and Justice (Los Angeles). What is characteristic of these coalitions is their largely informal character, their foundation in quasi-autonomous local action groups, and the absence of a top-heavy bureaucracy.

In their role as mediators, radical planners are in an excellent position to connect community groups with politically effective social movements.

However pragmatic they might be in some respects, coalitions no less than small action groups require the mediations of theory to be effective.

Strategic action (focusing)

Action must be focused so as not to dissipate its energies, and this means not merely having objectives in view but also possessing a sense of sequence and timing – what is usually called strategy. Strategies are necessary, because any innovative practice is bound to meet with resistance, and this resistance must be overcome.

For actors to devise a successful strategy, they must (1) be well grounded in *the relevant technical information*; (2) be aware of *the major constraints* on their choices, and what it would take to break them; (3) have a clear sense of the *political options* and of the costs and benefits attached to them; and (4), as the action itself unfolds, be *continuously informed,* as close to real time as possible, about the consequences of their actions and any changes in the objective conditions they confront.

These tasks are among the assignments for mainstream planners who apprise their clients of information that will improve the quality of their decisions. Radical planners are no different in this regard, though their role as information providers may not be formally defined. Since timing is of the essence, and since, in any event, there is no clear-cut division of labor between planning and practice, much of this gathering and evaluating of intelligence takes place informally, by word of mouth, and involves the members of the group in an ongoing dialogue. Appropriate strategies must be devised in the very eye of the storm.

Dialogue, mutual learning (transactive planning)

Radical practice is self-organized and depends for its effectiveness on interpersonal relations based on trust. It is this requirement, above all others, that determines the small size of action groups and their preferred dialogic mode of communication. In the course of transformative practice, more formal organizations, such as coalitions, may come into existence. But even they decompose into smaller groups whose members stand in a close personal relation to each other.[7]   Always? Idealistic.

The process of social learning, moreover, is premised on dialogue, which allows mutual learning between actor and planner to take place. I have called this process, which generally leads to a new synthesis of knowledge relevant for action and incorporates both experiential and formal codes, *transactive planning* (Friedmann, 1973). When the theory of transactive planning was first published in 1973, few planners knew what to make of dialogue in planning.[8]

Critics failed to appreciate how much planning actually gets done by word of mouth, and they could not conceive of a radical practice except by invoking huge Althusserian abstractions, such as a revolutionary class, in which no one has a need to talk at all.

Yet the evidence pertaining to the efficacy of small groups in which dialogue is practiced is conclusive. Writing from the feminist front, where group dynamics have been used extensively, Cook and Kirk report:

> [F]orming small groups allows women to get to know one another well; provides a basis of trust and mutual support for the action; makes decisions easier to reach; and avoids the need for leaders. It also makes it easier to absorb individuals into the action at the last minute, forming the basis for a future network and future action. (Cook and Kirk 1983: 73)

In Sweden, small-group organization has been introduced on an extensive scale into industrial production. Johnstadt concludes his evaluation of this technique with the following observation:

> In the beginning, group dynamics methods are purchased for the purpose of increasing productivity and profits; under the surface and in the long run, however, they will lead to a sharpening of political questions about the meaning of and justice in the way we live and work together. (Johnstadt 1980: 140)

In revolutionary China, the small group, or *hsao-tsu*, was made the basis for transforming and unifying the Chinese people in a largely successful attempt at mass mobilization (Whyte 1974).

Many other examples could be cited, from guerilla warfare to literacy training. In a review of the pertinent literature, Gil Court concludes that the small-group tactics of the social learning/social mobilization paradigm of planning are effective compared to other organizational strategies. "Rather than destroying the current system, it gradually questions and undermines the reality on which it is built. This may prove a far more effective strategy in the long run" (Court 1984).

If her conclusion is correct, radical planners will have to get used to the idea that their business is not primarily to write reports for their hierarchical superiors but continuously to inform their comrades during the course of the action itself. It is primarily through interpersonal transactions, grounded in dialogue, that the mediations of radical practice occur.

Transactive planning is not, of course, without problems of its own. Personalities may clash; personal trust may be unwarranted; the very nature of radical practice may lead to a cliquishness that fundamentally negates the style. But more often than not, the conditions for mutual learning are right, and planners, though not centrally engaged in the action itself, will be able to foster an environment conducive to interpersonal transactions at the level of planning.[9]

Dilemmas of radical planning

Although radical planners will not always be professionals – indeed, a traditional education may be more of a hindrance than a help – there is no question but that their practice requires certain skills and knowledge for their mediations. In carrying out their assignment, radical planners face extraordinary difficulties. It is the purpose of this section to elucidate some of these dilemmas and to hint at ways of overcoming them. I shall discuss them under three headings: critical distance, open inquiry, and the unity of opposites.

✗ Critical distance

I refer here to the planners' social involvement with the group that is the "carrier" of radical practice. Planners must be committed to the group's practice and to the global project of emancipation. At the same time, however, they should neither stand apart from the group's practice nor be absorbed by it. As mediators, they must maintain a *critical distance* from the group's practice.

We may visualize planners' social distance along a continuum: beyond a certain point, the closer they come to the action, the less useful are their mediations likely to be. The same holds in the other direction: the further away they move from the immediacies of the group's actions, the less they will be able to accomplish. We posit, then, an optimum critical distance between planners and the front line of action. Planners must be part of the action, but not entirely so.

It is quite easy, then, for planners to lose the correct location vis-à-vis the group's practice. A basis for their effectiveness is the trust they inspire as people. The position implied by "critical distance," however, suggests that if planners remain too distant and aloof, trust may be dissipated. Alternatively, even though trust may be gained by closer involvement with the action, planners' ability effectively to mediate theory in the thick of the action may plunge to zero. Why? How?

Open inquiry

The result of this requirement for effective mediation is the same as that of trying to find the proper social distance from engagement in practice. Planners are expected to bring the "whole world" to bear on local action. Inevitably, this involves a questioning mind. Are you doing things right? Is the theory according to which you are proceeding correct? Planners as mediators are inquirers who place the group's action in perspective through a fundamental questioning of its premises. They are the critical consciousness of radical practice.

self-assigned position of authority

This role can lead to situations that will render the planner's task well-nigh impossible. On the one hand, any group committed to action will want to protect itself against fundamental doubt. It does not need to have its hard-won practice undermined by marginally situated intellectuals. The questioning can go on indefinitely and may lose sight of its original purpose. An inquiry that does not respect boundaries and thus has very lax criteria of what constitutes warranted knowledge is obliged to consider even outrageous hypotheses: there is no stopping rule. As thinking goes on and on, from question to question, over an immense expanse, it can paralyze the will to act. But at what point does one say enough is enough, and bring the inquiry to a close?

The unity of opposites

One of the most difficult requirements for radical planners is the ability to live with contradictions. Yet one is tempted to say that contradictions define the very essence of radical planning practice.

To live with contradictions is to say that planners must hold in tension two opposing categories, *affirming both*, even where traditional logic tells us that only one of the terms can be asserted without running into unsolvable dilemmas. Some examples of contradictions follow:

- Theory *and* practice.
- Empirical analysis *and* normative vision.
- Critique *and* affirmation.
- Explanation *and* action.
- Future vision *and* present reality.

Our natural inclination is to substitute the conjunction *or* for every *and* in the list above. Alternatively, it is to wish the opposite term away and to coin perhaps some new words, indicative of a mixed reality – ugly terms such as "theo-practica." Neither of these escape routes is, in fact, open to planners. The problem has to be faced in all of its complexity and without giving way.

As an example of what I have in mind, let us look at the contradiction between critique and affirmation. In strictly logical terms, critique is something altogether different from affirmation. If standards are made explicit, it is relatively easy to get agreement on what, in given instances, is missing. To formulate these standards and apply them to observable reality is the essence of a good critique. Thus, given an unambiguous concept of open unemployment, it is relatively easy to measure actual unemployment in the economy. And given a concept of gender inequality, the measurement of inequalities in the treatment of women workers is fairly straightforward. People may interpret these measurements in various ways; the numbers themselves commit no one to action. It is quite another matter, however, to build a consensus on what ought to be done. Whereas critique is always about an existing or past event, affirmation concerns a future that is still open to choice. You must assert certain values, alert people to the seriousness of the situation, invent solutions, gauge their probable impact, test them for their feasibility, and consider strategies to overcome resistance. You are now in a different mode of thinking: *you affirm.* For this reason, good critics rarely make good poets and painters. Or even planners, for that matter.

And yet, radical practice and planning must begin with a critique of what, in the present, is so wrong and offensive that it justifies actions to restructure the system. What is the planner to do? Critique can be carried to the point where it virtually eliminates all options. Everything must go, cries the radical critic, and go at once, in one climactic upheaval. All merely partial actions are pronounced useless; worse still, they may be enlisted in the "enemy's" cause.[10] A bland critique, on the other hand, may be inadequate for motivating and sustaining radical practice.

In short, critique and affirmation must be linked in practice, but linked dialectically, in reciprocal action upon each other. That is the core meaning of a "unity of opposites."

A similar analysis can be carried out for each of the pairs of contradictory terms. Carried to an extreme, each term negates the possibility of the other. A theoretical extreme negates the possibility of practice (and vice versa); an extreme of empirical analysis negates the possibility of vision; too much explanation loses sight of the requirements of action; future vision without a link to the present becomes addicted to utopian speculations. But how much is too much?

The dilemmas of radical planning are, in the end, all of the same kind. How much is too much? What is the optimal social distance? When should a halt be called to critical inquiry? None of these questions allows of a formal reply. Yet neither can we say, with Wittgenstein, that if an answer does not exist, the question itself has no meaning. In fact, in the practice of radical planning, it is the absolutely central question. And because it is about practice, the answer to it must come from practice itself and not from pure thought. It is a question about practical reason (Ulrich 1983).

A tentative answer might be as follows (the very terms of the answer remain imprecise: we are now with Michael Polanyi [1967], in the arena of tacit knowing). With an epistemology of social learning, which is the theory of knowledge underlying radical practice, *action is always primary*. Questions are thus put to theorists from the side of practice and not the other way around. The imperative of action always has priority over the equal imperative of knowing.

So long as the planner keeps this order of priorities in mind, the dilemmas of radical planning practice can be resolved, though only in practice. As planner, you always work within a context that has its own limits of time and place, and you address specific actors with known characteristics. These are the practical conditions that help the planner to find the critical distance, to guide his or her inquiry, and to hold dialectical opposites in reciprocal relation.

Radical planning and the state

why "a planner" then?

Radical planning, always based on people's self-organized actions, stands in necessary opposition to the established powers and, more particularly, the state. For the state to engage in radical planning poses a contradiction in terms. Still, it would be wrong to ignore the state's existence or to treat it as an adversary only. Its presence is pervasive, and social advances achieved through a radical planning that bypasses the state will quickly reach material limits. To go beyond these limits, appropriate actions by the state are essential. Such actions must be fought over in political struggle for the legitimate claims of the disempowered (Piven and Cloward 1979; Peattie and Rein 1983). The ultimate aim of these struggles – the reassertion of political community in civil governance – will undoubtedly require a permanent restructuring of the state. But this can only be achieved through a step-by-step process of radical reforms and social learning in all of the domains of public action.

Three kinds of politics are relevant. The politics of empowerment takes place over claims staked out around the major bases of social power. One of these bases, time, involves a claim to greater access to a surplus of time over and above what is required for social reproduction. In Western, industrialized countries, this struggle is currently focused on such issues as time sharing, the thirty-five-hour week, flexitime, child care provision near the place of work, and extended maternity and paternity leaves. In Third World cities, struggles over time tend to be merged with those over access to space and the complementary investments that render that space socially useful. By correct planning for space use, settlement, and land in metropolitan areas, time, currently used up in subsistence activities, could become available as "surplus." Land for new urban settlements should be situated near the major sources of employment and enjoy good access to public transportation. The amount of land should be sufficient to allow, in addition to shelter, the development of urban gardens for self-provisioning

(Sanyal 1986). The land should be adequately served with water, electricity, and sanitary facilities at a cost affordable to people with very low incomes. Schools and other collective facilities should be planned as an integral part of low-income housing estates.

As this abbreviated catalogue makes clear, the state, whether national or local, must be involved in projects that directly address people's survival needs and liberate their energies for self-development. It is true that struggle over time and space, or indeed over greater access to any of the other bases of social power, will not, in itself, lead to empowerment. Genuine power comes only from successfully engaging in political struggles, and from using the gains in social power to engage in yet further struggles to enhance people's capacity for a development from within.

In view of the massive material needs of the disempowered, the potential costs imposed on the state are very large indeed. To divert the resources required from other, economically more lucrative uses will require a *politics of redistribution* at the national level. Such a politics is likely to favor the disempowered only when advocates for progressive redistribution can count on mobilized grassroots support. Linked to each other, the politics of empowerment and of redistribution illustrate the intimate association that exists between successful micro-actions on the one hand and a national politics on the other.

Finally, we must consider the *politics of place*, which sets out to defend people's life spaces against the rapaciousness of capital and bureaucratic fiat. Life space comprises the homes and neighborhoods and districts that sustain and support the self-production of life by individual households and communities. People have an inborn desire to preserve and improve its character. They will want to extract from the state assurance of continuity in local production against the rise and fall of business and technological cycles. They will want to control outside investments that, while they will benefit few within the community, are likely to be harmful to many. They will want to provide safeguards against speculative building.

The politics of place is typically conducted at the level of the local state, because the relevant policy instruments, such as zoning, rest in the hands of the state. And yet, these instruments are not likely to be used in the protection of people's life spaces unless the people themselves become engaged in defending them. The state may thus be visualized as a "terrain of struggle" in which different class interests contend over the direction of development and the distribution of the related costs and benefits. This is not to argue the state's neutrality. The state has interests of its own at stake, and it asserts these interests from time to time even as it strikes an alliance with this or that class fraction. But whatever the outcome, the state-as-actor can never become a radical state. For better or for worse, it always acts as a hegemonic force.

Surviving in a heartless world

To be an outsider, or "radical," is a difficult role to sustain. It means to swim against the stream, to mobilize for action, and always to struggle against the resistance of powerful forces. Of course, most so-called radicals do not perceive their actions to be radical at all. They are merely doing what comes naturally to them, fighting for what they believe to be right, for their own survival, for a better and happier existence.

Tenants going on strike tend to see their action as a last resort; they are not naturally radicals. People protesting a nuclear power plant, or organizing a peace march, see themselves as exercising their legitimate right as citizens under the Constitution. Women setting up a shelter for battered women are doing something to help their sisters; they may be angry, but they are not radicals. Energy activists fighting the private utilities for permission to tie alternative power generating sources, such as wind, into the larger territorial grid, are using a legal means to achieve their purpose. Neighbors planting a community garden to grow fresh produce for themselves are doing a neighborly thing in the time-honored tradition of barn raising. Bicycle enthusiasts lobbying the city council for grade-separated bike paths act like any other pressure group. Workers buying out an abandoned manufacturing plant, perhaps with local community assistance, are not challenging the system; they are battling to save their livelihood. Labor unions negotiating with employers for the thirty-five-hour week, flexible time arrangements, and child care provisions are doing what they have always done: engaging in collective bargaining. Black women forming a local development corporation that will help them get adequate housing for themselves and their children and common services specifically tailored to their needs as single-parent heads of households, all at a cost they can afford, are doing something that is of vital importance to themselves through an institutional mechanism that is already sanctioned.

Yet taken together and blown up to the proportions of society as a whole, these instances of a radical practice constitute a major challenge to the prevailing system. They will make people less dependent on global capital, increase their social power, and expose them to the lessons of political practice. A sense of commonality in the simultaneous pursuit of their separate interests is diffused through network publications such as TRANET (Transnational Network for Appropriate/Alternative Technologies) and journals such as *Coevolution Quarterly* (now discontinued). The time for an encompassing, integrative political ideology for the loosely textured radical practices of today may not be here as yet, but the potential for it exists, and once the movement acquires political potency, it will be quickly perceived as the real threat that it is.[11]

Let tenant activists elect a city council, as they did a few years ago in Santa Monica, California, and real estate and local business elites will see the pillars of capital toppling and raise millions of dollars to defeat the incumbents. Not surprisingly, the money is always with those who uphold the status quo. People have only themselves. Their real strength lies in the transactive relations of their dialogue.

Still, groups engaged in radical practice also need money. How shall they finance themselves? Even more to the point, how shall radical planners survive when neither the state nor private foundations pay for their work?

Radical practice does not come dear in terms of money. It is more demanding of time: time for countless meetings that may last long into the night, or for the "sweat equity" that many jobs demand. But time, which is almost always in scarce supply, can be "saved" for radical practice from other activities so long as people are prepared to help each other out. Mutual help, which has its own intrinsic satisfactions, must be organized and requires forethought. To rely on merely spontaneous enthusiasm is not enough.   *?*

As for money, if you want it badly enough it will often materialize. Small individual amounts can be pooled. Fund raising helps. Institutions, such as parish churches, can make meeting space available. Foundations can be persuaded to underwrite certain kinds of activity. Even the government may be ready to fund some "radical" projects, perhaps unaware of their connection to the larger agenda. Militant political action may succeed in putting condition on the use of public pension funds that will channel a larger proportion in the direction of radical projects. Often, there is a tipping point, with the public purse strings suddenly untied after a series of successful struggles, which have created a certain aura of respectability for the project. *Example?*

As for radical planners themselves, their circumstances may be as varied as the sources of financing I have described. Very often, radical planning is not a full-time occupation. In this event, planners come to earn their livelihood in the usual way, not unlike actors, painters, dancers, writers, and poets who work at relatively undemanding jobs while their real work lies elsewhere. In the relatively rare instances when radical planning constitutes the only source of income, the employer may be a radical "think tank," such as the Washington-based Institute of Policy Studies; a progressive labor union, such as the United Electrical Workers; or a church group such as the Maryknollers. Occasionally, radical planners may even work inside the bureaucracy as a kind of "fifth column" in support of radical practice outside. The material situation of radical planning is thus far from hopeless. But it is no way to get rich.

Concluding comments

Throughout this book, "planning" has been used in a heuristic sense. As such, it has served us well, as we explored the several modes of technical reason in the public domain. But when we came to radical planning, we discovered that we had to step outside the traditions of societal guidance and change the terms of our discourse. We had to substitute the dialectical relation of transformative theory and radical practice for linking knowledge to action. Because of this difference, what we have described as radical planning has little in common with the traditions of policy analysis or social reform. And yet, in the attempt to guide the course of human destiny through reason, to place the goal of history in *this* world and not in some transcendental heaven, there is a common root. Both transformative planning and societal guidance were born of the Enlightenment.

In closing my story with a discussion of radical planning, I have no wish to suggest that the other planning traditions have now been superseded. In the case of the peasant periphery, we observed that radical practice requires actions by a revolutionary state without which social mobilization for a self-reliant development cannot take place at all. And the planning by even a revolutionary state tends to have more in common with Saint-Simonian technocracy than with anarchist-inspired forms of radical planning, which are, by nature, oppositional.

Nor is the state in the so-called First World of industrial capitalism about to go away. To speak of its declining powers is not to argue the case for its imminent dissolution. And so, with the state continuing in the hands of technocrats, Saint-Simon lives on, along with a lingering belief in the technical mastery of unlimited progress.

But societal guidance from the top is not, as some liberal theorists would have it, the dialectical other of radical planning (Stöhr 1981). For the latter is not about participation in projects by the state. Its aim is the structural transformation of industrial capitalism toward the self-production of life, the recovery of political community, and the achievement of collective self-reliance in the context of common global concerns. In this context, our task is to wrest from the political terrain still held by state and corporate capital expanding zones of liberation in which the new and self-reliant ways of production and democratic governance can flourish. And for this project, the mediations of radical planning are essential.

Notes

1.   This account of transformative theory is drawn directly from the social mobilization paradigm of planning. Contemporary examples include certain varieties of feminist theory, particularly socialist feminism; the radical political theory implicit in *Democracy: A journal of political renewal and radical change*, edited by Sheldon Wolin and now, unfortunately, defunct; and the emerging theory of a "self-reliant" development.

2. Each of such practices teaches political lessons. In some, the state or corporate power is directly opposed. In others, their financial assistance will be sought, but their tutelage rejected. Some of the practices are purely local in character, such as tenant struggles (Heskin 1983), while others link up from city to city to build a national movement. What is still missing is the political link-up among single-issue social movements and hammering out a genuine alternative. But to imagine the possibilities of such an alternative can no longer be dismissed as a utopian fantasy.

3. This formulation is borrowed from Ravetz (1971: ch.3), who refers to science, in its inquiring aspects, as "craftsman work": "[W]ithout an appreciation of the craft character of scientific work there is no possibility of resolving the paradox of radical difference between the subjective, intensely personal activity of creative science, and the objective, impersonal knowledge which results from it" (Ravetz 1971: 75). We may recall that the craftsman view of science, not coincidentally, also informs the work of policy analysts, who have gone on record to reject subject matter as a relevant concern (Wildavsky 1979).

4. For a splendid critical review of Habermas's ideas on discursive thinking, see Ulrich (1983: ch.2).

5. For the epistemological grounding of this statement, see Ulrich (1983: 305–10).

6. One of the best studies of "survival strategies" in poor societies was sponsored by the Organization for Economic Cooperation and Development (OECD). The authors write:

> It is our thesis that the only political efforts which have some possibility of success are those in which: i) an appropriate degree of *awareness* of the social, political, and economic situation coincides with ii) the necessary *capacity to organise* protracted actions, with iii) a *realistic appraisal* of the reformist or revolutionary possibilities of the overall situation and with iv) the ability to hammer together the *indispensible alliances with other social groups and actors*. (Harari and García-Bouza 1982: 43)

Radical planners can play significant parts in all these aspects of the struggle. Perhaps the best-documented, most profound study of radical planning is by Max-Neef (1982). The experiences of this self-styled "barefoot economist" come from Latin America but their lessons have validity for all of us.

7. The emphasis on "trust" in transactive planning has been ridiculed by certain critics. One wonders whether they would prefer to put their trust instead in government statisticians, the public pronouncements of the president, the contrived images of television reporting, and the daily press. Trust is a necessary facet of all human relations. With so much conscious and unconscious deception in the management of public affairs, the personal trust among a small number of people who know each other, work with each other, and rely on each other would seem to be essential for moving the world's business.

8. For critiques, see Roweis and Scott (1977) and Camhis (1979).

9. Two recent doctoral dissertations provide positive proof that transactive planning based on dialogic relations can be made to work even in public settings, such as the management of wilderness areas. See McLaughlin (1977) and Stokes (1982).

10. The whole of the Frankfurt School of Critical Sociology might be accused of carrying its critique beyond the critical threshold. The mind, as Gramsci said, is inclined to pessimism. What is needed is to join its pessimism to the optimism of the will.

11. For a very different and much less sanguine evaluation of what he calls the "new populism," see Carl Boggs (1983). He writes:

> It would be illusory to view the new populism as a fundamentally new strategy that, because of its uniquely indigenous and pragmatic character, could be the basis of a revitalized oppositional movement of the 1980s. On the contrary, the new populism has a deep affinity not only for *traditional* American populism but for the very European social democracy it considers obsolete …. Hence, whatever is distinctive "American" language and priorities, the new populism seems destined to repeat earlier failures. The probability is that, where such movements succeed in their own terms, they will end up *stabilizing* the very corporate power structure they ostensibly set out to oppose ….

The decisive theoretical and strategic limits of the new populism are not a function of its emphasis on "community" over "workplace" organizing or even of the predominant role it assigns to "alliance" politics; it is difficult to imagine any social movement in the U.S. establishing a public presence without *some* kind of community-based, alliance-oriented radicalism – and, moreover, none of the new populist theories have abandoned a commitment to workplace struggles ….

The basic underlying problem is deeper and more complex. On the one hand, new populist theory contains no critical or transformative approach to power relations, or to domination. The vision of democratic structural reforms is not shaped by any radical conception of the state – that is, it anticipates no overturning of the old social and political hierarchies, no sustained attack on the authoritarian state apparatus, no development of qualitatively new forms of self-management. Lacking such a dialectic, the principles of "economic democracy" ultimately have to be fitted into the design of the corporate power structure. (Boggs 1983: 358–9)

Bibliography

Bluestone, B. and Harrison, B. (1982) *The Deindustrialization of America: Plant closings, community abandonment, and the dismantling of basic industry*, New York: Basic Books.

Boggs, C. (1983) 'The new populism and the limits of structural reforms', *Theory and Society*, 12: 343–63.

Camhis, M. (1979) *Planning Theory and Philosophy*, London: Tavistock Publications.

Cook, A. and Kirk, G. (1983) *Greenham Women Everywhere*, Boston: South End Press.

Court, G. (1984) 'Social learning', unpublished paper, Graduate School of Architecture and Urban Planning, UCLA.

Forester, J. (1980) 'Listening: the social policy of everyday life (critical theory and hermeneutics in practice)', *Social Praxi*, 7 (3/4): 219–32.

Friedmann, J. (1973) *Retracking America: A theory of transactive planning*, New York, Anchor Press.

——(1979) *The Good Society*, Cambridge, MA: MIT Press.

Haas, G. (1985) *Plant Closures: Myths, realities, and responses*, Boston: South End Press.

Harari, D. and García-Bouza, J. (1982) *Social Conflict and Development: Basic needs and survival strategies in four national settings*, Paris: OECD.

Heskin, A. (1983) 'Crisis and Response: a historical perspective on advocacy planning', *Journal of the American Planning Association*, 46 (1): 50–63.

Johnstadt, T. (1980) *Group Dynamics and Society: A multi-national approach*, Cambridge, MA: Oelschlager, Gunn & Hain.

Luria, D, and Russell, J. (1981) *Rational Reindustrialization: An economic development agenda for Detroit*, Detroit: Widgetripper Press.

McLaughlin, W.J. (1977) 'The Indian Hills Experiment: a case study of transactive planning theory', PhD dissertation, Colorado State University. (Available from University Microfilms International, Ann Arbor, Mich.)

Massey, D. and Meegan R. (1982) *The Anatomy of Job Loss*, London: Methuen.

Max-Neef, M. (1982) *From the Outside Looking in: Experiences in "barefoot economics"*, Uppsala, Sweden: Dag Hammarskjöld Foundation.

Metzgar, J. (1980) 'Plant shut-down and worker response: the case of Johnstown, Pennsylvania', *Socialist Review*, 10 (5): 9–50.

Morales, R. and Wolff, G. (1985) *Los Angeles Labor Union Responses to Plant Closings and Growth in the Immigrant Labor Force*, Los Angeles: UCLA Institute of Industrial Relations.

Oakley, P. and Marsden, D. (1984) *Approaches to Participation in Rural Development*, Geneva: International Labour Office.

Peattie, L. and Rein, M. (1983) *Women's Claims: A study in political economy*, New York: Oxford University Press.

Piven, F.F. and Cloward, R.A. (1979) *Poor People's Movement: Why they succeed. How they fail*, New York: Vintage Books.

Polanyi, M. (1967) *The Tacit Dimension*, Garden City, NY: Doubleday.

Ravetz, J.R. (1971) *Scientific Knowledge and its Social Problems*, New York: Oxford University Press.

Roweis, S.T. and Scott, A.J. (1977) 'Urban planning in theory and practice: a reappraisal', *Environment and Planning A*, 9: 1097–119.

Sandercock, L. and Melser, P. (1985) '"Like a building condemned": planning in the old industrial region', *Built Environment*, 11 (2): 120–31.

Sanyal, B. (1986) 'Urban Cultivation: people's response to urban poverty in East Africa', manuscript, Cambridge, Mass.: MIT Department of Urban Studies and Planning.

Stöhr, W.B. (1981) 'Development from below: the bottom-up and periphery-inward development paradigm', in W.B. Stöhr and D.R.F. Taylor (eds) *Development from Above or Below? The dialectics of regional planning in developing countries*, New York: John Wiley & Sons.

Stokes, G.L. (1982) 'Conservation of the Blackfoot River Corridor: an application of transactive planning theory', PhD dissertation, Colorado State University. (Available from University Microfilms International, Ann Arbor, Mich.)

Ulrich, W. (1983) *Critical Heuristics of Social Planning: A new approach to practical philosophy*, Bern: Verlag Paul Haupt.

Whyte, M.K. (1974) *Small Groups and Political Rituals in China*, Berkeley: University of California Press.

Wildavsky, A. (1979) *Speaking Truth to Power: The art and craft of policy analysis*, Boston: Little, Brown.

Study questions

This chapter is both a synthesis of the preceding chapters and a preview of Chapters 5 and 6. Radical planning can be defined in a number of ways, but here it refers to planning and acting by, for, and with civil society organizations and/or social movements whose aim is to bring about conditions that are supportive of the collective self-production of life. Abstractly stated, its central task is the "mediation of theory and practice in social transformation."

1. What is meant by a "transformative theory?" Discuss each of the five steps listed on page 62. How are these steps related to one another? Can you think of actual examples?
2. What is meant by the "unity of theory and practice" in radical planning? And how is such planning different from planning for societal guidance by the state, thus implying an "epistemological break" with past ways of thinking about and engaging in planning?
3. The following is a statement that suggests what radical planners actually do: "to shape transformative theory to the requirements of an oppositional practice in specific local settings, to create opportunities for the critical appropriation of transformative theory by groups organized for action, and to rework this theory in ways that will reflect firsthand experience gathered in the course of radical practice itself. In terms of social space, radical planners occupy a position tangential to radical practice at precisely the point where practice intersects theory." Please comment on this statement. Do you agree with it or not, and why? What else do you think radical planners do when they engage in practice? What is meant by practice "intersecting" with theory?
4. Here is another excerpt from the text: "It is through communicative acts that knowledge for radical practice comes to be provisionally established. I say provisionally, because the knowledge used in planning is inherently ephemeral, and nowhere more so than in the process of social transformation. Therefore, it is preferable to substitute the more dynamic concept of social learning, which is the way we critically appropriate experience for action, for the more solid [formal] 'knowledge' that suggests a fixed stock of accumulated learning." This is an argument for the centrality of social learning in planning for social transformation. The text continues in the next paragraph: "But in radical planning, the relevant knowledge, embedded as it is in transformative theory, is always and necessarily contextual: it points to action, considers strategy, endeavors to reach a critical understanding of the present and near future, and is informed by specific social values" that it seeks to actualize through its practice in the world. Please discuss this epistemological theory. Relate it to what was argued in Chapter 2 about social learning.

(handwritten margin note): why not be part of social mvmts? with an argument for better methodology?

5. This epistemology of radical planning is continued in the following quotation: "The provisional nature of knowledge in planning tells us that the theory of social transformation must never be allowed to harden into dogma but must remain open to even fundamental questioning and re-conceptualizations. The organizational counterpart to this epistemological commitment is a structure for radical practice that consists of a large number of autonomous (or quasi-autonomous) centers of decision and action whose coordination remains loose and informal." This is a claim about the network character of radical practice. Please discuss this claim with respect to the transformative aims of radical practice.

6. Radical thinking is thinking without frontiers. What are some of the boundaries that prevent this from happening? Take, for example, hierarchy. Planners may come with a university degree or institutional affiliation that can make open and unfiltered communication with the community with whom they are working difficult. What would it take to overcome this barrier to dialogue? How do we acknowledge the value of what community members know and bring to the table? Can hierarchy be bracketed in face-to-face encounters? Consider some other obstacles to "thinking without frontiers" and how to remove them so that an open dialogue can emerge.

7. Here's another quotation from the text: "The more fragmented experience appears to us, the less it holds the promise of meaning, the more alienated we become .... [But] when you set out purposes and try to achieve them, you suddenly discover a firm criterion that helps you to interpret the world: the definition of a problem, the search for an appropriate strategy, and a clear grasp of the values to be realized in practice. Action simplifies by excising irrelevant information. At the same time, it unifies thought by bringing disparate information and experience into relation." How does action "unify" thought? Can we also say that action concentrates the mind?

8. What is the difference between "advocacy planning" and radical planning?

Compare this chapter on the mediations of radical planning with Brian Walker and David Salt's recent book, *Resilience Thinking*, which is listed below, particularly pages 145–8. Although this book uses a different language and was written 20 years later, it advocates a type of approach to ecological resilience planning that is very much in tune with what is discussed in the present chapter as radical planning practice.

Selected additional readings

Walker, B. and Salt, D. (2006) *Resilience Thinking: Sustaining ecosystems in a changing world*, Washington, DC: Island Press.

Friedmann, J. (1987) *Planning in the Public Domain: From knowledge to action*, Princeton: Princeton University Press, ch 2. See also the Epilogue, this volume.

5

Rethinking poverty:
the dis/empowerment model

The following essay takes us into a different terrain from the remaining chapters of this volume. It avoids the high-order abstractions of the knowledge/action paradigm, by delving into one of the burning questions of our own day, which is how best to address massive global poverty, particularly in the countries of the Third World. Here is a challenge – some argue, the principal challenge – of economic development, the very purpose for which development policies should be designed. By the 1990s, however, it was already apparent that the neo-liberal policy regime that for the past 20 years had spread to the far corners of the world, far from eradicating poverty, was actually adding to the misery of the poor.

An intellectual movement for an alternative to mainstream economic policies as advocated, for example, by the World Bank and the International Monetary Fund, already exists. Its high-point was reached in 1976 with a flurry of discussions concerning the viability of a "basic needs" approach to poverty and to development more generally. Although championed by the International Labour Office (ILO) in Geneva, it was soon shelved and forgotten, because its chief promoters, the distinguished economists Dudley Seers and Dharam Ghai, had been unable to forge the necessary consensus within the wider development community. In the essay below, published in 1992, I took on the question of global poverty once more, but this time from a perspective different from the ILO.

Central to my thinking was the household economy – the *oikos* of antiquity, rather than the utility-maximizing individual of neo-classical economics. I defined the *oikos* as a household unit consisting of "all who live under a single roof and eat out of the same pot" and who collectively produce their own life and livelihood with whatever resources are at hand. Whereas most anti-poverty policies are concerned with income distribution, which is still the case today, I argued that a household's ability to improve the life-chances of its members depends chiefly on its access to the means for social reproduction which, while including income and credit, go significantly beyond financial resources to seven additional "bases of social empowerment." Importantly, households dispose over the capacities and skills of its members, and allocate them in different proportions to the production of both use and exchange values. Moreover, households are endowed with "social capital" in their relations to family, friends, and neighbors as well as social organizations, such as labor unions, religious institutions, farm cooperatives, and the like.

This, in brief, was the framework for an alternative development that, inspired by the work of the Hungarian anthropologist and social historian Karl Polanyi (1977), would be based on (poor) households' self-production of their life and livelihood. Limited support for this by the state and voluntary organizations was part of this model, which was primarily geared to making small improvements in the life of the poor, with particular emphasis on localities of rural village and urban neighborhood. For more fundamental outcomes, political change would be needed to elect leaders who are prepared to work towards a more equitable, people-centered development, the energy for which would come "from below."

What can we say today, looking back over the 20 years since I wrote this essay and the nearly 40 years since the debates began on a basic needs approach as central to the eradication of global poverty? A few brief observations suggest themselves. Non-governmental organizations have been proliferating throughout the world so that NGOs today number in the tens of thousands, many of them enjoying government support and international funding. They have gone into villages and neighborhoods to work with local folks primarily in rural areas on self-help projects, sometimes successfully, often not. Generally their work is uncoordinated, they are often in direct competition with each other for the limited funds that can be raised, while the state, in its eagerness to attract international capital, has generally looked elsewhere.

An example of a different sort comes from Bangladesh, where Muhammad Yunus was awarded the Nobel Peace Prize for his outstanding work with the Grameen Bank and its various business off-shoots. Starting in 1984, the Grameen Bank had pioneered what is today widely known as the micro-credit program. Over the years, Yunus and his associates have evolved a whole new philosophy about lifting people out of extreme poverty, by helping them to get started on a life informed by hope (Yunus 2007). Its focus is the social empowerment of the family household, and its criteria for a poverty threshold are in some respects similar to mine: a house with simple furnishings, pure drinking water, a primary education for all children of school age, minimum weekly loan repayments of around three dollars, a hygienic latrine, sufficient clothing to meet daily as well as seasonal needs, additional sources of income such as a vegetable garden or fruit-bearing trees, a small savings account in the Grameen Bank, enough food throughout the year for three square meals a day, and access to medical services when needed (op.cit., 111). But the Grameen philosophy was tailored to the basic needs of the

Bangladeshi peasantry. Similarly tailored efforts are needed in other parts of the world.

Bibliography

Polanyi, K. (1977) *The Livelihood of Man*, Pearson, H.W. (ed.), New York: Academic Press.
Yunus, M. (2007) *Creating a World without Poverty: Social business and the future of capitalism*, New York: Public Affairs.

From *Empowerment*

Originally published in 1992

Without the prevalence of real poverty in the world, there would be no need for an alternative development. Reforming the existing system would be sufficient to reduce vestigial injustices, to take care of social needs identified in public discourse, and to reduce environmental degradation by carefully dosed state interventions in markets. But massive poverty unquestionably exists as a worldwide issue, and so the issues of an alternative development must be addressed.

The trouble is, we think that we know about poverty, and that all that remains is to think up better ways to … do what? *Eradicate it? Reduce it? Alleviate it? Cope with it? Manage it?* Quite aside from being unsure what it is that we, who are not poor, want to do about poverty, we are wrong to think that combating poverty simply boils down to *knowing how* without, at the same time, being very clear about the *what* of poverty. We need to know what causes poverty, and whether poverty is one big or many small questions. There are urban and there are rural poor, and for a few, poverty may be a chosen way of life. Others, though they might live poorly by some standards, don't think of themselves as poor. Still others are poor only temporarily, while many are born into poverty and do not expect ever to escape their condition that they have come to accept as in some sense natural. Nor is poverty viewed everywhere, as it is in Western countries, as a radical evil that prevents the poor from "human flourishing."

These are some of the issues that need to be separated and clarified. What we are looking for is an understanding of poverty as a public issue that must be approached collectively.

Bureaucratic poverty

Poverty is traditionally defined by those who regard themselves as the social superiors of the poor. Hence it comes about that the poor are widely regarded with suspicion. The nineteenth century called them the dangerous classes, haborers of indolence and vice. These negative perceptions have not disappeared. To be poor is still widely perceived to be dirty, dumb, wanting in skills, drugged, prone to violence and criminality, and generally irresponsible. People with these traits must be controlled, institutionalized, and managed. They fill our jails, and when the jails are full, more jails are built. In the United States, where much existing poverty is also concentrated among certain ethnic groups, some of the poor are defined as members of an "underclass" who have few if any rights and are perceived as an immanent threat to the established order. At least one well-known commentator wanted to put them all into detention camps (Banfield, 1970).[1]

Social reformers have protested the identification of the poor with vice. They argued that the poor are not themselves to blame for their condition, which should instead be regarded as a result of unfortunate circumstances. In the reformers' rhetoric, the dangerous are turned into the unfortunate, or disadvantaged classes. Because abject poverty is degrading, they argued, poor people should be raised at least to the level of a decent minimum, with a roof over their heads, clothes to cover their nakedness, and food on the table. Other reformers concerned themselves with issues of work and employment. The poor were poor, they said, because there weren't enough jobs of the right kind. And so, not unreasonably, these reformers concentrated on policies for full employment and on "work and welfare" programs.

But, in the final instance, the guardian of the poor, at least in modern times, has always been the state, which, on behalf of the rest of society, is charged with managing the poor, controlling the dangerous classes, running the jails, and administering the welfare program under its authority. Labor has become divided, so that the poor are now the primary responsibility of the police and an extensive bureaucracy of social workers, parole officers, and other specialists. Ordinary citizens are thus relieved of their responsibility for the poor, confident that the problem is being handled by qualified professionals.

The state bureaucracy has evolved its own language to describe its relationship to the poor. Some of these terms have gained wide currency and now form part of the standard vocabulary of poverty:

- *Poverty line.* The level of minimum household consumption that is socially acceptable. It is usually calculated in terms of an income of which roughly two-thirds would be spent on a "food basket" calculated by welfare statisticians as the least-cost provision of essential calories and proteins. In setting this standard, however, statisticians do not count the labor time required for either least-cost food acquisition or the preparation of meals. Thus they tacitly assume the presence of women who are willing to undertake this work without pay, or women's subsidy. They are usually unwilling to acknowledge that time allocated to these activities could be used to earn additional household income.[2]
- *Absolute and relative poverty.* To fall below some minimum standard of consumption is to be regarded as absolutely poor, or indigent, and thus dependent on charity. But poverty also exists *above* this line, although that kind of poverty tends to be regarded differently, being judged in terms of the distance between the poor and non-poor or of relative income. Other descriptive categories used include the *chronic poor* and the *borderline poor.*

- *(Un)deserving poor*. This term carries over the traditional European view of the poor as lazy and improvident, inclined toward vice. The "deserving" poor are those who are willing to conform to the expectations of the non-poor, are clean and honest and responsible, willing to accept any kind of work for any wage offered. The deserving poor are pictured as docile and industrious. They alone, it is argued, have a right to charity that will help them "to stand on their own feet."
- *Pockets of poverty*. One of the beliefs informing the work of welfare bureaucrats is that the poor are comparatively few in number and that the problem is therefore manageable. The phrase "pockets of poverty" was invented to suggest that the problem is relatively insignificant. "Pockets", it is suggested, can be "mopped up." Mass poverty is another matter altogether. It is a term the welfare bureaucracy would rather avoid.
- *Target population*. This refers to specific groups of people that are the key object of government policies and programs. They may be female-headed households, children, landless rural laborers, small-farm peasants, victims of war or drought, and shantytown dwellers.

Those labeled as the poor have few options other than to acquiesce in the role assigned to them as the state's wards. For the most part, they are regarded as incapable of taking charge of their own lives. As in so many cases of service professionalism, welfare clients are treated as helplessly dependent on the authorities who have set themselves up as their caretakers. It is their clients who sustain and provide the raison d'être of a large and inevitably growing administrative apparatus that, although responsible *for* them, is never accountable *to* them.

The attention of international aid professionals is, for the most part, preempted by the "absolutely" poor. What this means, in practice, has been explained by M.S. Ahluwalia of the World Bank (Ahluwalia 1974) at a time when that organization was beginning to show some interest in poverty issues:

> The incidence of poverty in underdeveloped countries defined in absolute terms has powerful appeal for dramatizing the need for policy action in both domestic and international spheres. Estimates for this type have been attempted for some countries using arbitrary poverty lines for each country to measure population below these levels .... For each country we have estimated the population living below ... [annual] per capita incomes of US $50 and US $75 (in 1971 prices) ... the countries included ... account for about 60 per cent of the total population of developing countries excluding China. About a third of this population falls below the poverty line defined by US $50 per capita *and about half falls below US $75 per capita*. (1974: 10–11; my italics)

By World Bank reckoning, therefore, the difference of a mere $25 per capita more or less – the price of a good meal in Los Angeles – meant that between 15 and 20 per cent of the population was either counted or not among the "absolutely" poor; the difference amounted to more than 200 million people.[3]

Given the overwhelming magnitude of poverty in poor countries, 50 per cent according to World Bank estimates in the 1970s and 60 per cent according to our calculations for the 1990s, it becomes conceptually difficult to isolate the poor. In the poor countries of the world there are no administratively convenient "pockets of poverty." The poor form a majority. They are the peasants and popular urban sectors. They are the people, *el pueblo*.

The World Bank did not draw this conclusion, however. To do so would have led it to abandon its traditional approach to economic growth and "development." And this it was not prepared to do even under Robert S. McNamara's relatively enlightened reign from 1968 to 1981.[4] Instead it adopted the perhaps not unreasonable idea that a redistribution of income toward the poor might be easier to carry out if there were rapid economic growth. But, of course, the World Bank also noted, as economist Simon Kuznets had shown, that, in the initial phases of growth, income inequalities might actually widen. Operating within the mainstream of international economic assistance, therefore, the Bank proposed a triple strategy of *accelerating economic growth, reducing population growth*, and *redistributing income toward the poorest sectors of the population*. To the extent that it relied on redistribution, it aimed at increasing the consumption levels of the poor.[5]

Poverty and basic needs

In the mid-1970s, basic-needs approaches became the axis around which virtually all proposals for an alternative development turned. The question was put on the agenda by the International Labour Office (ILO) when it convened a global conference on employment, growth, and basic needs in 1976 (ILO 1976a, 1976b, 1977). At the time ILO efforts were paralleled by the World Bank's own strategy of "redistribution with growth" (McNamara, 1973; Streeten and Burki, 1978; Ayres, 1983). It was a brief period of efflorescence for an alternative development. By the end of the decade, however, the winds were blowing from another direction.

The basic-needs approach has been subject to multiple interpretations. The official view presented at the 1976 conference defined basic needs to include:

- minimum requirements of a family for private consumption (food, shelter, clothing, etc.);

- essential services of collective consumption provided by and for the community at large (safe drinking water, sanitation, electricity, public transport, and health and educational facilities);
- the participation of the people in making the decisions that affect them;
- the satisfaction of an absolute level of basic needs within a broader framework of basic human rights; and
- employment as both a means and an end in a basic-needs strategy. (Ghai 1977)

This, the ILO said, was a minimum definition. Even so, the public presentation of this vision stirred up a good deal of controversy. Some representatives of industrialized market economies and employers' delegates thought that the ILO was over-emphasizing structural change and redistribution as essential requirements to meet basic human needs. They considered rapid economic growth as the most important remedy instead (ILO 1977). Others saw in basic needs the key to a conception of alternative development that linked into the Cocoyoc meeting, the Dag Hammarskjöld Foundation's report, *What Now?*, and similar contemporary statements.

The debate over basic needs was highly conscious of the political implications of the proposed approach. National elites would not look kindly on efforts to reduce their share of the national product in favor of social classes that had been excluded from development (Bell 1974). A widely shared view held that elite acquiescence in a basic-needs approach would be a great deal easier to achieve if rapid economic growth were not itself being threatened.[6]

In the heat of this debate, the meaning of basic needs in more conceptual terms tended to get lost. But for an alternative development, more than code words are needed. If basic needs are relevant as a planning concept – and we have not yet established this – what should we take them to mean? The history of the concept takes us back to the first social survey ever, undertaken more than a century ago, in 1886, when Charles Booth presented his typology of the urban poor in London as a basis for devising public policies tailored to their condition (Hall 1988: 28–31). Booth's work initiated a long line of research into levels and standards of living, worked its way into the construction of poverty lines, was central to a revival of welfare economics in the post-World War II era, and finally issued in what came to be known as the social indicators movement of the 1960s and 1970s, which proposed a greatly expanded program of statistical research into social conditions at both national and metropolitan levels (Gross 1966; Perloff 1985; United Nations 1990).

The basic-needs concept was an outgrowth of this earlier research into levels and standards of living. It may be useful at this point to introduce the concept in a more formal way, for what we call "basic human needs" can have several meanings, each with different policy implications. Only one of these, however, was seriously considered as the basis for a new approach to development. I shall begin with the concept of *need*, a word that can be used in four different senses:[7]

1. *As an intense want* (needs-1). The social process through which needs-1 are identified is the market and related market research. The unit of "wanting" here is the individual in an actual or potential market transaction. Individuals may or may not have the means to satisfy their deeply felt wants, and when they are unable to do so they are frustrated or disappointed.
2. *As a functional relationship* (needs-2). We say that A is needed to accomplish B, as an appropriate tool is needed for hammering in a nail. The relationship is that of an appropriate means to an end. Needs-2 are typically identified by experts who base their decisions on either scientific-technical principles or experience. Thus when nutritional needs-2 fail to be met, degenerative diseases are likely to follow. Or when educational needs-2 are not met, a person's chances for employment and income may be reduced. In general, failure to meet functional needs-2 leads to an impairment in human/social performance relative to the end in view.
3. *As a political claim* (needs-3). This is a claim made by a group on resources that are managed in the common interest of a political community. Needs-3 (e.g. agricultural subsidies, research on AIDS, military weaponry, afforestation) are thus turned into a political argument. The political claim is for a (re)allocation of the collective resources in favor of the claimants. Political claims can be argued in terms of needs-2, but a more directly political argument may also be used, including needs-4.[8]
4. *As a customary right* (needs-4). Successful struggles for needs-1 and -2 may result in securing broadly based rights or entitlements, such as free public education, health services, clean drinking water, public transportation, social security, and so forth. Needs-4 are claims that have been politically accepted and institutionalized. They set up patterns of expectation among the population that, if broken, result in popular outrage over what is perceived to be an unjust infringement of their rights.

Major contenders for a basic-needs approach to development are clearly needs-2 and needs-3. The former are identified by professionals, the latter by people acting through the political process.[9]

Given the origins of the basic-needs approach to development within the international bureaucracy, it is not surprising that it was needs-2 that became the principal focus of attention. Needs in the sense of political claims was not a concept bureaucrats knew or with which they cared to work at least in relation to poverty programs.[10] The world's poor would thus continue to be patronized by the rich. Priorities would be set for them from outside their own communities. Aid levels (and forms of aid) would be determined unilaterally.[11]

When the welfare bureaucracy is asked to define what is basic about basic needs, it is in effect asked to set priorities for investment, production, services, and consumption. But how does it go about this task? One thing is clear from the start: basic needs must be affordable. The means for satisfying them must already exist, or they must first be created. Poor countries are unable to afford what countries that are rich might consider basic needs in their own societies. To have running water and electricity in every home is not a currently affordable option in Mozambique or Bangladesh. And there are other differences as well. People living in the tropics do not have to make provision for space heating; those living in temperate climates cannot survive their winters without it. In addition, tastes and preferences vary a great deal and must be included in the equation.

These considerations would seem obvious, and in the 1970s planners readily acknowledged that the responsibility to define basic needs and to set priorities for their attainment would have to be delegated to individual countries (Streeten and Burki 1978: 413). They did not, however, press this logic of devolution to groups below the nation level. If planning for basic needs is to be done separately for each country so that means may be adapted to ends and ends to means, both reflecting relative urgencies and scarcities, why should the same not be true for the country's regions, cities, towns, and villages?[12] Basic-needs planning is not simply a matter of declaring that, say, an average of 2,200 calories a day is necessary for a healthy and active life. An abstract datum such as this has to be translated into a national food security policy that ensures that the right kinds of food will be available to *every* household in the country. And to do this properly requires a territorially differentiated approach that goes beyond even food security to basic questions concerning development: the relative importance of markets; interregional and local transport systems; agricultural organization; the relative importance of investment in food production as exports; territorial self-reliance; and so on. These matters need to be considered in excruciating detail at all levels of territorial governance and planning and will ultimately have to enlist the will and energies of the people, without whose active collaboration nothing of lasting value can be accomplished. This, roughly, is what is called multilevel planning in India, except that the vertical integration of planning in such a system cannot be taken for granted, but involves a continuous *political* process in which different territorial, no less than sectoral, interests contend. In all this, it is far from certain that the interests of the absolutely poor – who are typically excluded from both politics and planning – will be given the kind of attention implied by the basic-needs approach.[13]

If nothing else, the intense debate over basic needs revealed the dilemmas facing development planners in the mid-seventies. These dilemmas were resolved, albeit temporarily, reflecting the current balance of power among contending interests. Among the more important conflicts were these:

- *Economic growth vs. (re)distribution.* To what extent does rapid economic growth, with its implied structural transformation of the national economy, require a markedly unequal distribution of income and wealth? The issue was "resolved" by the unleashing of market forces under the banner of neoliberalism in the 1980s. The redistributive role of the state was minimized, while income inequalities, along with unemployment and landlessness, increased and real wages declined precipitously.

- *Technocratic vs. political determination of basic needs.* Should basic needs be defined along functional lines by experts and planners, or should they be identified through open discourse by each territory-based community for itself? Basic needs must be worked into the allocation of common resources. Is allocative planning simply the outcome of a process of competitive "claiming" by organized groups of citizens within the limits set by a democratic politics, or of technical calculations? This issue was unambiguously resolved in favor of technocracy. The basic-needs discourse arose from within the international bureaucracy. It was virtually unthinkable that this bureaucracy should offer to subordinate its work to a democratic politics that at the international level did not exist. National planning would be done in imitation of international practice. The hoped-for revolution of basic needs was to be a revolution from the top.

- *Production vs. consumption.* Should planning for basic needs be oriented primarily to increasing individual household consumption, or should it be seen as directing resources toward improving the productive capacities of the poor in informal urban activities and small-scale peasant farming? This debate assumed that consumption could be split from production as a meaningful activity in its own right, just as it is in the national economic accounts. The resolution tended to favor production. At the insistence of the IMF, whose role in shoring up poor, unstable economies was greatly enlarged with the debt crisis of the eighties, many countries were obliged to eliminate consumer subsidies for food, urban transportation, and so forth, while social programs, especially for low-cost housing, were curtailed. Enthusiasm waxed over the rediscovery of informally organized work as an enterprising, indigenous form of petty-capitalism. Small-farmer strategies were also encouraged.

- *Markets vs. planned allocation.* The basic-needs approach would have required extensive government planning to favor those population sectors whose ability to participate in markets was extremely weak (we may recall that the

World Bank had estimated that 50 per cent of the population in poor countries had annual incomes of less than $75 per capita). Or, as Streeten and Burki (1978) put it, "The emphasis of basic needs on restructuring production, not necessarily in response to the preferences of the people with very unequal incomes in an imperfect market, implies a substantial role for government" (p. 414). But in the wake of economic crisis, planning by the state was becoming discredited, and the resolution favored markets. Thus it became fashionable to say that the state was part of the problem and to stress its corruption, incompetence, and political instability. Publicists like Peruvian Hernando de Soto argued that his country was still caught in the vise of a pre-capitalist economy organized along mercantilist lines, in which powerful domestic interests were protected by the state. What Peru needed was more of the free-wheeling, enterprising spirit so valiantly displayed by the tens of thousands of informal entrepreneurs on Lima's streets (de Soto 1989). International aid agencies echoed this passionate call for unfettered market competition in an open economy. The protective, redistributive role of the state had to be curtailed.[14]

As a result of this series of "resolutions" favoring accelerated economic growth, technocratic decision-making, production, and markets, the basic-needs approach has become virtually inoperative. References continue to be made to the "unmet needs" of the world's poor (World Commission 1987), but there is little action on this front.[15] And so the condition of the poor continues to deteriorate (Rodgers 1989).

But the debates of the seventies were not all in vain. They have left us with some firm conclusions about poverty that can lead us toward a major rethinking of the question. We have learned, among other things, that:

- basic needs are essentially political claims for entitlements;
- growth-maximizing strategies are not in themselves sufficient to satisfy these claims, even though rapid growth, as in the Republic of Korea, Taiwan, and Singapore, is compatible with relatively low indices of income inequality;
- poverty is a multidimensional phenomenon and does not signify merely a relative lack of income;
- greatly improved statistical systems are needed to assess people's quality of life and to contribute toward defining appropriate standards of living;
- the poor must take part in the provisioning of their own needs rather than rely on the state to solve their problems;
- to become more self-reliant in the provisioning of their own needs, the poor must first acquire the means to do so; and
- effective anti-poverty programs cannot be devised at the top for implementation downward through a compliant bureaucracy but must

emerge from the hurly-burly of politics in which the poor continuously press for the support, at the macro level, of their own initiatives.

All these lessons have contributed to a new perception of what it means to be poor. From the perspective of alternative development, the poor are no longer regarded as wards of the state but as people who, despite enormous constraints, are actively engaged in the production of their own lives and livelihood.

Poverty as (dis)empowerment

The (dis)empowerment model of poverty is a political variant of the basic-needs approach. It is centered on politics rather than planning as the principal process by which needs are identified and the means for their satisfaction pursued.

The starting point of the model is the assumption that poor households lack the social power to improve the condition of their members' lives. It places the household economy into the center of a field of social power in which its relative access to the bases of social power may be measured and compared (Figure 5.1). These critical terms require further explanation.

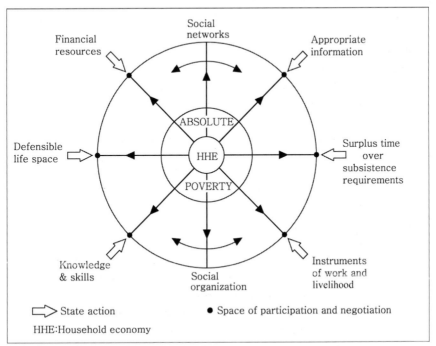

Figure 5.1: Poverty as lack of access to bases of social power

Social power is the power associated with civil society; it is limited by contrasting forms of state, economic, and political power. Each form of power is based on certain resources that can be accessed by a collective actor. The state has the law on its side and a monopoly over the legitimate use of violence. Corporations have substantial access to financial resources, the power to shift capital from one place to another, and the power to hire and fire. The political community – parties, social movements, political action committees – has the power to vote, to stage street demonstrations and rallies, and to pressure politicians through lobbying. The power of civil society, finally, is gauged by the differential access of households to the bases of social power.

There are eight bases of social power, the principal means available to a household economy in the production of its life and livelihood:

1. *Defensible life space.* The territorial base of the household economy, defensible life space includes the physical space in which household members cook, eat, sleep, and secure their personal possessions. In a wider sense, it extends beyond the space called "home" to the immediate neighborhood where socializing and other life-supporting activities take place, chiefly in the context of the moral economy of nonmarket relations. Gaining a secure and permanent foothold in a friendly and supportive urban neighborhood is the most highly prized social power of all, and households are prepared to make almost any kind of sacrifice to obtain it.

2. *Surplus time.* This is the time available to the household economy over and above the time necessary for gaining a subsistence livelihood. It is a function of many things, such as the time spent on the journey to (wage-paying) work; the ease with which basic consumption items such as food, water, and fuel can be obtained; the frequency of illness in the household and access to medical services; the time required for the performance of essential domestic chores; and the gender division of labor. Without access to surplus time, household options are severely constrained. It is the second most prized base of social power.

3. *Knowledge and skills.* This refers to both the educational levels and the mastery of specific skills by members of the household economy. Poor households correctly perceive that education and technical training for at least some of its members are essential for enhancing its long-term economic prospects. They are therefore willing to heavily invest their time, energy, and money in the development of the household's "human resources".

4. *Appropriate information.* This is reasonably accurate information bearing on a household's struggle for subsistence, including such matters as better methods of household production, improved sanitation practices, proven methods of infant care, standard health practices, available public services,

changing political configurations, and opportunities for wage-paying work. Without the continuing access to relevant information, knowledge and skills are virtually useless as a resource for self-development.

5. *Social organization.* This refers to both formal and informal organizations to which household members may belong, including churches, mothers' clubs, sports clubs, neighborhood improvement associations, credit circles, discussion groups, tenant associations, peasant syndicates, and irrigation associations. Organizations are not only the means for a more convivial life; they are also a source of relevant information, mutual support, and collective action. They connect the household with the outer society.

6. *Social networks.* These are essential for self-reliant actions based on reciprocity. They tend to increase with membership in social organizations but are not exclusively determined by such membership. Households with extensive horizontal networks among family, friends, and neighbors have a larger space of maneuver than households without them. Vertical networks, up through the social hierarchy, give households a chance to access other forms of power but may lead to dependent patron-client relationships.

7. *Instruments of work and livelihood.* These are the tools of household production: vigorous and healthy bodies (physical strength) and, for rural producers, access to water and productive land. They also include the tools used in the household's informal work (bicycles, sewing machine) and in the domestic sphere itself (stove, pail, kitchen implements, toilet facilities, etc.).

8. *Financial resources.* These include the net monetary income of households as well as formal and informal credit arrangements.

These eight bases of social power all refer to the means for obtaining other means in a spiraling process of increasing social power. In this sense, they are interdependent. Yet because they cannot be collapsed into a single dimension such as money, which mainstream doctrine regards as the principal means for household "empowerment," they are also to a degree independent of each other.

Relative access is a measure of the extent to which households command the basic resources for their self-development. Households can gain greater access to resources in numerous ways. Whatever the method – and a reallocation of available time resources among household members will invariably be involved – all households must have *some* access in order to survive at all.

Conceptually, access may be measured from the center of Figure 5.1, a virtual zero, to the outer rim of the diagram, which represents a non-quantifiable (theoretical) maximum. Households will be arrayed at different points along each of the eight spokes of the wheel, from virtual zero to the hypothetical limit. Obviously, no single yardstick can be used to measure access to the several bases of social power. Rough comparisons among households can nevertheless be made. In general, increasing access along any of the dimensions shown will improve a household's condition of life and livelihood, and therefore constitutes a measure of genuine development.

Relative access also allows us to conceptualize a level of *absolute poverty* consistent with the model's multidimensional view of poverty. People living at or below this "line" may be unable to move out of poverty on their own. Nevertheless, the model allows each household to make its own decisions on how to use its resources for gaining greater access to the several bases of social power. Most households initially tend to seek some firm grounding for their activities (in the countryside a piece of land; in the city minimally adequate housing). Surplus time is often a second priority, and both may be dependent on households' social networks and participation in popular organizations. Once these "basic needs" are minimally satisfied, however, households may set very different priorities for themselves, pursuing very different ends. At this point, collective action based on shared purposes is likely to yield to more individual-familistic action.

Households' struggles to gain greater access to bases of social power is partly a self-reliant effort and partly a political and thus collective struggle to put forward *claims* on the state for financial and/or technical assistance. But most households would not want the state to act unilaterally: they want meaningful help, not handouts that would return them to the status of wards. Households want not only to be consulted about but to take an active part in the provisioning of their needs. Figure 5.1 accordingly shows six spaces of participation and negotiation in which households can negotiate solutions to their problems with agents of the state.

Such spaces are not shown for either social organization or social networks, which are power bases of civil society from which the state is excluded. Acting in collaboration with others and beyond the state's reach, households can increase their chances of gaining access to the remaining bases of power. This is indicated by the lateral arrows fanning out from the vertical axis in Figure 5.1. The model of (dis)empowerment may thus also be viewed as an empowerment model or, more accurately, a model of *collective self-empowerment*. It is thus not only a model of poverty and deprivation but also a model of how poverty can be overcome and a genuine development promoted.

Even so, there are serious limitations to the prescriptive uses of the model. By making household action central to it, its spatial referent is the microsphere of the locality. It is at this level that households can perceive their interests most clearly and are also motivated and engaged. But the constraints on what can be locally achieved are severe, for poverty is a condition of systematic disempowerment whereby implied *structural conditions* keep the poor poor and confine their access to social power to the level of day-to-day survival.

Mainstream economic growth renders much of the population superfluous to the needs of capital accumulation. The constraints on the poor are therefore structural in the sense that the system of power relations that sustains capitalist production also acts to keep the poor disempowered. It fails to provide for the full employment in the formal economy; it fosters a pattern of land ownership that reduces small peasants to a condition of virtual landlessness; it shuts out the "underclass" from effective political participation. To move beyond survival, then, means that the dominant relations of power in society will have to change. This calls for something beyond an increase in access to the bases of social power. It calls for the transformation of social into political power and a politics capable of turning political claims into legitimate entitlements. Embattled as they are, social democracies of the West have acknowledged household rights to life space and surplus time for a long time. But the institutionalization of these rights was preceded by decades of hard struggle for worker housing, a 40-hour work week, a minimum wage, and child-care services.

The (dis)empowerment model of poverty is both descriptive and prospective. It helps us to look at poverty from the perspective of those who are trying to make ends meet and, if possible, to better their lives. The active center of this effort is the household economy. Poverty in this view is to be disempowered relative to certain bases of social power. But the model can also be turned inside out and so become prospective. Those who are relatively disempowered will want more power and are indeed engaged in a lifelong struggle to improve their situation with respect to one or more bases of social power. The basics of this struggle are shown as the horizontal and vertical dimensions of Figure 5.1: life space and surplus time, social organization and networks. Once these bases are minimally secured, households can devote their efforts to the remaining dimensions of social power: knowledge, skills, and information; tools of production; and financial resources.

Of course, as households address these issues they encounter extraordinary obstacles. The very poorest – famine victims, landless rural laborers, women-headed households in the squatter areas of big cities – may simply lack the *education* means to help themselves. They require help from religious organizations, labor unions, and even the state. But even for the less destitute, collective self-empowerment is rarely a spontaneous process of community action: external agents are critically important.   **?**

The principal purpose of this model is heuristic. The model can be used to help define more precisely the tasks of an alternative development. I will refer to these tasks as political claims, because this is how they appear in the context of social movements that seek to displace the hegemonic growth model with a meaningful alternative capable of attracting political support.

Notes

1. The term underclass has come into common usage in the United States, were major private foundations are sponsoring research under this heading. The term itself has never been properly defined. In a general way, it stands for the hard-core poor, most of

whom belong to disadvantaged ethnic groups. The underclass is America's locked-out minority.

2. In some countries this problem is avoided by simply calculating the poverty line in terms of absolute consumption, without income conversion. According to Rodgers (1989), measures of absolute consumption are "both easiest to use [as an indicator of poverty] and most widespread; and while [they] can be readily criticized, simplicity and data availability are virtues not to be despised" (p. 5).

3. Had the World Bank applied the equally arbitrary standard of $100 per capita, perhaps two-thirds of the population in the world's poor countries would have been "absolutely" poor.

4. Writing of the McNamara years, Robert L. Ayres thought that the underlying rationale for the World Bank's poverty projects were "political stability through defensive modernization. Political stability was seen primarily as an outcome of giving people a stake, however minimal, in the system. Defensive modernization aims at forestalling or preempting social and political pressures. If defensive modernization is successful, it results in conservatism among the newly modernized and thus to [sic] their contributions to political stability" (1983: 226).

5. To move the bulk of the poor from $50 to $75 per capita might require several decades of sustained economic growth. But what actually happened during the 1980s was a decline in the real incomes of the poor.

6. No one, of course, challenged the continued dominance of existing elites.

7. For the philosophical basis of the needs concepts, see Braybrooke 1987; Leiss 1976; Heller 1976; and Soper 1981.

8. Like all politics, the politics of basic needs requires a political community that sets up certain rules of governance and then defines who is to be included as a citizen member. The nation is the best known of political communities, but political communities also exist at household, city, district, region, and even supranational levels. As citizens we claim reciprocal entitlements to common resources. In return for our obligations to the community (to pay taxes, to render service, to defend the community against aggressors), we may press for certain rights or entitlements, such as free public education or subsidized transportation services for the elderly. The first, already enshrined as a right in virtually all countries, may be effectively denied to some, who find its financial demands unreasonable. To attend public school, for instance, children may be required to buy expensive uniforms and purchase textbooks, which would effectively (and inequitably) exclude many poor children from school. The second claim, for subsidized transportation, presents a different sort of argument, for seniors citizens would be competing with the claims of other groups within civil society. Because "rights" have not yet become established in the transport area, seniors would have to present themselves as, for example, aggrieved citizens who have served their community well and now wish to enjoy some privileges in return.

    Needs-3 are clearly not as "objective" as are functional needs. The grounds of argument are often subtle. Civic discourse objectifies needs-3 by requiring each claimant to present the best possible arguments in public. Needs-3 are therefore more than simply a reciprocal entitlement. They must be decided by a process that gives equal voice to all members of a polity, so that both obligations and rights may be decided through an open democratic process. According to Soper (1981), "all the definitions of [needs] and all appeals to the concept of 'human needs' are, and must necessarily remain, problematic .... [I]t is only when the question of human needs is posed in a form that recognizes this problematicity, that is posed in its full dimensions, and that means, importantly, in the acknowledgment of its *political* dimension" (p. 1; my italics).

9. Lee (1977) additionally identifies needs-1 as relevant for a basic-needs approach. Here, needs would continue to be set by experts (as with needs-2), but experts would have to pay attention to consumer tastes and preference, so that the market would clear any production geared to the satisfaction of needs-1.

10. To my knowledge, the only presentation of a case for needs-3 is an essay of my own (Friedmann 1979). For a related argument see Soper (1981).

11. International aid is, of course, never determined unilaterally in the strict sense, but the counterparts of international bureaucrats are principally national bureaucrats; the people themselves are never consulted.

12. To mention self-governance in this context is, of course, questionable. Although virtually all countries are capable of planning at regional levels, formal planning abilities tend to deteriorate quickly after that. All the same, the logic of devolution in setting economic priorities is not invalidated by the existing lack of appropriate institutional arrangements for local governance.

13. International agencies struggled mightily to define hierarchies of basic needs. Streeten and Burki (1978), for example, distinguish between what they call core needs (food, water, clothing, shelter) and all other needs. One supposes that the Streeten-Burki definition of core needs is influenced in part by the ability of international organizations to influence their provision – for example, urban housing for the poor – rather than by more philosophical considerations, where meeting food requirements may have to be weighed in a comparison with, perhaps, liberty.

14. De Soto's (1989) argument was especially appealing to free marketeers. It seemed to offer a way out of the otherwise embarrassing dilemma that the liberalization of the economy, combined with export-led growth, would further isolate the poor on their "reservations" – squatter communities on the outskirts of large cities – even as it would generate increasing numbers of landless laborers in a rapidly modernizing countryside. De Soto's argument, that the poor in the city's informal sector, far from leading unproductive lives, display enormous ingenuity and talent in generating a livelihood for themselves, was an appealing message in the ideological struggle. The poor could now be portrayed as the vanguard of a yet-to-arrive entrepreneurial capitalism, not only in Peru but in the rest of Latin America as well. Indeed, the subtitle of his book made an even more sweeping claim: "The Invisible Revolution in the Third World." De Soto was thus heralded as a major player by, for example, San Francisco's International Center for Economic Growth, which supported the publication of his book in English. The objective was to deconstruct the Keynesian state and to give rein to the free market. De Soto's book made it possible to put up a smokescreen around the devastating effects of such a policy on the poor.

15. Even the environmental movement, of which the Brundtland Report is an expression, is divided within itself. Deep ecologists, for instance, have an Earth First! attitude in which the real problem of humanity is humanity itself.

Bibliography

Ahluwalia, M.S. (1974) 'Income inequality: some dimensions of the problem', in H. Chenery *et al* (eds) *Redistribution with Growth: Policies to improve income distribution in developing countries in the context of economic growth*, published for the World Bank and the Institute of Development Studies, Sussex, New York: Oxford University Press.

Ayres, R.L. (1983) *Banking on the Poor: The World Bank and world poverty*, Cambridge, MA: MIT Press.

Banfield, E.C. (1970) *The Unheavenly City: The nature and future of our urban crisis*, Boston: Little Brown.

Bell, C.L.G. (1974) 'The political framework', in H. Chenery *et al* (eds) *Redistribution with Growth: Policies to improve income distribution in developing countries in the context of economic growth*. Published for the World Bank and the Institute of Development Studies, Sussex, New York: Oxford University Press.

Braybrooke, D. (1987) *Meeting Need*, Princeton, NJ: Princeton University Press.

de Soto, H. (1989) *The Other Path: The invisible revolution in the Third World*, New York: Harper & Row.

Friedmann, J. (1979) 'Basic needs, agropolitan development, and planning from below', *World Development* 7 (6): 607–13.

Ghai, D (1977) *Fixing Income and Price Targets for the Poor in India*, New York: Elsevier.

Ghai, D., Hopkins, M. and McGranahan, D. (1988) 'Some reflections on human and social indicators for development', Discussion paper No. 6, Geneva: United Nations Research Institute for Social Development.

Gross, B.M. (1966) *The State of the Nation: Social system accounting*, London: Tavistock Publications.

Hall, P. (1988) *Cities of Tomorrow*, London: Bart Blackwell.

Heller, A. (1976) *The Theory of Needs in Marx*, London: Allison & Busby.

International Labour Office (1976a) *Tripartite World Conference on Employment, Income Distribution, and Social Progress and the International Division of Labour: background papers, Vol. 1, Basic needs and national employment strategies*, Geneva: ILO.

——(1976b) *Tripartite World Conference on Employment, Income Distribution, and Social Progress and the International Division of Labour: background paper, Vol. 2, Basic needs and national employment strategies*, Geneva: ILO.

——(1977) *Meeting Basic Needs: Strategies for eradicating mass poverty and unemployment*, Geneva: ILO.

Lee, E.L.H. (1977) 'Some normative aspects of a basic needs strategy', in International Labor Office, *The Basic-Needs Approach to Development: Some issues regarding concepts and methodology*, Geneva: ILO.

Leiss, W. (1976) *The Limits to Satisfaction: An essay on the problem of needs and commodities*, Toronto: University of Toronto Press.

McNamara, R (1973) *One Hundred Countries, Two Billion People: The dimensions of development*. New York, Praeger Publishers

Perloff, H.S. (1985) 'Relative regional economic growth: an approach to regional accounts', in L.S. Burns and J. Friedmann (eds) *The Art of Planning: Selected essays of Harvey S. Perloff*, New York: Plenum Press.

Rodgers, G. (ed.) (1989) *Urban Poverty and Labour Market: Access to jobs and incomes in Asian and Latin American cities*, Geneva: ILO.

Soper, K. (1981) *On Human Needs: Open and closed theories in a Marxist perspective*, Brighton, Sussex: Harvester Press.

Streeten, P. and Burki, S.J. (1978) Basic needs: some issues, *World Development*, 6 (3): 411–21.

United Nations Development Program (1990) *Human Development Report 1990*, New York: Oxford University Press.

World Commission on Environment and Development (1987) *Our Common Future*, Oxford: Oxford University Press.

Study questions

In the prevailing neo-liberal economic order, the shift of planning from the state to a re-energized civil society seemed to me to be a logical trajectory. In this chapter, I focused attention on how development planning might be approached so that it would stand in the service of poor people's self-production of life and livelihood. Here the role of the state would be facilitative rather than dominant. The following questions deal with a series of new concepts that this alternate form of development planning would seem to require.

1. Discuss the four different meanings of "need" identified in the chapter and think about the implications of choosing any one of them as a basis for social policy.
2. The concept, "bases of social power," is defined here as "the principal means available to a household economy in the production of its life and livelihood." Please comment. In particular, think how poor households might produce their life and livelihood through an allocation of their human resources to different tasks involved in the process. In doing so, remember that "production" can refer to use values as well as exchange values, both of which are needed for living (though in different proportions at different times and places). You might say that use values refer more to the spiritual part of human existence, whereas exchange values cover many, though by no means all, of the material aspects of human life.
3. A related question is a distinction between life and livelihood. Where livelihood narrowly refers to the means of sustenance, the encompassing concept is that of life itself. Why is it important to make this distinction? Or would it be sufficient to deal exclusively with livelihood issues? What is lost by excluding life from a discussion of empowerment?
4. Why do we take the multi-person household and its "economy" as the basic unit for the production of life and livelihood rather than the individual as most economists would have it? Recall that we can also think of the household as the smallest political community of which the larger political community of city, nation, and so forth are composed.
5. Figure 5.1 identifies eight bases of social power. In a household perspective, which of these would be regarded as especially important? When answering this question, imagine yourself living in a poverty household in a specific country and locality. You may also want to draw an imaginary diagram that ranks this household on all of the eight power dimensions. Can you think of any additional "bases?" If you do, please justify your choice. See also question 6 below.
6. What is meant when we say that poverty can be thought of as a form of dis-empowerment? In this context, we can also speak of its opposite, which

would then be a form of self-empowerment. But any serious self-empowerment involves some sort of collective, cooperative action. Do you agree with this statement? And if you do, what forms of politically practice would be involved?

7. Many people and organizations have argued that the right to housing is a fundamental human right. This tells us something about the significance that almost all households would assign to a safe and functionally adequate life space without which human flourishing is inconceivable. Discuss this right in the context of the politics of self-empowerment. For more detail see the Human Rights Education Association website <hrea.org> on the "right to housing."

Selected additional readings

Polanyi, K. (1977) *The Livelihood of Man*, Pearson, H.W. (ed.), New York: Academic Press.

Roy, A. (2010) 'Poverty truths: the politics of knowledge in the new global order of development', in P. Healey and R. Upton (eds) *Crossing Borders: International exchange and planning practices*, London: Routledge.

Yunus, M. (2007) *Creating a World without Poverty: Social business and the future of capitalism*, New York: Public Affairs.

UN Habitat (2010) *State of the World's Cities 2010–2011*, London: Earthscan.

6

The rise of civil society

In anticipation of my imminent retirement from UCLA in 1996, my colleagues generously offered to organize a major conference on the theme of civil society. Though much debated by philosophers and political scientists, civil society was still a relatively unfamiliar term in the planning lexicon. As planners, we were more comfortable with references to "community," and some critics were wondering why it was necessary to replace a familiar vocabulary with a faddish new expression. Of course, in the sense of associational life, civil society was not a particularly new idea, having been noted already by de Tocqueville (1969) as a unique feature of American life in the early 19th century. Had it been merely a code word for civic associations of this kind, such as the Rotary Club or the Community Chest, perhaps a new vocabulary would not have been needed. What was distinctive in the contemporary use of civil society was a shift from a sociological terminology already assimilated into the language of planning to a term in political economy. For in its newly coined meaning, civil society referred primarily to the social mobilization of citizens for political ends.

Formal definitions in the literature varied. Here is one of them: "Civil society designates those social organizations, associations, and institutions which, being self-organized and autonomous, exist beyond the direct supervision of and dependence on the state." I had come across this usage in Brazil in the 1950s, when Paulo Freire was organizing peasant unions among farm workers in the Northeastern regions of the country. Peasant unions, like those for labor, were for the first time in Brazilian history making political demands, such as for fair wages, decent housing, and lands to farm on their own. A military coup put an end to this movement, however, and forced Freire into exile.

The current revival of civil society discourse was triggered by social movements that had erupted in Eastern Europe during the eighties and nineties and eventually led to the collapse of communist regimes in Poland, Czechoslovakia, and East Germany (Cohen and Arato 1992). What was of special interest for planners, however, was not the term itself, but the varied forms of discourse linked to it, such as discursive democracy, citizenship (especially citizen rights and obligations), civic spaces, social justice, voluntary organizations, and social movements. Here were openings for planners, especially insurgent planners, and their interventions through their writings and direct political engagement (Marcuse *et al* 2009; Douglass and Daniere 2009; Angotti 2008; Sandercock 2003; Hartman 2002; Flyvbjerg 1998, among others).

There is a tendency in the literature to portray civil society in a positive light, as being always on the side of angels. But as Janet Abu-Lughod (1998) has reminded us, civil society is neither good nor bad; it has many different faces and is as varied in its concerns as society at large. Religion is one of the axes of its multiplicity. Social class is another. And when we think of contemporary social movements, of which there are many, they range from the Greens in Europe and America to advocates of the right-to-life, Aboriginal movements worldwide, the gun lobby in America, the land rights movement in Brazil, gay and lesbian movements everywhere, the women's movement, and so forth, none of which are officially sponsored, all of which have their radical and conservative factions making political demands that are often deeply contested within civil society itself. Internationally, these movements are the most visible face of civil society. Less visibly, civil society is also deeply enmeshed in the life of local neighborhoods, where organizations are frequently referred to as community-based, non-governmental, or occasionally in international discourse, the Third Sector.

In any event, the essay reprinted below was one of the first attempts to introduce the concept in its plurality of meanings to planning and to show its implications for practice. In the late 1990s, neo-liberalism seemed triumphant, and planning through the instrumentality of the state bureaucracy appeared less attractive than it had once been. For a growing number of planners, civil society opened new horizons of what could be accomplished.

Bibliography

Abu-Lughod, J. (1998) 'Civil/uncivil society: confusing form with content', in M. Douglass and J. Friedmann (eds) *Cities for Citizens*, Chichester; New York: John Wiley & Sons.
Angotti, T. (2008) *New York for Sale: Community planning confronts global real estate*, Cambridge, MA: MIT Press.
Cohen, J.L. and Arato, A. (1992) *Civil Society and Political Theory*, Cambridge, MA: MIT Press.
de Tocqueville, A. (1969) *Democracy in America*, New York: Doubleday.
Douglass, M. and Daniere, A. (eds) (2009) *The Politics of Civic Space in Asia*, New York: Routledge.
Flyvbjerg, B. (1998) *Rationality and Power: Democracy in practice*, Chicago: University of Chicago Press.
Hartman, C. (2002) *Between Eminence and Notoriety: Four decades of radical urban planning*, New Brunswick, NJ: Center for Urban Policy Research.
Marcuse, P. *et al* (eds) (2009) *Searching for the Just City*, New York: Routledge.
Sandercock, L. (2003) *Cosmopolis II: Mongrel cities in the 21st century*, London: Continuum.

From *Cities for Citizens*

Originally published in 1998

In the late 1940s and early 1950s, when I was still a student of planning at the University of Chicago, the common understanding was that the freshly minted planner would go out and work for the state. The state itself, whether national or local, was thought to be beneficent, responsible for and final guarantor of the public weal. My intellectual mentors, Rexford Guy Tugwell and Harvey S. Perloff, were firm believers in social democracy, the legacy of the Rooseveltian New Deal: they espoused the ideal of a vigorous, interventionist state. For Tugwell in particular, New York patrician and admirer of Thorsten Veblen, planners were to rise above the backstage dealings of the vested, corporate interests that usually prevailed, to articulate, defend and uphold a public interest. Standing above the hubbub of politics, planners would somehow discover and give voice to the broad interests of people in a long-term future perspective. A development or master plan would enshrine this populist vision and, if sanctioned by the relevant political body, become the legal basis for shorter-range plans and capital budgets that, in a descending cascade of documents, would implement its vision (Padilla 1975).

Tugwell's was perhaps an extreme form of enlightened statism, but in the early postwar years, with the consolidation of Mr Attlee's welfare state in the United Kingdom and the specter of the Great Depression still vivid in memory, his views on the role and functions of the state and, in particular, of the federal state were widely shared.

Our present understanding of the role of government planning has undergone a sea-change since those halcyon days. A major turning point came with the civic struggles of the 1960s, when a number of social planners, led by Paul Davidoff, turned from being advocates of a presumptive public interest to advocacy of the disempowered sectors of our cities. Negotiating with City Hall and the Feds, they tried to become spokespersons for poor, inner-city neighborhoods (Peattie 1968).

In Western Europe, Latin America and the United States, urban social movements were being celebrated as a progressive force, reshaping cities and their provisioning for the poor and other marginalized groups. Generated from within working-class ethnic and racially distinctive communities, as well as by dispersed groups of women, gays and lesbians, the homeless, the frail and the disabled, these were valiant, but notably disarticulated, efforts to reclaim the city for themselves. Foreshadowing what would become an important theme of public discourse in the 1990s, Manuel Castells referred to them as citizen movements (Castells 1983: part 5). Planners were beginning to turn from their master visions of the city to spontaneous action in the streets (Piven and Cloward 1979).

A second turning point was the cyclopean process of economic restructuring that began in the mid-1970s and taught us a whole new vocabulary – deindustrialization, globalization, flexibilization – that would become central to our revisioning of the city. Planning academics were among the first to point out what was happening (Bluestone and Harrison 1980; Friedmann 1988; Storper and Walker 1989; Sassen 1991). But the restructuring process was merely the material expression of an underlying political change in the constellations of power, as capitalism shifted into a new phase of capital accumulation. At the ideological level, this meant, at least in the English-speaking world, an about-face to the rhetoric of nineteenth-century Manchester liberalism with its doctrines of rugged individualism, the minimal state and the uninhibited worldwide movement of capital and commodities, if not of labor. The Thatcher and Reagan regimes set the ball rolling for privatization, deregulation, welfare reform, decentralized government and, most recently in the United States, the mantra of the balanced budget. ✭

It seemed that the state, even at local levels, was going to get out of the business of planning altogether. It was this general retreat of the state from the twin onslaughts of restructuring and global accumulation that gave impetus to the voluntary, non-governmental sector of the economy, supported by private charities and foundations, though public funds were also important. In Los Angeles alone there are now hundreds of such organizations which, in one way or another, address the vast social needs of the city, many of them generated by the restructuring process itself. On a worldwide basis, their number rises to tens of thousands. As one might expect with this type of development, a new typology evolved to distinguish among them: community-based organizations; first-, second-and third-generation NGOs; intermediary organizations, and more (Korten 1990; Friedmann 1992; Carroll 1992). Voluntary organizations come in all shapes and sizes. Only one generalization can be made of them with assurance: however hard they may try, and some try very, very hard indeed, their collective efforts inevitably fall far short of the problems with whose symptoms they engage.

This, then, is what we have come to in four decades of planning, starting from a credo in a centralized, benevolent state which was assumed to have a far-sighted and comprehensive vision of the public good to the present welter of a triumphant market economy driven by global competition, an emasculated national state in retreat, a plethora of social movements vying for our attention and support, and a burgeoning sector of voluntary organizations competing fiercely among themselves for private and public resources that are becoming ever more scarce.

Although some would argue that this situation precludes any meaningful role for planners, this is not my view. The market economy doesn't solve urban problems; it creates them. Its pathetically narrow vision for the future comes down to the one syllable, "more." More is better than less. Growth is mandatory. Consumption is a civic obligation. But, in fact, the materialism of the consumer society has very little to do with the good life, which is rather about the quality of human relationships. As I see it, then, the challenge for us as planners is to redefine ourselves and our profession in ways that will make our work congruent with what I take to be the hallmark of the new political economy, the reemergence of civil society as a collective actor in the re/construction of our cities and regions, in search of the good life.

Defining civil society

In their important study, *Civil Society and Political Theory*, Cohen and Arato (1992) speak of the "contemporary revival of civil society." Civil society was first used in its modern sense by Hegel in his *Philosophy of Right* (1821) and, in a less philosophical manner, by Alexis de Tocqueville in his classic study, *Democracy in America*, published a decade later (Hegel 1967; de Tocqueville 1969). As with any concept in the human sciences, civil society refers to something we claim to perceive in the observable world that may serve us as a lens through which to view and interpret phenomena that otherwise would appear disconnected from each other. In that sense, the concept of civil society has heuristic value. While its specific meaning has remained fluid, as observers across a broad political spectrum began using it, its core meaning has remained constant. Civil society designates those social organizations, associations and institutions that exist beyond the sphere of direct supervision and control by the state. It is this core meaning that most often figures in the accounts of conservative critics. Basing themselves on Tocqueville's early observations of Americans' propensity to form themselves into a plethora of voluntary associations, these critics see civil society as essentially composed of institutions – neighborhood, family, church and voluntary associations – that "mediate" between the individual and the state (Berger and Neuhaus 1977). Intellectual radicals, on the other hand, such as Ernesto Laclau and Chantal Mouffe (1985), emphasize political mobilization and active resistance to a hegemonic discourse rather than Tocquevillian mediations. The Left, accordingly, dwells on social movements, self-management and the practices of direct democracy (Keane 1988a).

When civil society was first introduced into theoretical discourse, it served primarily to argue for the preservation of a sphere of freedom against a potentially despotic state (Keane 1988b: 35–72). And it was popular resistance to dictatorship that led to its current revival. Although most contemporary authors point to the Polish Solidarity movement and the Lutheran Church in former East Germany as catalysts in the popular struggles to bring down

communist regimes during the 1980s, it was earlier resistance movements in
South America, especially in Brazil, Argentina and Chile, which first led to
the reappearance of civil society in the sociological literature. As we shall see,
however, important as the theme of resistance is, the discourse of civil society
has not been confined to it but has been expanded to include such topics as
participatory democracy (Barber 1984), the social meaning of citizenship
(Parliament of the Commonwealth of Australia 1995) and justice in
postmodern society (Young 1990).

Planners have held themselves aloof from these debates. At the same time,
many of us have been at the front lines of the actual struggles for greater citizen
participation, community-based development, and for the aims of new social
movements, from feminism to ecology. This very activism on the part of our
profession may have prevented us from seeing the larger picture and from
taking part in the theoretical debates. Being so close to the action, we have
failed to recognize the new configurations of power within which we will have
to reset our sights and learn to be different sorts of planners from the professional
self-image we have promoted in the past.

At this point, I feel obliged to set out my own take on civil society, and how
I propose to use the concept in the remainder of this chapter. I will therefore
ask you, at least for now, to see the world from my particular angle of vision.

Literature on civil society is informed by two very different philosophical
presuppositions. The first, derived from a critical reading of the Scottish
Enlightenment – Francis Hutchinson, Adam Ferguson and Adam Smith –
centers civil society in the individual human being who is endowed with
reason, including a capacity for moral reasoning. Some proponents of this view
argue that the Enlightenment's synthesis of the individual and society fails us
today because contemporary urban societies have replaced trust in institutions
and interpersonal relations with mutual suspicion: the apparent solidarity
which was once believed to have existed has come unraveled (Seligman 1992:
168–70). A more generous reading is given by the British anthropologist
Ernest Gellner (1994) who sees individual liberty guaranteed by civil society
against Leviathan. The epistemological core of both these analyses is the
individual as an abstract, self-interested, reasoning being.

The second position starts with the given of the individual person's social
nature. We are born into a group – the family, the clan – which we need for
our physical survival, and we become individuated only gradually, learning to
speak and act as we become conscious of ourselves and others to whom we
relate in a variety of ways. As social beings, we are communicative beings. This
position leads us away from liberal philosophy towards a thinking that regards
social relations as primary. We find this thinking in the young Karl Marx, in
Antonio Gramsci, and in the recent work of Cohen and Arato (1992). My
own position follows in this tradition (Friedmann 1979; 1989).

Accordingly, civil society appears as one of four partially autonomous and overlapping spheres of action and valued social practices, and it can only be grasped in relation to this ensemble.[1] Civil society's "opposition" to the state is central to this understanding and was already present, one might say, at the hour of its birth, when the two social and political revolutions that marked the final decades of the eighteenth century broke out in the North American colonies and in France. But civil society must also be seen as standing in "opposition" to the corporate economy, the sphere of capital writ large which, over the course of the nineteenth century separated itself from civil society to become a distinctive sphere of action and valued social practice of its own (Polanyi 1957). The sphere of capital has become essential to economic growth; at the same time, its relentless commodification of all social relations threatens to undermine the very foundations of civil society. The fourth sphere of action, finally, is the political community or the terrain of political conflict and struggle which, as a social construct, we need for our common understanding of democracy where civil society reasserts its sovereignty from the state. This is the terrain of political parties, clubs, social movements and the like, which represent the public face of civil society. When these four overlapping and intersecting spheres of action are inscribed within territorial bounds, they may be said to constitute a social formation.

[margin note: Four spheres of social action]

Central to the organization of civil society, and the basis of all other forms of social organization and collective action, is the household whose moral economy, like that of civil society as a whole, works primarily on the basis of reciprocity and trust, though compulsion is also part of it (Cohen and Arato 1992 n 81: 724). In a wider sense, it is also the blood line – the family or clan – whose members do not share life under the same roof, but are linked by descent or marriage. Despite deep intrusions by both the state and corporations and its general fragility, the household may still be viewed as a relatively autonomous sphere of action and valued social practice, and its work is essential for the production (and reproduction) of the life and livelihood of its members. Linked to households are religious organizations – tabernacles, churches, synagogues, mosques – to the extent that they are not part of the state apparatus, as well as all manner of formal and informal associations, clubs, fraternal orders, cooperative ventures and similar social bodies that animate the life of civil society and are largely beyond the reach of the state.

Along with the other spheres of action, civil society is lodged within the territorial limits of a state, region, city or neighborhood, but its linkages and networks extend increasingly beyond these boundaries to the rest of the world through electronic media, the migration of kin and friends, and associational bonds. Another caveat is that civil society must under no circumstances be read as a homogeneous sphere. Deep divisions run through it, creating an internal dynamic that is based on social class, gender, religion, ethnicity, so-called race, access to household resources and other social markers. These divisions are major sources of conflict both within civil society and on the wider political terrain. The discourse on civil society as such takes us only a few steps into a better understanding of political economy. Beyond them, we need to particularize and refine our observations.

Finally, I want to draw a distinction between organized and mobilized civil society. What I have described so far – households, associations, churches – constitutes, so to speak, the basic scaffolding of civil society. This is the private domain of our lives. Mobilization, on the other hand, always occurs around a specific purpose that, by its very nature, is political in a sense quite different from the politics of everyday life. All social movements may be seen as mobilizations of certain sectors of civil society, whether for protest or some other limited purpose in the public domain. Social mobilizations are necessarily of finite duration and occur, so to speak, in the interstices of organized civil society. They are not part of its structure. It is also important to note that mobilizations may be directed not only against the state but also against segments of civil society itself. This, for example, is the case with current American debates on "family values" and the "right to life," in which militants from different sides of these issues join battle over "right conduct" in American civil society – the political community – as a whole.

The role of households

Let me turn to what I would argue is the primary social role of households, the daily (re)production of life and livelihood. This may seem unexceptional to you, but it is, in fact, contested by the contrary assumption (promoted by corporate capital) that households are best understood as units of consumption or, more precisely, as loose aggregates of self-interested age- and gender-graded individuals who are out to maximize their individual utilities as soon as they can speak and act for themselves. Certain consequences flow from this contrary assumption. First, under what I shall call the consumer hypothesis, poverty is treated as a condition of insufficient income or low spending power. Second, and as a correlate to this, anti-poverty measures should aim at raising household incomes through direct transfers and/or pushing so-called welfare dependants into low-paying jobs. Although it would be foolish to deny the importance of monetary income, it would be similarly mistaken to reduce households to the essentially passive status of consumers instead of seeing them as being fundamentally engaged in the production of their own life and livelihood.

Some feminists have been extremely skeptical of taking patriarchal households as units for any reason, whether for consumption or production, preferring to see them as a terrain of conflictive relations of power between men and women. I wouldn't for one moment deny the reality of the patriarchal order and the need for an emancipatory politics. But however biased actual household and other relations of power may be, favoring men, the prior claims of life and livelihood must be acknowledged. Household relations, especially among the poor, take place largely outside the exchange economy, and in this sense they may be called moral relations that, in the last instance, are based on reciprocity and trust (Ekeh 1974; Lomnitz 1977). The moral economy of the household does not preclude the existence of a gendered division of labor in which women are tethered to domestic tasks. Nor does it deny the possibility that the actual bonds that tie members of households to each other are, to some degree, based on material necessity, exploitation and fear of physical violence. All this notwithstanding, relations of reciprocity do exist within most households. They are based on dyadic, face-to-face transactions, and a measure of unspoken trust and dialogue is their specific mode of transaction. The moral economy, we can venture to say, makes possible the exchange economy. It extends outwards from households through networks of close personal relations into the world of work, including those voluntary activities in the community without which civilized life would be unthinkable.

Poor people's households are especially dependent on keeping the moral economy in working order. They must draw each of their members into the tasks necessary for life and livelihood. They depend on multiple sources of income, including the monetary contributions of all income earners within the household and remittances from family members living elsewhere. But poverty cannot be reduced to a mere condition of low income (Wratten 1995). In structural terms, it is also a result of low access to the resources that are necessary for household production. I call them the household's bases of social power (Friedmann 1992), and they include a secure life space (roughly equivalent to housing), surplus time over and above the time required for the reproduction of life and livelihood, social networks, knowledge and skills of appropriate kinds, information, social organizations, good health, instruments and tools of domestic production, and finally also financial resources, including both income and credit. Unless household access to these bases of social power can be improved, poor households will continue to be disempowered; poverty will be perpetuated.[2]

Planners engaged in anti-poverty work are directly involved in improving household access to these structural bases of social power, and they frequently choose to work in local neighborhoods, attached to both community-based and non-governmental organizations to accomplish their task. But access to household resources on a societal scale depends to a great extent on provisioning by the state. Poor people's politics has therefore focused on struggles for low-cost housing, rent control, affordable mass transit, childcare, cooperative banking, the clean-up of their immediate environments, the provision of conveniently located health facilities and similar household resources. Planners involved in these struggles at municipal, county, state and federal levels have often had to perform the triple role of community activist, technical expert and political strategist.

But beyond the specifics of local action and the politics surrounding household resources is a level of politics that raises fundamental questions of rights or entitlements: human rights in their most universal dimension (including, importantly, the rights of women and children) and, more specifically, citizen rights. I would like to speak briefly to the latter.[3]

Citizen rights

Citizen rights derive from full membership in a distinct political community (Kymlicka and Norman 1994). And, as Michael Walzer reminds us, "the primary good that we distribute to one another is membership in some human community: ... it determines with whom we make ... choices, from whom we require obedience and collect taxes, to whom we allocate goods and services" (Walzer 1983: 31).

The question of citizenship and its attendant rights (and reciprocal duties) has recently been revived in countries as far apart as Brazil, Germany and Australia. In Brazil, which threw off the yoke of a long period of military dictatorship with a new constitution in 1988, current debates about citizenship concern primarily grassroots participation in political decision-making. They are largely about the political meaning of citizenship. Rebecca Abers tells us about one significant Brazilian experiment, the process of participatory budgeting in the southern city of Porto Alegre (Abers 1998). From this it is only a small step before other demands, grounded in the idea of citizenship and especially local citizenship, are made. A booklet issued in 1991 by FASE, a Brazilian NGO, contains a critical analysis of the government's plans for the environmental clean-up of the Baixada Fluminense, Rio de Janeiro's vast, insalubrious periphery. It is subtitled: *Direito à cidade, direito à vida (right to the city, right to life)* (Florêncio *et al* 1995). Four years later, in another FASE publication, the authors subtitle their collection of essays reporting on seven years of popular struggle, *Cidadania e Gestão Democrática* (Citizenship and democratic management)" (Florêncio *et al* 1995). Their report uses the term citizen in a dual sense, referring both to membership in the political community of all Brazilians that guarantees them the right to voice, and to residence in a locality – the state and city of Rio de Janeiro and, more specifically, of the Baixada Fluminense – which confers legitimacy to their claimed rights to a clean environment, to rivers whose floods are contained, and beyond that to basic urban infrastructure and services, and last, though not least, to decent, wage-earning jobs.

The theme of local citizenship in this sense is also taken up in a series of pronouncements concerning the status of foreign immigrants in Frankfurt, Germany. Since German citizenship is automatically passed on through the blood line, and naturalization is difficult, the third of Frankfurt's population that is "without a German passport," while clearly making its full contribution to the economy, is politically excluded. Foreign workers and their families, regardless of their period of residence in Germany, lack citizen rights. Although various initiatives have been afoot at the national level to extend German citizenship to long-term immigrants on easier terms than in the past, it is the local rhetoric that I found particularly compelling. Under the leadership of Daniel Cohn-Bendit, the member of Frankfurt's city council who was in charge of multicultural affairs for the city, a campaign was waged over a period of years, beginning in the late 1980s, to extend the "right to the city" to the Turkish, Greek, Moroccan, Italian, Croat, Bosnian, Sri Lankan and other non-German immigrant families and individuals. Though legally without the right to vote in public elections, they eventually gained the right to representation in the city council, thus gaining both visibility and voice (Friedmann and Lehrer 1997). It seems to me that this extension of the meaning of citizenship to the local, regardless of nationality, has much to commend it in an era of hypermobility and vast international popular movements, an era that is marked by the "hollowing out" of the national state and the concomitant rise of virtual city-states conducting the world's business among themselves in networks of dense urban clusters that extend from the shores of the Rhine to China's Pearl River delta (Jessop 1994; Taylor 1995). Local citizenship also recalls Walzer's principle of political justice: "that the processes of self-determination through which a democratic state shapes its internal life, must be open, and equally open, to all those men and women who live within its territory, work in the local economy, and are subject to local law" (Walzer 1983: 60).

Curiously, it is Australia, itself an archipelago of city-states – Sydney, Melbourne, Brisbane, Adelaide, Perth – which has begun an official inquiry into the meaning of citizenship (Parliament of the Commonwealth of Australia 1995). A working paper commissioned by the Parliamentary Committee charged with the inquiry distinguishes between a legal or formal meaning of citizenship and a broader social meaning. The latter is the inquiry's main subject and turns on four issues:

1. the quality of full membership and active participation;
2. in a just and mutually supportive political community;
3. including the individual and collective rights and responsibilities – legal, social, economic, cultural and environmental – that go with such membership; and

4. the public and private policies and resources needed to sustain it (Parliament 1995: 5–6).

This strikes me as an unusually broad conceptualization. It stresses active participation in a political community that is just and mutually supportive and embraces all sorts of rights and responsibilities, including cultural and environmental. This holistic approach to citizenship which, in the final analysis, is the right to have rights, represents an attempt on the part of the committee to respond to what it called the "excesses of economic rationality and small government ... and a reassertion of the importance of communitarian values against the official rhetoric of competitive individualism" (Parliament 1995: 45).

Let it be noted that the Australian inquiry is not only about rights – important as they are – but equally about an ethics of responsibility. "The ethical content of citizenship," write the authors, "the idea of civic duty, is crucial. Without individuals and organisations prepared to participate and take responsibility, without a concept of the public interest, without the values of tolerance and compassion, and some sense of solidarity and belonging, citizenship would be impossible and 'democracies become difficult to govern, even unstable'" (Parliament 1995: 69). To illustrate the inquiry's exploration of the extended meaning of citizenship and its effort to recover a sense of the public good rooted in daily life, here is a partial listing of a suggested code, incorporating 18 points of what the report calls "The duties of the good citizen" (Parliament 1995: 67):

*   To nurture, love, and educate one's children.
*   To moderate one's own demands and consumption in the interests of the broader community.
*   To pay one's taxes as fairly assessed without artificial avoidance.
*   To vote in elections.
*   To look after the environment.
*   To be tolerant of differences within society.

Though not intended to be prescriptive, these so-called duties do suggest a much wider meaning of citizenship than is common in the United States. The Parliamentary Committee hopes to open up a public debate about what it means to be a responsible member of a multicultural political community, to be an Australian "citizen" in these terms. It spells out one possible version of what I have called the valued social practices of the Australian community in the political sense.

What strikes me about this list of citizen duties – and I have cited only 6 of its 18 mandates – is, first of all, their implicit hope for some agreement on "valued social practices" and therefore the formation of an inclusive national political community beyond ethnicity, "race," regional loyalty or any other social division and, second, the grounding of so many "duties" in the life space where our everyday lives unfold. Citizenship, I would agree with James Holston, is multiple, ranging from membership in the human community and the national polity down to city and neighborhood (Holston 1995). These several citizenships are layered; they confirm specific rights but also impose multiple responsibilities, which is their ethical content. When ethical imperatives conflict, as they often do, we are obliged to choose. Choice is unavoidable, often difficult, and its results are frequently ambiguous. Only one thing we cannot do: step outside the human and political communities that fill the world in a seamless web of valued social practices. Stepping outside them, we are shunned as outlaws.

Civil society: insurgent and for itself

In a recently published essay, James Holston introduces the term "insurgent urbanism" to describe a mode of practice by sectors of civil society (Holston 1995). He writes:

> when citizenship expansions and erosions focus on urban experience, they constitute an insurgent urbanism which informs this development in several ways. First, they present the city as both the text and the context of new debates about fundamental social relations. In their localism and strategic particularism, these debates valorize the constitutive role of conflict and ambiguity in shaping the multiplicity of urban life. In a second sense, this heterogeneity works against the modernist absorption of citizenship in a project of state-building, providing alternative possible sources for the development of new kinds of practices and narratives about belonging to and participating in society. This "working against" defines what I called an insurgent citizenship, and its spatial mode of insurgent urbanism. This insurgence is important to the project of rethinking the social in planning because it reveals a realm of the possible that is rooted in the heterogeneity of lived experience, which is to say, in the ethnographic present and not in utopian futures. (Holston 1995: 48)

Throughout this extensive passage, it is worth noting, Holston avoids the currently fashionable term "resistance." Civil society, which is a society of citizens, is engaged in something larger than sporadic rearguard actions against Leviathan. According to Holston, it is engaged in "providing alternatives, possible sources for the development of new kinds of practices, narratives about belonging to and participating in society." Civil society does, indeed, resist, protest, make demands on the state and stake out new claims. It also struggles against the corporate Leviathan when it pressures Hollywood to reduce the violence of its films or the tobacco companies to make their advertising less appealing to children. But more important than any possible resistance, civil society is simply engaged in being "for itself."

Traditional Marxist terminology doesn't capture this moment of being for itself. It speaks of the work of households as social reproduction, meaning the reproduction of labor power, as though the whole truth of households were exhausted by their functional relation to capital. But surely we are not victims of "false consciousness" when we celebrate anniversaries, hold street parties, watch Little Leaguers slide into first base, or organize, as did the working-class women of Lima, Peru, in the 1980s, a city-wide "daily glass of milk" campaign for their children (Pease García 1992: 168–9). Civil society is ultimately for itself. Within the constraints of structural imperatives, it is in its attention to small things that the quality of our life is found. We make the city serve our needs by molding the physical appearance of streets into distinctive neighborhoods. In less visible ways, we mark it on cognitive maps of historical landmarks that commemorate sites of insurgent citizenship. Moira Kenney (1994) has recently drawn such a map for the gay and lesbian community of Los Angeles. Dolores Hayden's book, *The Power of Place,* is also relevant here (1995). Some of our neighborhoods are a result of forced segregation. But others, like San Francisco's Castro District or Los Angeles' Koreatown, are better understood as affinity environments where particular cultural rituals can be freely celebrated. They are districts that, to a considerable extent, are shaped by the very people who live in them, who lend them their distinctive character and who, over the years, have left a residue of memories behind. Are they insurgent spaces in Holston's sense? Perhaps. But they are also the work of civil society when it is working "for itself."

There is a darker side to this story, however, when civil society turns against itself in its rage against differences within its own ranks. This is the tragic litany of racism, intolerance, terrorism and persecution of those who are judged to be different from us by some arbitrary distinguishing mark, whether of birth place, language, skin color, sexual practice or religious belief. Driven to excess, intolerance of difference leads to the marginalization of whole groups of people, to apartheid, ethnic cleansing, genocide and, worst of all, the Holocaust.[4]

We cannot say, then, that civil society is inherently "good" or, for that matter, inherently "bad." But wherever they are found, intolerance and evil must be resisted. Ethnic cleansing is evil. Social and political exclusions are intolerable. People must be held to the valued practices and ethical standards of the nested communities to which we all belong. Human rights – to the extent we all agree what they are – take precedence over all other rights; they are foundational (An-Naʻim 1992). The political and civic rights enshrined in the American Constitution take precedence over specific social rights or entitlements by virtue of its people's membership in a political community. But social rights in the United States are still very few. Essential for the flourishing of human life, they constitute an agenda of political struggle: the right to a decent standard of living, the right to housing, to education, to the highest standards of physical and mental health, and the right to work.[5]

These and any similar rights must apply to all who belong to a given political community. Democratic citizenship does not give us license to exclude from the enjoyment of its privileges anyone with a legitimate claim to membership. It does give us license to pursue a civil, that is, a civilized life. In the final analysis, this is the aim, if indeed it has an aim, of civil society.

 what does this mean?

Notes

1. Valued social practices refer to norms of individual and social behavior that form the culture and subcultures within each of the spheres of action.
2. Other forms of empowerment, including political and psychological, are equally necessary for the good life.
3. For a wide-ranging discussion of human rights, see An-Naʻim (1992).
4. See, for example, the hair-raising account of the rebirth of neo-Nazism in East Berlin (Hasselbach and Reiss 1996).
5. These rights are taken from the International Covenant on Economic, Social, and Cultural Rights of the United Nations (Parliament 1995: 62).

Bibliography

Abers, R. (1998) 'Learning democratic practice: distributing government resources through popular participation in Porto Alegre, Brazil', in M. Douglass and J. Friedmann (eds) *Cities for Citizens: Planning and the rise of civil society in a global age*, New York: John Wiley & Sons.

An-Naʻim, A.A. (ed.) (1992) *Human Rights in Cross-Cultural Perspectives: A quest for consensus*, Philadelphia: University of Pennsylvania Press.

Barber, B. (1984) *Strong Democracy: Participatory politics for a new age*, Berkeley: University of California Press.

Berger, P.L. and Neuhaus, R.J. (1977) *To Empower People: The role of mediating structures in public policy*, Washington DC: American Enterprise Institute for Public Policy Research.

Bluestone, B. and Harrison, B. (1980) *Capital and Communities: The causes and consequences of private disinvestment*, Washington, DC: The Progressive Alliance.

Carroll, T.F. (1992) *Intermediary NGOs: The supporting links in grassroots development*, West Hartford: Kumarian Press.

Castells, M. (1983) *The City and the Grassroots: A cross-cultural theory of urban social movements*, London: Edward Arnold.

Cohen, J.L. and Arato, A. (1992) *Civil Society and Political Theory*, Cambridge, MA: MIT Press.

de Tocqueville, A. (1969) *Democracy in America*, New York: Doubleday.

Ekeh, P.P. (1974) *Social Exchange Theory: The two traditions*, Cambridge: Harvard University Press.

Florêncio, J. *et al* (eds) (1995) *Saneamento Ambiental na Baixada: Cidadania e gestão democratic*, Rio de Janeiro: FASE and Inter-American Foundation.

Florêncio de Oliveira, J. *et al* (1991) *Saneamento Básico na Baixada: Direito á cidade, direito á vida*, Rio do Janeiro: FASE.

Friedmann, J. (1979) *The Good Society*, Cambridge, MA: MIT Press.

——(1988, original 1982) 'World city formation', in J. Friedmann, *Life Space and Economic Space: Essays in Third World planning*, New Brunswick, NJ: Transaction Books, ch. 3.

——(1989) 'Collective self-empowerment and social change', *Ifda Dossier*, 69: 3–14.

——(1992) *Empowerment: The politics of alternative development*, Oxford: Blackwell.

Friedmann, J. and Lehrer, U. (1997) 'Urban policy responses to foreign in-migration: the case of Frankfurt-am-Main', in M. Douglass and J. Friedmann (eds) *Cities for Citizens: Planning and the rise of civil society in a global age*, New York: John Wiley & Sons.

Gellner, E. (1994) *Conditions of Liberty: Civil society and its rivals*, New York: Penguin.

Hasselbach, I. and Reiss, T. (1996) 'How Nazis are made', *The New Yorker*, January 8: 36.

Hayden, D. (1995) *The Power of Place*, Cambridge: MIT Press.

Hegel, G.W.F. (1967) *Hegel's Philosophy of Rights*, trans. T.M. Knox, New York: Oxford University Press.

Holston, J. (1995) 'Spaces of insurgent citizenship', in L. Sandercock (ed.) *Making the Invisible Visible: New historiographies for planning, planning theory*, Milan: Franco Angeli.

Jessop, B. (1994) 'Post-Fordism and the state', in A. Amin (ed.) *Post-Fordism: A reader*, Oxford: Blackwell.

Keane, J. (ed.) (1988a) *Civil Society and the State: New European perspectives*, London: Verso.

——(1988b) 'Despotism and Democracy: the origins and development of the distinction between civil society and the state 1750–1850', in J. Keane (ed.) *Civil Society and the State*, London: Verso.

Kenney, M. (1994) 'Strategic visibility: gay and lesbian place claiming in Los Angeles', Ph.D. dissertation, Department of Urban Planning, UCLA, Los Angeles.

Korten, D.C. (1990) *Getting to the 21st Century: Voluntary action and the global agenda*, West Hartford, CT: Kumarian Press.

Kymlicka, W. and Norman, W. (1994) 'Return to the citizens: a survey of recent work on citizenship theory', *Ethics*, 104 (2): 352–89.

Laclau, E. and Mouffe, C. (1985) *Hegemony and Socialist Strategy: Towards a radical democratic politics*, London: Verso.

Lomnitz, I. (1977) *Networks and Marginability: Life in a Mexican shantytown*, New York: Academic Press.

Padilla, S.M. (ed.) (1975) *Tugwell's Thoughts on Planning*, San Juan: University of Puerto Rico Press.

Parliament of the Commonwealth of Australia (1995) 'Discussion paper on a system of national citizenship indicators', Canberra: Senate Legal and Constitutional References Committee.

Pease Garcia, M. (1992) 'The Glass of Milk Campaign', *Rethinking the Latin American City*, Baltimore: John Hopkins University Press.

Peattie, L. (1968) Reflections on advocacy planning, *Journal of the American Institute of Planning*, 31 (4): 331–8.

Piven, F.F. and Cloward, R.A. (1979, original 1977) *Poor People's Movements: Why they succeed. How they fail*, New York: Vintage Books.

Polanyi, K. (1957, original 1944) *The Great Transformation*, Boston: Beaver Press.

Sassen, S. (2001) *The Global City: New York, London, Tokyo*, 2nd edn, Princeton, NJ: Princeton University Press.

Seligman, A. B. (1992) *The Idea of Civil Society*, Princeton, NJ: Princeton University Press.

Storper, M. and Walker R. (1989) *The Capitalist Imperative*, Oxford: Basil Blackwell.

Taylor, P.J. (1995) 'World cities and territorial states'. in P.L. Knox and P.J. Taylor (eds) *World Cities in a World System*, Cambridge: Cambridge University Press.

Walzer, M. (1983) *Spheres of Justice: A defense of pluralism and equality*, New York: Basic Books.

Wratten, E. (1995) 'Conceptualizing urban poverty', *Environment and Urbanization*, 7 (1): 11–36.

Young, I.M. (1990) *Justice and the Politics of Difference*, Princeton, NJ: Princeton University Press.

Study questions

This chapter imports the concept of civil society, which plays a central role in contemporary political theory, into the field of planning. What I seek to demonstrate is how adopting this concept can change planning practice as its several connotations reverberate across all dimensions of our field. I should like to suggest five sets of questions for discussion.

1. How is civil society defined and used in this chapter? A distinction is made between an insurgent civil society and a civil society "for itself" that is primarily engaged in its own affairs. What is the basis for this distinction? And what specifically is meant by "insurgent" in this formulation? In the present context, insurgency is related to social movements and, more specifically, urban social movements as defined by Manuel Castells (see suggested readings, below). Some planners also speak here of planning "from below." But is this the same as speaking of insurgencies? If not, what does it mean to say "from below"? Others have pointed out that, as a collective actor, civil society is neither to be praised nor condemned, and far from being a homogeneous body of citizens, is often divided within itself. Think of some examples where this division is particularly pronounced. As you know, all significant political issues are contested and sometimes fought over bitterly in what Habermas calls the public sphere. If we grant that all planning is inherently political, can we then call interventions by civil society in the public sphere as part of planning?

2. Underlying this discussion is the more fundamental question of what it means to be human. In North American societies we usually speak of ourselves as individuals, emphasizing the individual quality that makes each one of us a distinctive and unique human being. What we often fail to acknowledge, however, is that in some fundamental ways we are also social or, as Aristotle would have it, political beings. Virtually everything we do depends on interacting with others, and our social relations can be said to be intrinsically a part of who we are. That is why we continually connect with each other, and why dialogue is central to our being in the world. Discuss this issue in relation to what is called the moral economy that comprises the next set of questions.

3. The moral economy is introduced here as a pervasive presence alongside of and even within the exchange economy that is the usual coin of discourse in planning. The moral economy has its origin in the household, where it is based on relations of reciprocity and trust. But it also enters both civic and political spheres where it plays a major role that we sometimes refer to as volunteering, that is, doing things without getting paid. Think of examples of the moral economy from your own lives and discuss these with

the examples given by others in your group. In the larger scheme of things, which do you think is more important for your work getting done: efforts that are compensated or those that are not, representing a voluntary contribution? (Note that the moral economy figures importantly also in the Epilogue to this volume).

4. Another theme touched on in this chapter is that of citizenship with its multiple claims of belonging, from the political community of the household on up to the larger communities of neighborhood, city, region, and country, until they reach the global human community to which we all belong. Do you think that these different political communities have equal claims on our loyalty, and what happens when these loyalties come into conflict with each other, as they often do? But loyalty claims are only one aspect of citizenship. Another and ultimately more important issue are the rights and obligations attendant upon citizenship. Rights are claimed within particular communities and may be granted or not, but they may also be taken away. Human rights are claimed globally, whereas in specific countries civic, social, economic and other rights are typically inscribed in constitutional documents. By marginalized groups within a national society, they are often asserted politically. But what happens at more local levels where specific rights may not be guaranteed or acted upon, as for example the right to housing? Even more ambiguous is the question of civic obligations, particularly at local levels. Political theory has little to say about the duties of citizens. And yet, rights and obligations are usually said to go hand-in-hand. So then, what obligations do we have as citizens and denizens of local communities? To take a current example, in an era of impending climate change, what obligation do we have with regard to the use of water, electricity, and carbon-based fuel? Or do you think we should perhaps discard the notion of civic duties altogether, except for such obvious mandates as obeying the law and paying taxes?

5. Over the past half century, planners have significantly shifted from working with and for the state to working with local communities and civil society organizations. And although the latter claim considerable autonomy from the state, confronting the multiple problems of local communities, some kind of collaboration with the state is often essential. Or put it this way: on the one hand, civil society may rise up in protest against the state and its agents while, conversely, the state's helping hand is needed, for example, for improving life in local communities. How is this contradiction resolved in both theory and practice? How can "seeing like a state" (James Scott) be reconciled with "seeing like a community?" Is collaboration with the state a winning strategy, as Patsy Healey might want to argue?

Selected additional readings

Abers, R. (1998) 'Learning democratic practice: distributing government resources through popular participation in Porto Alegre, Brazil', in M. Douglass and J. Friedmann (eds) *Cities for Citizens: Planning and the rise of civil society in a global age*, New York: John Wiley.

Beiner, R. (ed.) (1995) *Theorizing Citizenship*, Albany: State University of New York Press.

Friedmann, J. (2002) 'Citizenship: statist, cosmopolitan, insurgent', in *The Prospect of Cities*, ch. 4, Minneapolis: University of Minnesota Press.

Castells, M. (1983) *The City and the Grassroots: A cross-cultural theory of urban social movements*, London: Edward Arnold.

Holston, J. (eds) (1999) *Cities and Citizenship*, London: Duke University Press.

Seligman, A. (1992) *The Idea of Civil Society*, Princeton: Princeton University Press.

Mouffe, C. (ed.) (1992) *Dimensions of Radical Democracy: Pluralism, citizenship, community*, London: Verso.

Scott, J.C. (1998) *Seeing Like a State*, New Haven: Yale University Press.

7

Planning theory revisited

The end of the millennium was approaching, and I was invited to give the Nijmegen Academic Lecture in the Faculty of Policy Science, University of Nijmegen in the Netherlands, a country that, as Andreas Faludi once put it, had a "soft spot in the heart for planning." I wanted to accomplish a number of things with this talk. First, I thought it was important to remind my audience of mostly European planning scholars about the origins of Anglo-American theory that was not yet well known on the continent. Second, I wanted to spell out some of the reasons why planning theory has had such a difficult time to become established in a profession of practitioners, many of whom approach work pragmatically without worrying about the theoretical foundations of their practice. There are other, more serious difficulties as well, such as how we should define planning as a specific object for theorizing. Different definitions would point in very different directions.

I had difficulties choosing an appropriate theme for my talk. Living at the time in Australia, I visited Europe only infrequently and had never done any research there. Throughout my professional life, I had applied myself to development work in poor countries. But could what I had learned there be of compelling interest to an audience of European scholars who were chiefly interested in spatial planning at the urban scale? Then, too, there was the difficulty of choosing a mode of theorizing from among four alternatives: normative, empirico-positivist, critical, and paradigm-shifting. Which of these was it to be? In 1997, there was hardly anyone who was making these sorts of fine distinctions, and a theoretical contribution along these lines would probably be met with only polite interest. What I finally decided on was a broad-brush overview of American planning theory. Yet, I also wanted to go beyond what I had done in *Planning in the Public Domain*, partly as a self-critique of that book and partly to show how, as a profession, we had already moved beyond what I had written more than a decade earlier.

I had always pretended that my lifelong pursuit of planning theory was nothing more than a personal hobby. It was only now, in official retirement, that I had come to realize that theory is, in fact, essential to a profession that, if it is to be relevant in practical affairs, must constantly redefine itself and its mission. As we all know, and have known it all our lives, the urban world never stands still. And so I side with Susan Fainstein that we need to bring the city "back in" when we theorize planning – something I had not done before. Planning theory is not a universal theory, and we must constantly reinterpret what we do in the light of our own experiences.

Over the years, our field has expanded in many different directions; it now has university chairs not only in physical planning and design but also in social policy, transportation, housing, public health, regional and community development, disaster management, conflict resolution, international development, infrastructure, and the environment. To hold these vastly different policy concerns together under the sheltering roof of "spatial planning" requires both an historical appreciation of our enterprise and a vision of what it might become. Planning theory is one of the few means we have at our disposal to hold us together as a family of practitioners, and I see a historically informed visioning of planning education and practice as one of the important roles for a theorist. As Donald Schön once admonished us, we must become reflective practitioners. Critically reflecting on our practices is the only way to move forward.

Planning Theory Revisited

Originally published in 1998

I believe that I may have been among the small number of postgraduate students to sit in on the first ever seminar in planning theory. It was at the University of Chicago, and the year was 1948. Our instructor was Edward Banfield who was later to become a professor of urban politics at Harvard. At the time he taught us, he was still working on his doctorate in political science. Banfield was a protégé of Rexford Tugwell, who chaired the Interdisciplinary Program of Education and Research in Planning where I was studying. Tugwell was a believer in the collective wisdom of planners, and a sworn enemy of corporate power. He was also the first in my country to raise planning thought to the level of theory. Although his essays on the subject were published, they were not widely read (except by his students), and when Banfield put together his syllabus, Tugwell's writings did not figure importantly. The prominent names, as I recall them now, were Karl Mannheim, particularly his recently translated book, *Man and Society in an Age of Reconstruction*, and Herbert Simon's *Administrative Behavior*, which was destined to turn Public Administration into a policy science. Other names, familiar now from the post-war debates about the role of government in the economy – this was still, after all, the Age of Keynes – included Friedrich von Hayek and Barbara Wooton. We also pondered John Dewey's *The Public and Its Problems*.

From the beginning, then, planning theory was being conceptualized as a bi-continental, Euro-American enterprise. And such it has remained. But what I would like to stress is that this new subject, planning theory, really had to be cobbled together from elements that were originally intended for altogether different uses. Tugwell and Mannheim both shared a concern with the place of planning in society (where planning meant, for the first, a directive role for the state and, for the second, a democratic *via media* between fascism and communism). Neither was specifically writing with city planning in mind. Tugwell had come from a chair in institutional economics at Columbia University, via some years as Assistant Secretary of Agriculture under President Roosevelt, who, during his first term, counted him as a member of his "brain trust." After leaving Washington, he was appointed Chairman of the New York City Planning Commission under Mayor La Guardia, ending his public career during the war as the last appointed Governor of the Commonwealth of Puerto Rico. Karl Mannheim, who had written the first version of *Man and Society* in Holland as an émigré from Nazi Germany in 1935, was best known for his earlier work on the sociology of knowledge. Herbert Simon, who would eventually move on to other endeavors in organization theory and artificial intelligence, had come out of Public Administration. Both Hayek and Wooton were economists. And John Dewey, the eminent philosopher, was a major figure in American pragmatism, one of whose central ideas – learning by doing – was widely adopted by educators in the post-World War II era.

I myself was very excited by all of these ideas and how they might be brought together to serve an enterprise we called planning and that remained, at least at the University of Chicago, unadorned by any constraining adjective. Banfield who eventually abandoned planning for political science, having formed a rather bleak view of planning practitioners and of humanity in general, decided that the most promising theory would have to be based on Herbert Simon's synoptic model of rational decision-making. For better or worse, this identification of planning with rationality served as its template for years to come and continues to inform the writings, most prominently, of Andreas Faludi and Ernest Alexander.

We have travelled quite some distance since those tentative beginnings. In our own day, planning theory has achieved a certain kind of legitimacy. Luigi Mazza of the Milano Polytechnic University started the first journal with the explicit title of *Planning Theory*, and virtually all American planning schools now offer one or more core courses on the theme. There are also several collections of readings, such as the recently published *Explorations in Planning Theory* by Mandelbaum, Mazza and Burchell, and two eagerly awaited new publications from Leonie Sandercock, *Making the Invisible Visible: Multicultural planning histories* and *Toward Cosmopolis: Planning for multicultural cities and regions*, as well as Bent Flyvbjerg's *Rationality and Power*, a story (finally told in English) of redevelopment planning in Aalborg. One might be justified to conclude from this evidence that planning theory has finally arrived and is likely to stay around indefinitely as a defining field of academic endeavor.

But things are never so simple. A couple of years ago, I wrote a short article for the *Journal of Planning Education and Research* – one of our house journals back in the United States – on "Teaching Planning Theory." My hope was to codify and delimit what, to me, appeared to be the virtually boundless field of planning theory as it had evolved. I identified five – today I would say six – discourses that seemed to me to cover perhaps 90 per cent of the relevant writings: applied rationality; societal guidance; behavioral (positivist) approaches; communicative practice; social learning; and radical planning or emancipatory practice. The journal editors invited comments from a number of distinguished academics, only to discover that no two of us could agree on the nature of the beast we wanted to theorize. None of those who wrote comments wanted to be "fenced in" by any definition of planning discourse, however loose and encompassing it might be. Definitions were somehow perceived as limiting their freedom to call theory whatever they wished it to mean. We did minimally agree that planning theory could serve as a code word among us, but the consensus stopped there. We were riding off on different horses, each galloping into the sunset in a different direction.

I do not want to overstate the unwillingness of our theory tribe to arrive at agreement. In particular, I want to acknowledge one currently very popular model in planning theory that is based on John Forester's work, which he has drawn, in turn, from Jürgen Habermas' high-flying theoretical writings on communicative action – another distinguished Euro-American collaboration. But this unhappy experience – my inability to get even a handful of my colleagues to acknowledge that we are engaged on a common project with a tradition and history of its own – led me to think about some of the reasons for this failure. And as I mused on this 50-year-old hobby of mine, which I call thinking about planning, I confess that I discovered a number of difficulties inherent in this undertaking. Let me mention four of them: the problem of defining planning as an object to be theorized; the impossibility of talking about planning disconnected from actual institutional and political contexts; the several modes of doing planning theory – normative, positive, critical, and paradigm-shifting – and the dilemma of choosing among them; and last but not least, the difficulty of incorporating power relations into planning discourse.

[handwritten: Four challenges to defining planning theory]

Before going into more detail on each of these, let me just say that it is never going to be easy to do theory inside a profession that prides itself on being grounded in practice. In the so-called academic disciplines, discourse is of course mostly about theory, and sociologists, anthropologists, geographers, psychologists and all those other "-ists" risk being ostracized from their respective clans should they be bold enough to seriously venture into policy applications. Social scientists live for theory! Ability to theorize establishes the pecking order in their disciplines. But this is not the case in practical professions such as planning, where theorists are generally looked upon askance and tend to write mainly for each other. What use are they and all that jargon-laden scribbling they do? I shall return to this question [see also Chapter 10 this volume]. For now, let me just say that the life of a planning theorist had best be dissembled, should s/he seek practitioners' admiration.

But back to the four "difficulties" that, I claim, we encounter whenever we engage in planning discourse. To start with, what exactly do we talk about when we talk about planning? We use words like "to plan" "the planner," "the planning process," but, quite apart from whether formal definitions would be helpful in answering my question, these terms are actually quite confusing. Who are the planners when they are engaged in doing planning? (For the sake of argument, I shall suppose here that we are limiting ourselves to city planners or urbanists, which is already a choice with baneful consequences for theory.) Professionals with a tertiary degree in the field? Architects specializing in urban design? The city engineer? Housing experts? Public officials who occupy positions in municipal planning offices? And should we distinguish city planners proper from, say, transportation or environmental planners? Are social planners in or out? What about planners who are not engaged in drawing up any sort of plan (strategic or otherwise) but are involved in the resolution of conflicts about urban issues of one kind or another? Do certain lawyers qualify, even though they have no planning degree? And what of city managers? There is no end to this sort of questioning, but whatever our answers are, they will make a significant difference to what and how we "theorize."

We also lose ourselves in another part of the labyrinth, whenever we ask a question about the "planning process." Some of our schools actually teach subjects by that name. They teach what, in Britain, would be called "statutory planning," that is, the formal procedures required by law for obtaining, for example, a zoning variance, and the legal appeals that are open to the petitioner in the case of a denial. But statutory planning is only the tip of the iceberg when it comes to large planning decisions on freeway routing, docklands redevelopment schemes, major facility locations and similar "mega"-projects that will have major impacts on the form and functioning of cities. Decisions on these larger matters are the life of politics; they may involve the national government and even international financial institutions; at best, they bear only a formal resemblance to what is ordinarily called the planning process. They involve more than the public bureaucracy and their "petitioners." The real process is rather a tug of war that may extend over several decades and involve all sorts of people, not least from the concerned sectors of civil society.

Planning theorists have tried desperately to escape this labyrinth by abstracting from real-life situations. When I left the University of Chicago in 1955, the prevailing notion was that our profession was all about making "rational decisions" in the mode of Herbert Simon, as interpreted and further reduced to a set of explicit rules by Edward Banfield. One either accepted this formulation or despaired of it. Banfield and his colleague, Martin Meyerson, later President of the University of Pennsylvania, despaired of rationality in human affairs and eventually turned their back on planning. Others, like Andreas Faludi, continued to work within this framework, while modifying it to turn it into something other than the Weberian "iron cage" that the original formulation had suggested. Outside of the planning field, decision-making remained the focus, but "rationality" now acquired new meanings, such as "incrementalism" (Charles Lindblom) or "mixed scanning" (Amitai Etzioni). My own "eureka" came one day in the late 1960s when I woke up one morning with the inspiration that planning could be modeled as the relationship between *knowledge and action*. That seemed to open up new avenues for research, much of which I summarized in two books, *Retracking America: A theory of transactive planning* (1973) and *Planning in the Public Domain* (1987).

But, of course, no theoretical object remains forever unchallenged. Paradigms shift, as we know, either because their potentials are exhausted (they no longer pose interesting questions) or because other topics are in the ascendancy. John Forester, to whose continuing work I have already referred, focuses on dialogue and communicative processes. His particular interest is in mediation, and how a structured process of talking through conflicting positions can help the interested parties to move, step by step, to an agreement. Most recently, Leonie Sandercock has been promoting the idea of alternative planning histories, those told by oppressed and marginalized social groups engaged in city-building processes. Her work clearly de-professionalizes planning and shifts attention to political conflict. Her primary interest is not Forester's "getting to yes" but social justice for those whose voices have been silenced. Her work opens up a vast field for research into planning that has barely been scratched.

But what makes this planning.

The theoretical object of planning thus remains open and necessarily contested. This is the first of my four difficulties, which continue to make any agreement in planning theory nearly impossible. We are too busy disagreeing to build up and refine a single theory of planning.

The second difficulty is the illusion that planning theory is some sort of Platonic universal, inhabiting the realm of pure ideas that float across planet Earth, shining their benevolent light upon humanity. In this post-modern age – I do apologize for using this overexposed epithet – we are used to consigning all universal theories to the Inferno. But I mean something quite tangible and specific. Planning theories are not only embedded in Euro-American planning traditions, they also suggest a way of thinking that is quite alien, to cite but one example, to Asian academic life. For instance, it would be virtually impossible for me to give this lecture to a knowing, appreciative audience in China or Japan. Asian audiences would perhaps expect to be informed about American (or European) planning practices, our own real-life experiences with planning, and about what works for us, and why. They would be shy on abstract musings about rationality, dialogue, the alternative histories of oppressed minorities and women, and the anguish we sometimes display about "getting our values right." They would rather learn about technical aspects of transportation planning, or how to organize land markets in countries that are still nominally socialist.

I have no wish to single out Asian planners, of whom there are now large numbers, from Delhi to Beijing and beyond. Admittedly, some ideas do travel even if they are changed in the process. I would nevertheless maintain that my proposition generally holds true. Even the Euro-American collaboration on theory is, to some extent, illusory. Take, for example, the role of the local state in the USA and in the Netherlands. Different political cultures produce very different kinds of planning. In my country, the Dutch planning system is much admired because it seems to have teeth in it and to be effective in controlling land uses and moving forward to a truly sustainable development. I rather suspect that I would hear far more critical voices about Dutch planning from

Dutch planners here in Nijmegen. One is always more critical at home. Speaking as an American, I would say that official, statutory planning in my own country is largely a farce. What counts with us more is the politics of city-building, and that is not quite the same thing. I am not in a position to come to a judicious conclusion about the actual practices of either Dutch or American planning, but I can say this much: theorizing that will help to improve the practice of planning in Holland would have to be tailored to the traditions of that country, just as American planning theory reflects conditions on the other side of the Atlantic. *Pace* post-modernism, Euro-Americans still enjoy, or pretend to enjoy, abstract theorizing; it is a sort of intellectual game with us. But the pay-off comes only when we can limit our assertions to the contexts of particular socio-cultural and political traditions. The call is out for many planning theories, not one.

The third difficulty arises from the fact that we have very different expectations about the role of planning theory and considerable trouble in choosing among them. Some of us think of theory as primarily *normative*: how to improve the practice of planning. That was my intent when I wrote about a theory of transactive planning in the early 1970s; it is also John Forester's explicit purpose. For others, theory has primarily *explanatory, even predictive value*. Case studies of planning – one might think here of Peter Hall's provocatively titled *Great Planning Disasters* – tend to fall into this category. They may not be high-powered theory, but they are grist for the mill. A more recent example is a case study by Rebecca Abers of participatory municipal budgeting in the southern Brazilian state capital of Porto Alegre. When her dissertation is published, it will be a contribution to the theory of popular participation in planning. Still another set of planning theorists, most of whom write from a political economy perspective, devote their time to deconstructing mainstream planning. Some of David Harvey's and Manuel Castells' earlier work, which was in a Marxist mode, or Christine Boyer's Foucauldian *Dreaming the Rational City*, belong to this category. Finally, there are scholarly efforts aimed at changing our thinking about planning altogether, which is how I would describe Leonie Sandercock's recent attempt to bring social planning into a broader accord with conditions prevailing in the contemporary city. The problem that arises is the difficulty we have in choosing among these several modes. To begin with, the categories I mentioned do not neatly delimit different modes of theorizing. What starts out as a descriptive account of planning, for example, soon turns into a critique, and every critique already implies a preferred normative theory. Or theoretical writings that propose a shift in how we should look at planning frequently range across the entire spectrum of theory modes. To our colleagues in the social and human sciences, this seems a very odd approach to what they would describe as theory-building, and as a result, they pay little attention to what we do in our own backyard. On the other hand, wanting to confine ourselves abstemiously to only one mode of theorizing, keeping our distance from other possible modes, has a devastating effect on the significance of what we manage to say. Theoretical austerity is clearly not the way to go. But writing in the plentitude of passion, across the entire gamut of modes of theory, runs the danger of saying too much too soon.

Perhaps the biggest problem we face in theorizing planning is our ambivalence about power. The rational planning paradigm studiously avoided talking about any form of power other than the power of mind. This was also Aaron Wildavsky's position in his well-known text, *Speaking Truth to Power*. The belief was that reason would prevail, and even when it failed, planners could always take the moral high ground. After all, were they not rational, and rationality was good? The knowledge/action paradigm did little better. It not only failed to acknowledge the knowledge/power relation that has come to be associated with the writings of Michel Foucault, it also had little to say on how new visions might be implemented, because implementation requires an acknowledgment of power as a central issue. Or consider the communicative action paradigm with its Panglossian view of the power of dialogue to bridge the gap between those who command substantial power and those who do not. Whenever planners have written about power it has been mostly in the sense of enabling the powerless to do things for themselves. Thus also Forester. The main literatures on power – whether of the state, money, or civil society – have thus been imported from outside our field. This situation has led to a great deal of conflict within the profession. Our more practical-minded colleagues have tended to dismiss planning theory precisely for its failure to countenance power. The quickest way to dismiss someone's earnest efforts is to label them idealistic or – God forbid – utopian. A recent example is an essay by Bent Flyvbjerg, provocatively entitled "Empowering Civil Society: Habermas, Foucault, and the Question of Conflict," in which he launches a fierce attack on Habermasian idealists, such as John Forester. It is nevertheless to Flyvbjerg's credit that he has ventured forth on the long trek towards integrating discourses on power, from Machiavelli to Gramsci and Foucault, with the still-sanitized multiple discourses of planning theory. The recent work of Orin Yiftachel (Ben Gurion University in Israel) should also be acknowledged in this context.

So this is my long answer to the question of why we experience such difficulty in getting anyone to listen seriously to us when we talk planning theory. All the same, we will go on doing what we do. Is this a contradiction? Allow me to suggest why I believe that we'll probably continue to engage in this Quixotic enterprise. First, we will keep on writing planning theory, because it's fun … at least, for some of us. Vladimir Nabokov loved to collect butterflies. We, who are not Nabokov, go hunting for exotic species of ideas, more specifically, ideas about the practice of what still goes by the name of planning. More importantly, as a practical activity in the world, planning is in constant need of rethinking, and I take it to be one of our tasks to assist in this enterprise. Third, the many skeptics notwithstanding, theory does help to improve practice. One of the extant myths among self-styled practical folk is that they have no need for theory. But, in fact, as Donald Schön has shown, practitioners constantly work with theoretical assumptions and it is the theorist's job to make these assumptions visible and thus to help practitioners reflect on them. Fourth, planning does not exist in an intellectual vacuum. There is a lively play of ideas "out there," which needs to be translated in ways that are meaningful to planners both academic and practical. The Mannheims, von Hayeks, Poppers, Deweys, Simons, Gramscis, Habermases, and Foucaults do not simply reveal themselves to planners; they require trustworthy and capable interpreters. At the same time, we would all be the losers, if all we ever did was talk to our kith and kin about the boring empirical details of our daily grind. Fifth, planning as practice needs to continuously reinvent itself, and this requires a knowledge of its history and a certain conceptual agility. Sixth, one of the ways to introduce students to what we do, and to socialize them into the mysteries of our field, is to give them a strong dose of theory and history along the way. Planning is indeed less and less about technical matters. One can always get a demographer to make yet another population forecast or an architect to design street furniture, and there are plenty of economists and engineers to run feasibility studies. But the critical appreciation and appropriation of ideas is a rare talent that is becoming increasingly important in a world hungry for chaos theory because chaos is what our senses perceive when we read the daily newspaper on waking up in the morning.

In the time remaining to me, I want to talk about some of the things I would do differently today than when I worked on the manuscript for *Planning in the Public Domain* in the early 1980s. Or to put it another way: in what ways have I moved beyond this text? I shall talk about three recently resurrected themes: the production of the urban habitat; the rise of civil society; and the inevitable question of power.

Trying to get an historical overview of how we in Europe and America have thought about the relation between knowledge and action, I deliberately abstracted from any specific applications of planning. Critics were quick to point this out to me as one of the book's more significant failures. More recently, in an article on planning education which appeared last year in the *Journal of Planning Education and Research*, I took a very different turn. In view of what many of my colleagues, as they looked on market triumphalism, regarded as a crisis for planning, I was searching for a *substantive domain* that would secure professionals holding a planning degree a legitimate place among the more established professions, from architecture to law and engineering. What, I asked, was our unique competence as planners, the body of knowledge which no one else could legitimately claim as their own? If we were unable to identify such a domain, then, indeed, planning, as a field of professional study, was perhaps not worth saving. My provisional answer was that planners have or should have a grounding in knowledge about the socio-spatial processes that, in interaction with each other, produce the urban habitat.

Now, that the urban habitat is somehow produced is not an especially novel idea. Henri Lefebvre was the first to formulate a productivist view of the city, in language that, because of its Marxist tinge, made his writings popular with some geographers and urban sociologists, most notably Manuel Castells and Edward Soja. The concept itself is simple enough: along with other animals, we humans build the nests in which we live and work, and where we reproduce ourselves. However, and this is the key that opens the question to debate, *we cannot make our habitat as we would wish*. The human, and more specifically, the urban habitat, takes form as multiple forces interact with each other in ways that are not fully predictable. In the article to which I referred, I mention six of these *socio-spatial* processes: briefly, urbanization, regional economic growth and change, city-building, cultural differentiation and change, the transformation of nature, and urban politics and empowerment. This is not the occasion to go into detail. Suffice it to say that, in their complex and dynamic interrelationships, these six processes produce the multi-dimensional habitats we inhabit.

In this context, one meaning of planning refers to the conscious *intervention* of collective actors – roughly speaking, state, capital and organized civil society – in the production of urban space, so that outcomes may be turned to one or the other's favor. It is, therefore, obvious that planners need to have a good understanding of how these city-forming processes work before we impose on them a normative structure or, what is currently more likely, mediate among the interests affected. This formulation posits the city-forming process first before there can be any serious talk of strategic intervention. Please note my use of the military term of strategy; each collective actor will seek to influence outcomes in the ways desired by them by pursuing different *strategies against their real or imagined opponents*. (But what is desired at the start of an enterprise may actually change in the process, so that "goals" are never completely given in advance, as was once required by the decision models of the early 1950s.)

Theorizing planning by incorporating city-forming processes into the planning paradigm, rather than talking about planning outside of any historical and spatial context, is thus one of the ways by which I would want to amend *Planning in the Public Domain*. And there are two additional ways, both of which I have already touched upon in this description of how the urban habitat is formed.

The inclusion of civil society as one of three collective actors shaping our cities would not have been possible a mere generation ago. Although we often used terms like "community" when we talked of local planning, the term was typically used in a passive, general sense. But over the last decade, spurred by civil protests in Latin America and Eastern Europe, there has been a revival of interest in the 18th century concept of a civil society. I cannot rehearse the rather extensive literature here. Suffice it to say, that civil society carries a heavy freight of political meaning in a world that seems to be moving, however slowly, towards a more inclusive, participatory model of democracy.

Civil society refers to that part of social, as distinct from corporate, life that lies beyond the immediate control of the state. It is the society of households, family networks, civic and religious organizations and communities that are bound to each other by shared histories, collective memories and culturally specific forms of reciprocity. As a political concept, however, democratic theory posits civil society as a counter-pole to the state, the ultimate source of a people's sovereignty. In this sense, civil society is composed of citizens, that is, of the members of a political community who claim not only the right to hold the state accountable for its actions but also the right to claim new rights for themselves. Among these are the right to *voice*, the right to *difference*, and the right to *human flourishing*.

These three rights are at the source of civil society's deep involvement with the production of the urban habitat. Market and state do not explain it all; we must also reckon with civil action, which is sometimes proactive but at other times is a filled with anger, protest, and defiance.

This new perception of the role of civil society, along with the partial retreat of the state from its traditional responsibilities, has dramatically changed what planners do. In this new scenario, they are no longer exclusively concerned with the central guidance of market forces or regulation. The new, emerging form of planning is more entrepreneurial, more daring and less codified. Typically, it is collaborative, as Patsy Healey has reminded us, concerned with large-scale projects more than with the entire system of spatial relations in the city, it seeks to forge a limited consensus through negotiated settlements among contesting parties; it is a provider of strategic information to all participants in the planning process. In these terms, planning moves ever closer to the surface of politics as a mediating hand within society as a whole. Its expertise is increasingly being sought not only by the state, where planning powers formally reside, but also by the corporate sector and even by organized groups within civil society itself.

I have taken these thoughts from the editors' introduction of a new collection of essays, entitled *Cities for Citizens: Planning and the rise of civil society in a global age*, which Mike Douglass of the University of Hawaii and I have put together for publication early next year. These essays represent a collective effort to talk about the second major new theme in the discourse on planning theory.

The third theme is power. I have already talked about how reluctant planning theorists generally are to incorporate dimensions of power into their work. We have consequently had little to say on the implementation strategies of specific actors, being more concerned with the extent of their formal adherence to particular planning-theoretic models.

I think it is important, when we talk about power, to distinguish between power that is used to coerce, constrain and control the actions of others and that which is enabling people to do the things they would like to do individually and collectively. Michel Foucault's name is associated with the first view of power, and his popular writings are filled with emancipatory passion. My own recent work, considerably more modest in influence and scope, reflects an enabling view of power. In *Empowerment: The politics of alternative development*, I speak of the individual, social and political empowerment of the oppressed sectors of society. Mine is the obverse of Foucault's preoccupation with the micro-politics of dominance and coercion. It is rather a planner's affirmation of how marginalized groups can begin to assert themselves in everyday life.

Others, and I have already mentioned the Danish scholar Bent Flyvbjerg, are more concerned with unveiling the real relations of power in the interplay of city-building processes. That, too, is an important and necessary task. All told, I would like to urge those of us who are committed to the further development of planning theory to build relations of power – and especially enabling power – into our conceptual framework. This will be done more readily once we ground our theorizing in the actual politics of city-building, acknowledging that the production of urban space involves the interaction of conflicting interests and forces, not least the growing force of organized civil society itself.

I must refrain from a summing up of my quick return to the past. There can be no conclusions. We are, after all, engaged in a continuing search to improve the practice of planning through the power of theory. And that is an ongoing effort that must remain open to the future.

Bibliography

Douglass, M. and Friedmann, J. (eds) *Cities for Citizens: Planning and the rise of civil society in a global age*, New York: Wiley & Sons.

Friedmann, J. (1973) *Retracking America: A theory of transactive planning*, Garden City, NY: Anchor/Doubleday,

Friedmann, J. (1987) *Planning in the Public Domain: From knowledge to action*, Princeton, NJ: Princeton University Press.

Friedmann, J. (1992) *Empowerment: The politics of alternative development*, Cambridge, MA: Blackwell

Schön, D.A. (1983) *The Reflective Practitioner: How professionals think in action*, New York: Basic Books.

Study questions

We can agree that planning theory has come of age, though perhaps it is too early to say whether the subject has reached maturity. And yet, mature or not, we seem unable to reach a consensus on what to teach as planning theory. Is this a paradox? Can we even agree on what the important questions are that planning theorists should think about? I won't attempt to answer these questions, because perhaps it is too soon before we can attempt this, which only a mature field of intellectual and practical endeavor can do.

Let us therefore proceed with the essay at hand, which starts with a bit of history of how the Euro-American discourse on planning theory got underway and then tries to explicate why we have been unable to reach a consensus until now. Consider the following four questions:

1. In reference to planning as a field of practice, the discourse of "theory" comes in four distinctive guises. The first concerns the study of planning itself as a subject of empirical inquiry. There are not many academic studies of this sort, and most of them deal with the question of politics in relation to a given urban setting. The second tells us how, in the opinion of the author, planning ought to be practiced; it is thus a normative theory. The third looks at planning in the context of a particular society, adopting a critical stance informed by values that are in conflict with those attributed by the author to the planning processes under review. Critical planning theory, you might say, is a form of applied social ethics. Finally, there is what I have called paradigm-shifting theory, which is a rare species of theorizing that leads to a different way not only of conceptualizing planning but of changing its practices in the world as well.

   Discuss these four modes of planning theory and think of specific examples to illustrate them.

2. Does planning as a professional field have "ownership" of a particular substantive domain? And if it has, how would you characterize it? In the essay above, I call it "the production of the urban habitat" (see Friedmann in the additional readings below). Today and speaking more broadly, I would change this phrase and speak instead of the production of the *human habitat*. While it is certainly the case that professional planners have no special expertise concerning the human habitat, we can turn the question around and argue that *all those concerned with the production of the human habitat are, for that very reason, engaged in its planning, that is, in shaping its future.* Inverting the question allows civil society to be included in the planning pantheon and places the emphasis on collaboration and the resolution of conflict (see Chapter 6).

   Please comment on this proposition and what is implied when we accept the argument I'm making.

[Handwritten margin note: Then why is there a "planner"? Why not just Planning]

3. Professional planners, at least in the academy, have for the most part been uncomfortable about addressing the question of power. This is strange because practitioners are certainly aware of how power is wielded in City Hall and elsewhere in the city. But somehow, most planning theorists have not addressed this knowledge gleaned from practice. A notable exception is Bent Flyvbjerg for whom questions of power and conflict in planning are central (see the reference below).

   Consider why this is the case. As you think about the question of power, distinguish between "power to" and "power over," or enabling and coercive power. Mention some other kinds of power – for instance, "the power of love" or charismatic power – and how they might or might not relate to planning. Discuss the varieties of power that planners may use in their practice.

4. Planning theorists frequently appear to be writing universal theory, as though their formulations could be understood and acted upon anywhere in the world. But if we accept the idea that planning cultures are multiple (see Chapter 9), it is necessary to limit the relevance of particular theoretical writings to specific places or regions of the world. We should therefore always situate theory in particular circumstances and, where possible, illustrate our abstractions with case studies. But the temptation to generalize is often difficult to resist.

   Please discuss this dilemma for writers of theoretical import in planning.

Selected additional readings

Flyvbjerg, B. (1998) *Rationality and Power: Democracy in practice*, Chicago: University of Chicago Press.

Forester, J. (1989) *Planning in the Face of Power*, Berkeley, LA: University of California Press.

Friedmann, J. (1996) 'The core curriculum in planning revisited', *Journal of Planning Education and Research*, 15: 89–104.

Krumholz, N. and Forester, J. (1990) *Making Equity Planning Work*, Philadelphia: Temple University Press.

Schön, D.A. (1983) *The Reflective Practitioner: How professionals think in action*, New York: Basic Books.

Wildavsky, A. (1979) *Speaking Truth to Power: The art and craft of policy analysis*, Boston: Little Brown.

8

The good city: in defense of utopian thinking

Not so long ago, in the bad old days, most planners, when asked what values informed their work, would have answered that they were champions of the public interest. But if pressed further, they would have retreated into generalities and soporific clichés. The public interest was essentially an a-political construction empty of specific content, at best a vague imaginary of suburban, middle-class life. In the sprawling American metropolis – the 21st century cosmopolis – multicultural by the very fact of its demographic composition and further divided by (pre)conceptions of race and ethnicity, who was to say where, in any given situation, the public interest might lie? Moreover, for many decades now, many professionals who had been educated as planners no longer worked exclusively in the municipal bureaucracy but also in non-profits on behalf of dozens of different causes: bicycle paths, food security, urban agriculture, the social integration of new immigrants, the re-naturalization of old stream beds, youth programs, affordable housing, combating homelessness, community development and similarly focused programs chiefly undertaken by agents of civil society in urban neighborhoods. They were active on behalf of causes each of which required special justification in its fund-raising efforts. Slow to respond to the new realities, professional organizations eventually recognized that planners who had initially been drawn into the profession "to do good competently" needed a more compelling expression of professional values than a mere wave in the direction of an eviscerated notion of the public interest.

Even so, with most planners claiming to be working to improve the conditions of people's lives, was it possible to be more specific by calling up some concrete images that would give substance to their claims? Some academics were giving voice to the poor and demanded a more equitable, a just city. Others argued the case for deliberative democracy. A third group rallied under the banner of ecological sustainability. A fourth promoted the practices of multiculturalism. And so on. All of them seemed worthy causes and went some way to respond to the hunger, especially among younger people, for an encompassing vision of the future and a source of hope.

The following essay was inspired by Tan Le, a 21-year-old Vietnamese-Australian woman who in her acceptance speech as the 1998 Young Australian of the Year had called for a vision that would carry "the connotation of value, meaning and purpose – and of something beyond our reach that is nevertheless worth striving for and aspiring to." Appropriately published in the millennium year, I wanted to respond to Tan Le's *cri de coeur*. To do so, I reached back to some of my earlier writings, especially *The Good Society* (see Chapter 3), by emphasizing the social nature of human beings in place of the reductive model of the utility-maximizing individual of economic theory or, in everyday language, the consumer as citizen. I also felt it necessary to posit a foundational value that would have wide appeal, if not universal validity. With respect to the first, I argued that humans are in essence dialogic beings, in a reformulation of Aristotle's assertion that to be fully human we have to be politically engaged, and that the well-being of the polis is our highest calling. With respect to the second, I proposed "human flourishing" as a fundamental right, subject to the constraints imposed by the wider communities of which we are a part. With these two foundational values in place, I set out to construct a more elaborate image of what the "good city" might be.

The Good City

Originally published in 2000

Utopian thinking: the capacity to imagine a future that departs significantly from what we know to be a general condition in the present. It is a way of breaking through the barriers of convention into a sphere of the imagination where many things beyond our everyday experience become feasible. All of us have this ability, which is inherent in human nature, because human beings are insufficiently programmed for the future. We need a constructive imagination that we can variously use for creating fictive worlds. Some of these worlds can be placed in the past, others in the future, and some, like Dante's *Divina comedia*, even in afterlife.

There are other ways of deploying this capacity than in the imagining of utopias. Religion is one of them, and for many people religious faith satisfies their thirst for meaning. Belief in hegemonic ideologies is a secular counterpart to religion. American ideology, repeated *ad nauseam* by our leaders and reinforced by the media, incorporates the idea of bliss in a consumer society, so that a better world is seen to be chiefly one of greater material affluence for individuals. This is the ideology we are selling around the world. Along with belief in a never-ending abundance of material goods, it includes the rhetoric of representative democracy, and blind trust in the powers of technology to overcome whatever problems that might be encountered along the way to a "free society." Intensely nationalistic feelings may also satisfy the need for ordinary lives to have a transcendent meaning.[2] The question of "why are we here in this world" arises precisely because the human condition is to be open to the future, and it requires a response on our part.

Beyond the alternative constructions of religion, ideology and nationalism, there are many good reasons why we might wish to engage in utopian thinking. For some of us, it is merely an amusing pastime. For others it serves as a veiled critique of present-day evils. For still others it may be, in the phrase of Sir Philip Sidney's comment on Thomas More's *Utopia* in 1595, a persuasive means of "leading men to virtue" (Manuel and Manuel 1979: 2). In the peculiar form of dystopias, it may alert us to certain tendencies in the present which, if allowed to continue unchecked and carried to a logical extreme, would result in a world we find abhorrent. The twentieth century has produced many literary dystopias (not to mention the many actual dystopias in the real world), from Aldous Huxley's *Brave New World* to the cyberpunk novels of William Gibson and others (Warren and Warren 1998). But most important of all, utopian thinking can help us choose a path into the future that we believe is justified, because its concrete imagery is informed by values that are precious to us.

Utopian thinking has two moments that are inextricably connected: critique and constructive vision. The critique is of certain aspects of our present condition: injustices, oppression, ecological devastation. It is precisely an enumeration of these "evils," however, that implies a code of moral values that is being violated. The code may not be written out, or it may merely be suggested symbolically by invoking slogans such as "freedom," "equality," "solidarity." But it is there nonetheless. The moral outrage over an injustice implies that we have a sense, however inarticulate, of justice. And so on, for each of our terms of condemnation.

Now it is true that negative and positive images are not necessarily symmetrical with respect to each other. Most of us might agree that great material inequalities are unjust, yet differ vehemently about what might constitute a "just" distribution of incomes or other material good. But differences about social justice are ultimately political, not philosophical arguments. In any event, they are unavoidable, because if injustice is to be corrected (or, for that matter, any other "evil"), we will need the concrete imagination of utopian thinking to propose steps that would bring us closer to a world we would consider 'just'.

Such visionings are always debatable, however, both in their own terms and when measured against alternate proposals. That is why I call them political. Where the uncensored public expression of opinions is allowed, they should become the substance of political argument. Utopian thinking is thus not at all about fairytales but about genuine futures around which political coalitions can be built.

There are always limitations on purposive action – of leadership, power, resources, knowledge. But if we begin with limitations rather than with images of the desirable future, we may never arrive at utopian constructs with the power to generate the passion necessary for a social movement that might bring us a few steps closer to the vision they embody.

The utopian tradition in planning

With considerations of this sort, we find ourselves back on the familiar ground of planning. City and regional planning (or spatial planning) has an enduring tradition of utopian thought (Friedmann and Weaver 1979; Weaver 1984; Friedmann 1987). The evocation of the classics requires no references: Robert Owen, Charles Fourier, Pierre Joseph Proudhon, William Morris, Peter Kropotkin, Ebenezer Howard, Lewis Mumford, Frank Lloyd Wright, Percival and Paul Goodman are all names in common currency among the tribe. In more recent decades, we can mention the illustrious names of Kevin Lynch and, for some of us also E.F. Schumacher and Ivan Illich. Still closer to our time and, indeed, contemporary with us, I could mention Jane Jacobs (1961), Dolores Hayden (1984) and Leonie Sandercock (1997). Given this chain of utopian writings stretching over 200 years that have influenced the education of planners and, to a greater or lesser extent, have also shaped their practice, it would be hard to argue that even the mainstream of the planning profession has kept itself aloof from utopian thinking.

In a recent essay, Susan Fainstein poses the question of whether we can make the cities we want (Fainstein 1999). In her account, the important values that should inform our thinking about cities include material equality, cultural diversity, democratic participation and ecological sustainability in a metropolitan milieu. Fainstein's background is in political economy, and so it is not surprising that she should give pride of place to the question of material equality (or rather inequality) and follow, if not uncritically, David Harvey's lead in *Justice, Nature and the Geography of Difference* (1996). I will come back to this particular prioritization of social values when I present my own answer to Fainstein's challenge.

But before I do this, I would like to recall an argument I made 14 years ago in *Planning in the Public Domain* (Friedmann 1987). The second and third parts of this volume attempt to sketch an intellectual history of planning, but, at the same time, aim to go beyond this history in advocating a transformative planning that, because it is based on the mobilization of disempowered groups in society, I called radical. The central focus of radical planning in this sense is political action by organized groups within civil society (which is the more familiar "community" of planning discourse but situated in a different theoretical setting). Its radicalism derives from actions that, with or without and even against the state, are aimed at universal emancipation. "A key principle in radical, transformative practice," I wrote, "is that *no group can be completely free until freedom [from oppression] has been achieved for every group.* Thus, the struggle for emancipation leads to results that will always be partial, and contradictory, until the final and possibly utopian goal of a free humanity is reached" (*ibid*: 301).[3] I then went on to examine what planners who opt for emancipatory struggles do. Among the many things I considered are elaborating a hard-hitting critical analysis of existing conditions; assisting in the mobilization of communities to rectify these conditions; assisting in devising appropriate strategies of struggle; refining the technical aspects of transformative solutions; facilitating social learning with engaged radical practice; mediating between the mobilized community and the state; helping to ensure the widest possible participation of community members in all phases of the struggle; helping to rethink the group's course of action in the light of new understandings; and becoming personally involved in transformative practice (*ibid*: 303–7). I wanted it to be understood that utopian thinking, at least so far as planners are concerned, is historically grounded in specific emancipatory struggles. Planning

[margin note: Planner's action in radical planning]

of this sort stands in the grand utopian tradition. In her most recent work, Leonie Sandercock calls it an insurgent planning (Sandercock 1998).

In the present essay, my intention is somewhat different. Rather than talk [*dif. approach*] about political struggles to resist specific forms of oppression, my aim is to delineate some elements for a positive vision of the "good city." And I want to do so in the manner of an achievable utopia rather than paint a scenario set in a distant, indeterminate future.

A century during which the vast majority of the world's population will have to live in urban environments cries out for images of the good city. I have purposely phrased this need in the plural. Taking the world as a whole, the diversity of starting conditions is so great that no single version of the city will suffice. Fifty years from now, the world's urban population will be roughly double the existing numbers of 2.9 billion. We can thus look ahead to a historically unprecedented age of city-building. And city-builders need not only blueprints for their work, but *guiding, normative images*. The following remarks are addressed to planners and to anyone else who wishes to confront the multiple challenges of the age.[4]

Imagining the good city I: theoretical considerations

Before proceeding, however, some preliminaries must be considered. First, in [*Key Q's*] setting out an account of the good city, whose city are we talking about? Can we legitimately assume the possibility of a "common good" for the city? Second, are we concerned only with process or only with outcomes, or should outcome and process be considered jointly? And finally, how is a normative framework such as we are considering to be thought of in relation to professional practice?

Whose city?

We have been bludgeoned into accepting as gospel that to speak of a common good in a given polity is either propaganda or an act of self-deception. The attacks on the common weal have come from all ideological directions. Pluralists see only group interests that strike temporary bargains in the political arena. Marxists argue on roughly similar grounds that the "common good" is a phrase used by the hegemonic class, i.e. the bourgeoisie, to hide purposes that are nothing more than an expression of class interest. Postmodern critics who see only a world of fleeting kaleidoscopic images, dissolve the "common good" into a thousand discursive fragments, dismissing any attempt to raise one of them above any of the others as an unjustifiable attempt to establish a new "meta-narrative" in an age from which such narratives have been banned.

Against all of these intellectually dismissive critics, I would argue for the necessity of continuing to search for the "common good" of a city if only because, without such a conception, there can be neither a sense of local identity nor a political community. In democratic polities, there has to be minimal agreement on the structure of the community and on the possibility of discovering a "common good" through political discourse. An administered city is not a political community and might as well be a hotel managed by some multinational concern. In that case, the answer to the question of "whose city" is very clear. But in a putative democracy, the city is ultimately "the people," and the cliché notwithstanding, it is the people – the local citizens – who must find a way among themselves to define, time after time, in what specific action agendas the "common good" of the city is to be found. It seems to me that it makes a world of difference whether we seek to justify an action by grounding it in a specific conception of the "common good," a conception that always remains open to political challenge, or merely to assert it without voices of dissent, or worse, omit any reference to it altogether.

Process vs. outcomes

This opposition of terms has a long pedigree. Democratic proceduralists believe in process, partly because they assume that the differences among the parties in contention are relatively minor, and because today's majority will become tomorrow's minority, and vice versa. Everybody, so to speak, gets their turn in the long run. Opposed to them are Kantian idealists for whom good intentions are sufficient to define what is good. A third position is held by those who are so persuaded of the rightness of their own ethical position that they are impatient with democratic procedure and pursue their ends by whatever means at hand. Among them are a few who believe in the theory of the "big revolutionary bang." Transformative change, according to this theory, requires a sharp break with the past, a break that is often marked by violence, because the *ancien regime* must be "smashed" before the revolutionary age can dawn.

My own position is to deny this separation of ends and means, outcomes and process. Process, by which I specifically mean democratic procedures, is no less important than desirable outcomes. But democratic procedures are likely to be abandoned if they do not lead, in the longer term, to broadly acceptable outcomes. Moreover, process in a liberal democracy, also includes the non-violent struggles for social justice and other concerns that take place outside the formal institutional framework. So, on the one hand, we need an inclusive democratic framework that allows for the active pursuit of political objectives even when these are contrary to the dominant interests. On the other hand, we need to be clear about the objectives to be pursued. The imaginary of the good city has to embrace both these terms.

Intention and practice

The good city requires a committed form of political practice, which I call transformative. It was Hannah Arendt who formed my concept of action or political praxis (she used the terms interchangeably). She writes: "To act, in its most general sense, means to take an initiative, to begin ... to set something into motion ... It is in the nature of beginning that something new is started which cannot be expected from whatever may have happened before. The character of startling unexpectedness is inherent in all beginnings and in all origins" (Arendt 1958: 177–8). To act, in other words, is to set something new into the world. And this requires an actor, or rather a number of such, because political action of the transformative kind always involves a collective entity or group. There are certain conditions of action. The group must first be brought together and mobilized. This requires leadership. It must also have the material, symbolic and moral power sufficient to overcome resistance to its projects. In the longer term, the group's actions, and the counter-actions to its initiatives, lead to results that are boundless and therefore require continuous social learning. The group must be passionately committed to its practice or it will be defeated in the first rounds of struggle (Friedmann 1987: 44–7).

The good city II: human flourishing as a fundamental human right

If they are not to be seen as arbitrary, principles of the good city must be drawn from somewhere, they must be logically connected to some foundational value. Such a founding principle should be clearly and explicitly formulated, so that it can be communicated even to those among us who are not philosophically inclined but make their living as carpenters, domestic workers or on construction jobs. I would formulate this principle as follows:

> *Every human being has the right, by nature, to the full development of their innate intellectual, physical and spiritual potentials in the context of wider communities.*

I call this the right to human flourishing, and regard it as the most fundamental of human rights. Despite this, it has never been universally acknowledged as a right that is inherent in being human. Slave societies knew nothing of it; nor did caste societies, tribal societies, corporate village societies or totalitarian states. And in no society have women ever enjoyed the same right to human flourishing as men. But as the fundamental, inalienable right of every person, human flourishing is ingrained in the liberal democratic ethos.

Human flourishing underlies the strongly held belief in contemporary western societies, and particularly in America, that privilege should be earned rather than inherited. Accordingly, human beings should have an equal start in life. Over a lifetime, individual and group outcomes will, of course, vary a good deal because of differences in inborn abilities, family upbringing, entrenched class privilege and social oppression. Still, the idea of a basic equality among all citizens underlies the mild socialism of western countries with their systems of public education, public health, the graduated income tax, anti-discriminatory legislation and so forth, all of which seek some sort of leveling of life chances among individuals and groups.

As this reference to political institutions makes evident, the potential of human flourishing can only be realized in the context of wider communities, so that right from the start, we posit humans, not as Leibnizian monads but as social beings. It is unconscionable, therefore, as Margaret Thatcher is reported to have done, to dismiss the concept of society as a mere fiction. Alone, we cannot survive without the unmediated support of others, from intimate family on up to larger structures and emotional bonds to individuals and groups. Without them, nothing can be accomplished.

The social sphere imposes certain requirements of its own, and these may appear as constraints on willful action. Although as individuals we are ultimately responsible for what we do, we are always constrained (1) by our social relations with family, friends, workmates, and neighbors, in short, by a culturally specific ethics of mutual obligation within civil society and (2) by the wider sociopolitical settings of our lives that inhibit human flourishing. The two are intertwined in many ways;[5] it would require a separate essay, however, to even begin to disentangle them and to do justice to the powerful constraints we, and especially women, encounter in the sphere of relations I call civil. Instead, I will turn to the sociopolitical sphere which is my primary focus.

Briefly, my argument is that local citizens do not merely use the city to advance their personal interests – some will do so more successfully than others – but, as citizens of a political community, which is the city in its political aspect, also contribute to establishing those minimal conditions – political, economic, social, physical and ecological – which are necessary for human flourishing. I refer to these conditions – and remember that I call them minimal conditions – as the common good of the polity, or the good city, because human flourishing is inconceivable without them. In this understanding, the "common good" of the city appears as something akin to citizen rights, that is, to the claims that local citizens can legitimately make on their political community as a basis for the flourishing of all its citizens. Making these claims, and at the same time to contribute to their realization in practice, is one of the deep obligations of local citizenship.

for those excluded?
Friedmann speaks to "Friedmanns"

The good city III: multipli/city as a primary good

Human flourishing serves as a template for judging the performance of cities. But to assist us in this detailed, critical work of assessing the extent to which a city provides an adequate setting for human flourishing, further guidelines are needed. I propose to do this by suggesting a primary good – multipli/city – together with certain conditions that would allow multipli/city to be realized in practice.

By multipli/city, I mean an autonomous civil life relatively free from direct supervision and control by the state. So considered, a vibrant civil life is the necessary social context for human flourishing. Multipli/city acknowledges the priority of civil society, which is the sphere of freedom and social reproduction – and it is for its sake alone that the city can be said to exist. Political economists might disagree with this ordering. They will tend to describe the city in terms of capital accumulation, external economies, market exchange, administrative control, and the like, and urban populations in terms of their incorporation into labor markets and social classes. From an analytical perspective, I don't object to these characterizations. But if our project is the good city, a different, explicitly normative approach is needed.

In its political aspect, civil society comprises the political community of the city. But there are other aspects of a richly articulated civil life, including religious, social, cultural and economic life, all of which can be subsumed under the concept of a self-organizing civil society.[6] Michael Walzer calls civil society "a project of projects," foreshadowing my characterization of multipli/city. The relevant passage is worth quoting in full:

> Civil society is sustained by groups much smaller than the *demos* or the [*Pre-cursor to 'Big Society' which Britain used to & social programs* — handwritten margin note] working class or the mass consumers or the nation. All these are necessarily pluralized as they are incorporated. They become part of the world of family, friends, comrades and colleagues, where people are connected to one another and made responsible for one another. Connected and responsible: without that, "free and equal" is less attractive than we once thought it would be. I have no magic formula for making connections or strengthening the sense of responsibility. These are not aims that can be underwritten with historical guarantees or achieved through a single unified struggle. Civil society is a project of projects; it requires many organizing strategies and new forms of state action. It requires a new sensitivity for what is local, specific, contingent – and, above all, a new recognition (to paraphrase a famous sentence) that the good life is in the details. (Walzer 1992: 107)

Throughout history, city populations have grown primarily through migration, and migrants come from many parts. Some don't speak the dominant language of the city; others practice different religions; still others follow folkways that are strange to the city. They come to the city for its promise of a more liberated, fulfilling life, and also perhaps, as refugees, escaping from the danger of physical harm. They do not come to the city to be regimented, to be molded according to a single concept of correct living. Nor do they seek diversity as such. Rather, they want to live by their own lights as undisturbed as possible, so that diversity appears as simply a by-product of the "project of projects." But cities are not always hospitable, and mutual tolerance of difference must be safeguarded by the state so long as certain conditions are fulfilled: respect for human rights and the assumption of the rights and obligations of local citizenship. In a broadly tolerant society, one may perhaps hope for a step beyond tolerance, which is to say, for mutual acceptance and even the affirmation of difference.

Reflected in a thickly quilted mosaic of voluntary associations, multipli/city requires a solid material base. A destitute people can only think about survival, which absorbs nearly all the time and energies at their disposal. A substantial material base, therefore, must provide for the time, energy and space needed for active citizenship. Four pillars support the material foundations for the good city. First in importance is socially *adequate housing* together with complementary public services and community facilities. As innumerable struggles in cities throughout the world have shown, housing needs, along with water and affordable urban transit, are viewed as a first priority of individual households. By common consent, the greatest social disaster (in peacetime) is to be homeless. *Affordable healthcare* comes second, particularly for women, infants, the physically and mentally challenged, the chronically ill and the elderly, as a prime condition for human flourishing. *Adequately remunerated work* for all who seek it is the third pillar. In urban market societies, a well-paying job is a nearly universal aspiration not only for the income it brings but for the social regard that attaches to regular work in capitalist society. Finally, *adequate social provision* in housing, medical care, human services and income must be made for the weakest citizens, if their own efforts are insufficient to provide for what is regarded as the social minimum.

Each of these four pillars has given rise to a vast literature, both technical and philosophical, and it is not my intention here to review it. I do want to take up a point of difference, however, that I have with the old socialist Left that has consistently argued that justice – social justice – demands "equal access to material well-being." The old Left has always given priority to material inequalities as their rallying cry. And though it is undoubtedly true that unconstrained capitalist accumulation leads to greater material inequalities, gross differences in income and wealth are, in fact, found in all social formations since the beginnings of urban society five millennia ago. My disagreement is, therefore, with a vision that regards material questions as primary and thus as the appropriate focus of popular struggle. All large-scale attempts to level inequalities, as in Maoist China, have had to employ barbaric methods to suppress what appears to me to be precisely a primary good, which is a flourishing civil life. It is certainly true that since the neutralization of the so-called Gang of Four, major inequalities have again surfaced in urban China, but alongside this are also the beginnings of a civil society reborn (Brook and Frolic 1997). As much as I welcome the second, I have no wish to justify the first, which brings about its own evils of exploitation and corruption. Still, the two phenomena are not independent of each other, as they point to a general relaxation of government control over social and economic life. And even though I argue here for "four pillars" to provide the material foundations of the good city, I regard them as chiefly a means to a more transcendent end, which is a vibrant civil life. Genuine material equality, Maoist-style, is neither achievable nor desirable. Whereas we will always have to live with material inequalities, what we must never tolerate is a contemptuous disregard for the qualities of social and political life, which is the sphere of freedom. A good city is a city that cares for its freedom, even as it makes adequate social provision for its weakest members.   *Discourse around freedom is contentious...*

The good city IV: good governance

☆Important point to compare

If process is as important as outcome, as I argued at the beginning of this essay, we will have to consider the processes of governance in the good city. Governance refers to the ways by which binding decisions for cities and city-regions are made and carried out. It is thus a concept considerably more inclusive than traditional government and administration and reflects the fact that increasingly there is a much wider range of participants in these processes than was traditionally the case.

   Three sets of potential actors can be identified. First, there are the politicians and bureaucrats, representing the institutions of the local state. It is because of them that decisions concerning city-building are made "binding." The state stands at the apex of a pyramid whose base is defined, respectively, by corporate capital and civil society. The role of corporate capital in city-building has become more pronounced in recent years, encouraged by privatization and the growing emphasis on mega-projects in city-building, from apartment blocks, new towns, office developments and technology parks to toll roads, bridges, harbor reclamation schemes and airports. The role of civil society has been a more contested issue. Beyond rituals of "citizen participation" in planning, civil society's major role, in most cities, has taken the form of protest and resistance to precisely the mega-projects dear to both state and capital.[7] Civil society has also put pressure on the state for more sustainable cities, for environmental justice and for more inclusive visions of the city.

It is tempting, in a utopian exercise, to invert the order of things and, as in this case, to place local citizens at the top of the governance pyramid. This would be broadly in accord with democratic theory as well as with my earlier claim that the city exists for the sake of its citizens, who are bound to each other by mutual if tacit agreement, thus forming a political community. But I hesitate, because I am not convinced that city-regions on the scale of multiple millions can be organized like town meetings or the Athenian *agora*. Nor do I believe in the vaunted capacity of the internet – even supposing universal access – to overcome the problem of scale. Democratic governance requires something more than a "thumbs up" and "thumbs down" to public intervention on any given issue, which would be no more meaningful than a telephone survey at the end of a public debate which asks the question: "Who won?"

An alternative would be simply to scale down city-regional governance until governance becomes coextensive with what I have elsewhere called "the city of everyday life." Thomas Jefferson had a name for it: "the republic of the wards" (for a summary, see Friedmann 1973: 220–22). More recently, there have been calls (in the United States) for "neighborhood governments" (Kotler 1969; Morris and Hess 1975; King and Stivers 1998). And there is even a Chinese-Taiwanese version of this idea, citing the writings of Lao Zi (Lao Tzu) (Cheng and Hsia 1999), as well as a striking example from southern Brazil (Abers 1998). Evidently, there is something very attractive about this devolution of powers to the most local of local levels – the neighborhood, the street. But a city-region is more than the sum of its neighborhoods, and each level of spatial integration must be slotted into a larger whole, which is the prevailing system of governance. The question, then, is how to articulate this whole so as to further the idea of multipli/city and the four pillars of a good city.

I do not claim great originality for my criteria of good governance. But I would like to think that they have some cross-cultural validity, because they address what are ultimately very practical issues that must be dealt with in cities East and West, North and South. Still, in any attempt to apply them, differences in political culture must be borne in mind. I would propose, then, the following six criteria for assessing the performance of a system of city-regional governance:

- *Inspired political leadership*: leaders capable of articulating a common vision for the polity, building a strong consensus around this vision and mobilizing resources towards its realization.
- *Public accountability*: (1) the uncoerced, periodic election of political representatives and (2) the right of citizens to be adequately informed about those who stand for elections, the standing government's performance record and the overall outcomes for the city.

- *Transparency and the right to information*: governance should be transparent in its manner of operation and, as much as possible, be carried out in full view of citizen observers. Citizens should have the right to information, particularly about contracts between the city and private corporations.
- *Inclusiveness*: the right of all citizens to be directly involved in the formulation of policies, programs and projects whenever their consequences can be expected to significantly affect their life and livelihood.
- *Responsiveness*: the primordial right of citizens is to claim rights and express grievances; to have access to appropriate channels for this purpose; to have a government that is accessible to them in the districts of their "everyday life"; and to timely, attentive and appropriate responses to their claims and grievances.
- *Non-violent conflict management*: institutionalized ways of resolving conflicts between state and citizens without resort to physical violence.

★ Does this really address the power of corporate capital?

The "utopian" character of these criteria becomes immediately apparent as soon as we invert the terms and picture a form of governance that displays a bungling leadership without vision, deems it unnecessary to render public accounts of its actions, transacts the state's business in secrecy, directs resources to groups favored by the state without consulting with affected local citizens, responds to expression of grievance with a mailed fist, and resolves conflicts with the arrest of opposition leaders and the brutal suppression of citizen protest.

This litany may no longer apply to North American or West European forms of city-regional governance, except perhaps in times of extreme tension – I am thinking of Paris and Chicago in 1968. *?* But in much of the rest of the world, and especially in Asia where urbanization is now in full swing, the dystopia of governance still prevails, and criteria of good governance, especially at local levels, are a considerable novelty. And in any event, good governance always hangs on slender threads. The last State of Victoria's Minister of Planning in Australia, responsible for planning and development in the City of Melbourne, suspended public consultation and declared public information on major city projects as no longer a requirement. This was the same Minister who, a few years earlier, suspended elected local councils and replaced them with city managers appointed by the state. He then proceeded to redraw council boundaries and issue administrative instructions on the privatization of council responsibilities. In the Australian State of Victoria, at least, good governance was, until recently, in jeopardy, and so perhaps it is not irrelevant, after all, even in a putative democracy, to be reminded of what some criteria of good governance might be.

A summing up

As human beings, we are cursed with a consciousness of our own death. This same consciousness places us in a stream of irreversible time. Minute by minute, lifetime by lifetime, we move through a continuing present – like the Roman god, Janus, forever facing in two directions – reading and re-reading the past and imagining possible futures even as we deal with the practicalities of the day. Shrouded in both darkness and light, as Gerda Lerner reminds us, history as memory helps us to locate ourselves in the continuing present while imagining alternative futures that are meant to serve us as beacons of warning and inspiration (Lerner 1997: Chapter 4). In our two-faced gaze, we are a time-binding species whose inescapable task in a fundamentally urbanized world is to forge pathways towards a future that is worth struggling for.

In this essay, I have set down my own utopian thinking about the good city. It is a revisiting of a problem terrain on which I worked, on and off, during the 1970s (Friedmann 1979). At the time, I was thinking through what I called a transactive model of social planning to which the practice of dialogue would be central. These concerns subsequently expanded into my interest in social learning and the traditions of radical/insurgent planning. My investigations then led me further to examine the micro-structures of civil action, such as the household economy, culminating in a theory of empowerment and disempowerment (Friedmann 1992). Today's communicative turn in planning (Innes 1995) is a more mainstream version of some of these ideas.

The good city, as I imagine it, has its foundations in human flourishing and multipli/city. Four pillars provide for its material foundations: housing, affordable healthcare, adequately remunerated work and adequate social provision. And because process cannot be separated from outcome, I also delved into the question of what a system of good governance might look like, attempting a thumbnail description of such a system. The protagonist of my visioning is an autonomous, self-organizing civil society, active in making claims, resisting and struggling on behalf of the good city within a framework of democratic institutions.

Physical planners and urban designers will miss a discussion of the three-dimensional city, but this is not my domain, and I refer them to the well-known "urban design manifesto" by Allan Jacobs and Donald Appleyard (1987), where these matters are taken up in a context not very different from the value premises that underlie the present essay. Also missing from my account is any reference to a "sustainable" city, which I am prepared to leave to the experts who will want to talk, more knowledgeably than I, about resource-conserving cities, blue skies and clear water.

So my image of the city remains incomplete, and I think that is proper, because no one should have a final say about the good city. Utopian thinking is an ongoing, time-binding discourse intended to inform our striving. It is no more than that, but also nothing less.

Notes

1. According to the distinguished Israeli sociologist, S.N. Eisenstadt (1998: 123), America forged a civil religion out of disparate elements including "a strongly egalitarian, achievement-oriented individualism, republican liberties, with the almost total denial of the symbolic validity of hierarchy; disestablishment of official religion beginning with the federal government; basically anti-statist premises; and a quasi-sanctification of the economic sphere."

2. Utopian thinking may also be denied altogether. In destitution and other situations in extremis, survival has priority and leaves no room for utopian thinking, despite wish-dreams of cornucopia. Finally, there are those who make a virtue of problem-solving via "muddling through" in Charles Lindblom's (1959) provocative formulation, where our choices are guided by nothing more than a simple pleasure-pain calculus. Market fundamentalists are similarly averse to charting the long-term future.

3. I would like here to quote from a recent essay by Gerda Lerner (1997: 197), which expresses a similar conviction: "As long as we regard class, race, and gender dominance as separate though overlapping systems, we fail to understand their actual integration. We also fail to see that they cannot be abolished sequentially, for like the many-headed hydra, they continuously spawn new heads. Vertical theories of separate systems inevitably marginalize the subordination of women and fail to place it in the central relationship it has to the other aspects of the system. The system of hierarchies is interwoven, interpenetrating, interdependent. It is one system, with a variety of aspects. Race, class and gender oppression are inseparable; they construct, support and reinforce one another."

4. Some other notable attempts to imagine normative frameworks for city-building include Allan Jacobs and Donald Appleyard's 'Toward an urban design manifesto' (1987), Richard Rogers' *Cities for a Small Planet* (1997), and an interesting utopian experiment in Germany, involving four cities (Stadt Münster 1997). Called an "Agreement concerning the quality [of life] for a league of cities of the future," this program includes specific discussions under five headings: (1) economizing land management practices; (2) forward-looking environmental protection; (3) socially responsible housing programs; (4) transportation policy guidance for a sustainable urban future; (5) promoting an economy that will ensure a firm foundation for the city's future within a sustainable and resource-conserving framework.

5. For a devastating look at the entanglement of political and civil spheres in twentieth century China, see Chang (1991).

6. For a discussion of civil society, see Keane (1988), Seligman (1992) and Walzer (1992). Friedmann (1998) has attempted to introduce the concept into the discourse on planning.

7. But see the case studies of 'deliberative democracy' which are cited in Fung and Wright (1998).

Bibliography

Abers, R. (1998) 'Learning democratic practice: distributing government resources through popular participation in Porto Alegre, Brazil' in M. Douglass and J. Friedmann (eds) *Cities for Citizens: Planning and the rise of civil society in a global age*, Chichester: John Wiley & Sons.

Abu-Lughod, J. (1998) 'The world system perspective in the construction of economic history', in P. Pomper, R.H. Elphick and R.T. Vann (eds) *World History: Ideologies, structures and identities*, Oxford: Blackwell.

Arendt, H. (1958) *The Human Condition*, Chicago: The University of Chicago Press.

Brook, T. and Frolic, B.M. (eds) (1997) *Civil Society in China*, Armonk, NY: M.E. Sharpe.

Chang, J. (1991) *Wild Swans: Three daughters of China*, New York: Anchor Books.

Cheng, L. and Hsia, C-J. (1999) 'Exploring territorial governance and transterritorial society: alternative visions of 21st-century Taiwan', in J. Friedmann (ed.) *Urban and Regional Governance in the Asia Pacific*, Vancouver: University of British Columbia, Institute of Asian Research.

Eisenstadt, S.N. (1998) 'World histories and the construction of collective identities', in P. Pomper, R.H. Elphick and R.T. Vann (eds) *World History: Ideologies, structures, and identities*, Oxford: Blackwell.

Fainstein, S.S. (1999) 'Can we make the cities we want?', in S. Body-Gendrot and R.A. Beauregard (eds) *The Urban Moment*, Thousand Oaks, CA: Sage.

Friedmann, J. (1973) *Retracking America: A theory of transactive planning*, Garden City, NY: Anchor Press/Doubleday.

——(1979) *The Good Society*, Cambridge, MA: The MIT Press.

——(1987) *Planning in the Public Domain: From knowledge to action*, Princeton, NJ: Princeton University Press.

——(1992) *Empowerment: The politics of alternative development*, Oxford: Blackwell.

——(1998) 'The new political economy of planning: the rise of civil society', in M. Douglass and J. Friedmann (eds) *Cities for Citizens: Planning and the rise of civil society in a global age*, Chichester: John Wiley & Sons.

Friedmann, J. and Weaver, C. (1979) *Territory and Function: The evolution of regional planning*, Berkeley: University of California Press.

Fung, A. and Wright, E.O. (1998) 'Experiments in deliberative democracy: introduction', (http://www.ssc.wisc.edu/~wright/experiments6-1.html).

Harvey, D. (1996) *Justice, Nature and the Geography of Difference*, Oxford: Blackwell.

Hayden, D. (1984) *Redesigning the American Dream: The future of housing, work, and family life*, New York: W.W. Norton.

Innes, J. (1995) 'Planning theory's emerging paradigm: communicative action and interactive practice', *Journal of Planning Education and Research*, 14(3): 183–9.

Jacobs, A. and Appleyard, D. (1987) [1996 edn] 'Toward an urban design manifesto', in R.T.L. Gates and F. Stout (eds) *The City Reader*, New York: Routledge.

Jacobs, J. (1961) *The Death and Life of Great American Cities*, New York: Random House.

Keane, J. (1988) *Democracy and Civil Society*, London: Verso.

King, C.S. and Stivers, C. (1998) *Government Is Us: Public administration in an anti-government era*, Thousand Oaks, CA: Sage.

Kotler, M. (1969) *Neighborhood Government*, Indianapolis: Bobbs-Merril.

Lerner, G. (1997) *Why History Matters: Life and thought*, New York: Oxford University Press.

Lindblom, C. (1959) 'The science of muddling through', *Public Administration Review*, 19(2): 79–99.

Manuel, F.E. and Manuel, F.P. (1979) *Utopian Thought in the Western World*, Cambridge, MA: The Belknap Press of Harvard University Press.

Morris, D. and Hess, K. (1975) *Neighborhood Power*, Boston: Beacon Press.

Rogers, R. (1997) *Cities for a Small Planet*, London: Faber and Faber.

Sandercock, L. (1997) *Towards Cosmopolis: planning for multicultural cities*, London: John Wiley & Sons.

——(1998) (ed.) 'Insurgent planning', special issue of *Plurimondi*, Italy: Bari.

Seligman, A.B. (1992) *The Idea of Civil Society*, Princeton, NJ: Princeton University Press.

Stadt Münster (1997) *Experimenteller Wohnungs- und Städtebau: Qualitätsvereinbarung für ein Bündnis Städte der Zukunft*.

Walzer, M. (1992) 'The civil society argument', in C. Mouffe (ed.) *Dimensions of Radical Democracy: Pluralism, citizenship, community*, London: Verso.

Warren, R., Nun, S. and Warren, C. (1998) 'The future of the future in planning: appropriating cyberpunk visions of the city', *Journal of Planning Education and Research*, 18(3): 49–60.

Weaver, C. (1984) *Anarchy, Planning, and Regional Development*, London: John Wiley & Sons.

Study questions

(handwritten: Is this Utopian ↓ thinking?)

The subtitle of this chapter is "in defense of utopian thinking." Do you think it is worth thinking about what our cities might become in 20 or 30 years' time? Or is it enough for planners to deal with the city in partial, fragmented terms? If planners are merely pragmatic problem solvers, utopian thinking would probably be of little value to their professional lives. What do you think? Should we have a well thought-out vision of the future and, if so, to what purpose?

Human flourishing is posited here as a fundamental human right. As the text says, it is a right "by nature." Why do you think I invoke here the theory of natural right, a theory that is out of step with contemporary notions of human life? Is it not the case, you might ask, that all rights are claimed, won, and defended in specific historical circumstances and are therefore socially constructed? But what would you say if I told you that the assertion of the natural origin of what I claim to be a fundamental human right was put there for emphasis, and to give a sense of *gravitas* to the claim?

Why was it necessary to qualify human flourishing by saying that it must be constrained by the context of wider communities? How does this context change the meaning of this fundamental human right? And in the case of conflict between individual interests and our obligations to others, how would you resolve this tension?

The idea of a "common good" runs throughout this essay. And yet we have difficulties describing it, and many writers ranging across the political spectrum deny its very existence. What is your view? In the text, I argue that human flourishing depends on certain conditions, which I list as different aspects of the city. We might argue about these conditions, and which would favor *(handwritten: Is this true?)* flourishing and which might not, but the fact that we can argue about these matters implies that there is indeed a "common good" worth talking about, even though we may disagree on its particulars. Is it not also the case that all political communities exist as such precisely because they hold certain things in common, be it institutions, histories, landscapes, language, and so forth? To deny this heritage would mean the dissolution of any meaningful human community.

Multipli/city is proposed as a primary good together with certain conditions that would allow this good to be realized in practice. Civil society is proposed as the sphere of freedom and social reproduction. This is an image of civil society "for itself" rather than being engaged in politically struggle. It is said to be an autonomous sphere, which is described in the text as a "quilted mosaic of voluntary associations." But civil society requires a material base for its sustenance that is described in the essay as the four pillars of a civil life. These "pillars" suggest the reappearance of the idea of "basic needs," that is, a certain minimum standard of living which should be accessible to all with respect to at least housing, healthcare, paid work, and social provisioning. This is sometimes also referred to as "the social minimum." By introducing multipli/city, the argument moves from philosophical ideas to material realities, which are anything but utopian. Please comment.

The fourth topic introduced to the discussion of the good city is the question of good governance. The thread of democratic thinking runs throughout this essay. Actually existing democracies differ greatly among themselves, and none conform to an ideal model. But whatever it may be ideally, democracy is a form of government that is inclusive, guarantees basic civil rights, treasures the rule of law, and is accountable to its citizens. The word governance, on the other hand, means something more than a form of government. It refers specifically to the participation of citizens in rule-making. Some criteria of good governance are spelled out with an eye to their applicability at local levels of government. Some of them sound fairly conventional; others, such as "responsiveness" make substantially new claims. Discuss some of these and how we might redeem them in the everyday life of the city.

What would you like to add to this portrait of the good city? Or might we also say, what is missing from this unfinished sketch? Look at some of the additional readings shown below.

Selected additional readings

Amin, A. (2006) 'The good city', *Urban Studies*, 43(5–6): 1009–23.

Jacobs, J. (1961) *The Death and Life of Great American Cities*, New York: Random House.

Marcuse, P. *et al* (eds) (2009) *Searching for the Just City: Debates in urban theory and practice*, New York: Routledge.

Sandercock, L. (2003) *Cosmopolis II: Mongrel cities of the 21st century*, London: Continuum.

Thayer, R.L. Jr (2003) *Life Place: Bioregional thought and practice*, Berkeley: University Of California Press.

Wood, P. and Landry, C. (2008) *The Intercultural City: Planning for diversity advantage*, London: Earthscan.

9

The many cultures of planning

The first World Congress of Planning took place in Shanghai in June 2001. There was a brief moment of euphoria, as some Western planners thought the Congress held the promise of "one world, one planning," and that planning had become, or was in process of becoming, one discipline, one universal profession. It must soon have become apparent, however, that the global discourse was far from unified, and that planners often talked past each other, not quite knowing whether or not they made sense to their polyglot audience. English was the lingua franca of the Congress, but not everyone was conversant in the language, and the translation of specialized terms at this academic meeting must have tried the skills of the simultaneous interpreters who labored bravely and anonymously in the background. How, for example, was a Chinese planner to explain to a colleague from, say, Barcelona, Spain, the intricacies of local institutions in the hyperactive metropolis that is Shanghai, and vice versa, when the entire municipality of the capital of Catalunya is smaller than a single urban district of the Shanghai municipality with its population of 14 million registered denizens and another 4 million temporary migrant workers, and do this in a language that is foreign to them both? To say the least, it must have been a challenging task.

Musings of this sort gave me the idea of writing a paper on the varieties of planning cultures around the world. This was a quixotic undertaking from the start. I had very little knowledge of how planning was actually performed across the 200-plus countries in the world, never mind the thousands of cities that were engaged in some form of planning. Even to think about doing this single-handedly was a rash, almost absurd idea. But all I wanted to accomplish with this essay was to provoke my one-world colleagues, and so I scoured the available literature on global planning practices, collecting brief vignettes that I believed were reasonably accurate representations of at least some facets of planning in the countries, regions, and cities I surveyed. I had no systematic procedure for selecting my accounts, but aimed at producing a crazy quilt of planning stories that would help to make my point that "planning cultures" were indeed real and multiple. If we were going to make ourselves understood in cross-cultural conversations about planning, we would have to be mindful of these differences.

This point of departure is perhaps not immediately obvious to American planners, many of whom are still fairly parochial in their thinking, having been nurtured in their own planning culture (and its language) with little knowledge of how planning is institutionalized and enacted beyond the borders of their own country or even the city where they happen to be employed. I would therefore like to spell out some of the main axes of cultural difference in planning practice.

At the macro-level, there is, first, the institutional context; for instance, the form of government, whether (as a first crude approximation) a country has a unitary form such as China (PRC), Japan, and France or a devolved federal structure, such as Canada, the USA, and India. Overlaying these formal institutional arrangements are local regimes with varying degrees of autonomy. In Europe, the pattern is further complicated by the role of the European Union which, although it has no formal powers over local planning, nevertheless exerts a significant influence over spatial planning in the 27 countries of the Union. Moreover, in this global catalogue of differences, some countries are capitalist and wealthy, others are in transition from a centrally planned to a market economy and are governed by authoritarian regimes, notably China, Vietnam, and the Russian Federation, while Africa is for the most part poor, disorganized, and agrarian, and the Middle East exhibits a varied tapestry ranging from Wahabi Saudi Arabia's absolute monarchy to Turkey's secular, democratic regime.

What planners do for a living is also very different as we move across the world. In rich countries with strong civil societies and liberal democratic regimes, government planners need to enter into conversation with civic organizations that are frequently quite skilled in mobilizing public opinion, whether to make special planning provisions, for example, for women, children, and the disabled, push for sustainability and environmental justice agendas, and so forth. On the other hand, urban life in Africa is largely organized informally, an indigenous civil society is all but invisible, and people are far too busy scraping together a livelihood to bother much about the niceties of "planning."

In most places, however, planners are expected to produce master plans with time perspectives of 10 to 20 years and which sometimes have statutory form. Such plans are a legacy of the past, when city authorities were preoccupied with making cities well behaved and orderly. In slowly urbanizing or actually de-urbanizing countries such as the Czech Republic, for example, long-range plans can make sense because changes are generally small and incremental. In hyper-urbanizing countries, on the other hand, such as China and Vietnam, events on the ground happen at twice the speed of producing master plans, rendering plans perpetually out of date and ineffectual.

Finally, there are major differences in planning education. In Japan, for instance, planning is taught in faculties of engineering. On the European continent, it is typically seen as a branch of architecture, focusing on urban design. Although this may be changing, the legacy of this educational tradition is hard to erase. In Canada and the United States, where the majority of planning schools started up in the decades following World War II, the emphasis is more on applied social science and policy analysis, with physical planning being only one of a number of sub-disciplines that include environmental, transportation, and community development planning, among others. India, Australia, and New Zealand have followed mostly the British model of planning education, which is highly bureaucratized. South Africa and many other countries that are trying to work their way out of poverty are emphasizing entrepreneurial development planning.

The evidence, I think, is overwhelming that today's global map of planning is amazingly diverse. This is not to say, however, that existing differences are necessarily forever. The Shanghai World Congress was only the first in a continuing series of such meetings. American planning journals are paying increasing attention to what is happening elsewhere in the world, and the same trend can be noted around the globe. China publishes both *Urban Planning International* (in Chinese) and the *China City Planning Review* (in English), and there is a very active International Association for China Planning that operates out of the Massachusetts Institute of Technology and maintains close contacts with Chinese counterparts through annual conferences, joint research projects, and other activities. European and North American planning organizations are also in close contact with each other through joint meetings, journals, and exchanges. As well, a number of jointly edited Anglo-American planning journals published in the UK, such as *Planning Theory*, the *International Development Planning Review*, *Urban Studies*, and *Planning Theory and Practice* are having a growing influence on the profession. I believe that these cultural exchanges, which would not have been possible 20 years ago, and are now mediated by the ever-expanding worldwide net of professional contacts and the internet, may lead to a gradual convergence of planning cultures over the next few decades. Whether for good or ill remains to be seen.

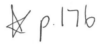

From "Globalization and the Emerging Culture of Planning"

Originally published in 2005

The mantra of globalization poses two problems for students of cities. The first is its obsession with economic relations to the exclusion of other possible perspectives, for example, social, cultural, and political. The second is that it tends to render invisible the very real effects that global economic relations have on the daily lives of ordinary people. Not only do global economic relations – what Manuel Castells has dubbed the "space of flows" – ultimately have to come down to the ground into the "space of places" but, when they do so, they inevitably impact the everyday life of a city in numerous ways (Castells 1996).

For nearly 20 years now, research has been carried out to study these effects in major cities of the world, particularly in those that are closely linked into transnational networks (Friedmann and Wolff 1982; Friedmann 1986; Knox and Taylor 1986; Sassen 2001, 2002b; Smith 2003). There is little agreement about which cities should be designated world or global cities, that is, as strategic nodes in the dynamic inter-city flows generated by financial transactions, trade, migration, and information (Taylor *et al* 2002: 99). Moreover, attempts at rank-ordering "world cities" have shown that their relative position is by no means stable, that new cities may join the roster from time to time, while other cities either drop out from the list or lose their relative standing. The number of such cities is in any event quite small. Sassen, for example, suggests that there might only be some 40 cross-border nodes, with heavy emphasis on the North Atlantic global subsystem, while the Globalization and World Cities Research Group under Peter Taylor identifies 50 "world cities", with another 67 showing "some evidence" of world city formation (Sassen 2002a; Taylor *et al* 2002: 100). Be that as it may, the present essay will focus on cities and adjacent regions that play a significant role in articulating the global system of transactions and are subject, in one way or another, to the restructuring of urban space that insertion into the global economy inevitably entails.

This leaves us with the question of what is meant by the culture of planning. The term was first introduced in 1993 by three European planners who undertook what they described as a "journey into the planning cultures of four countries": Switzerland, Germany, Italy, and France (DISP 115, 1993; Keller *et al* 1996). More recently, Bishwapriya Sanyal of the Massachusetts Institute of Technology convened a symposium, which produced a series of case studies of planning cultures (Sanyal 2005). A firm definition of the term, however, eluded their authors. For present purposes, I propose to define planning culture as the ways, both formal and informal, that spatial planning in a given multi-national region, country or city is conceived, institutionalized, and enacted. Because planning in this sense continues to be primarily a responsibility of the state even as it draws upon the contributions of other societal actors, it is deeply embedded in the political culture of the country and/or individual cities and, as such, is always historically grounded. This is not to say that planning cultures are engraved in stone. Globalization, for one, is bringing about major changes in the institutional structure, processes, influence, and scope of planning. It is the intent of this essay to point to some of these changes that already appear, so to speak, to be "in the air," redefining what we have traditionally understood by spatial planning.[1]

Before proceeding, however, I want to dispel the widely held notion that as a field of professional activity, planning practice is more or less the same regardless of where it is practiced. In other words, that like civil engineering, planning is a profession devoid of social, political, or cultural content except for its own specific professionalism. If this were true, planners in Chongqing would talk the same professional talk and act in ways not very different from planners in Zurich or, for that matter, in Jakarta or Cairo. In short, planners the world over would share the same professional *habitus* or disposition to act, giving rise to a uniform planning culture (Bourdieu 2002; Friedmann 2002). But, in fact, we know that, despite the growing volume of international communication within the profession, which is beginning to draw planners together into a globe-spanning, discursive community (Stiftel and Watson 2004), major differences exist in the ways that planning is conceived, institutionalized, and carried out.

In this chapter, some of these differences will be highlighted to illustrate the proposition that planning cultures worldwide can exist only in the plural, even as global restructuring is challenging them in similar ways. After a quick journey to planning as practiced in a number of multi-national regions, countries, and cities, preliminary conclusions will be drawn to underscore both similarities and differences in actually existing planning cultures across the globe.

It would be foolish to attempt a systematic delineation of planning cultures within the limited space devoted to the topic here. My intent is no more than to point to some distinctive characteristics of how spatial planning is done in a variety of cultural and political settings globally. No attempt has been made to provide a systematic coverage, either thematically or geographically. My enterprise was limited by the recent literature available to me in English. And although I wanted to get a reasonable coverage, I also wanted good stories that would tell us something significant about the variety of planning cultures globally. The following glimpses are therefore geographically uneven both in scale and coverage. They include a number of *national* perspectives (Japan, China, India, the United Kingdom, and the United States); a *continental* perspective highlighted with references to particular cities in Africa; an attempt to devise a normative framework for spatial planning in the countries of the European Union; and a series of interesting stories about specific *cities* (Yaroslavl/Russia; Rotterdam; Vancouver/British Columbia). Clearly, there are enormous gaps in this survey. For example, I found no suitable sources for Middle Eastern, Latin American, and Pacific Asian countries whose stories would have added variety, if not novelty, to my account. European planning traditions, of which there are many, are also represented by too few examples. Be that as it may, the following accounts represent the empirical basis of my interpretation of actually existing planning cultures in the world today.

Planning in Japan

Shift from centralized control in early 20th cent. to more localized, participatory engaged

Modern planning in Japan began in 1919 with the promulgation of the first city planning law.[2] This law was based chiefly on German precedents and was the work of a small group of elite bureaucrats in the Home Ministry, professors at the University of Tokyo, and a few others.[3] For most of the 20th century, therefore, planning was regarded as a function of the central state which subordinated the variety of local conditions and concerns to the overriding interests of the nation: rapid industrialization in the early days, colonial conquest (to 1945), reconstruction from the devastations of the war, accelerated economic growth, and efforts at economic revival since the early nineties. The costs of achieving these goals – environmental pollution and its associated health costs, the rapid depopulation of rural areas, regional imbalances, crammed and expensive housing – were patiently borne by a population that, by and large, acquiesced in these priorities. Japan's civil society has been described as extremely weak, and until quite recently, has had little influence on local planning matters, while city governments have been subservient to policy directives of central ministries and more specifically in regard to planning, to the Ministry of Construction.

Major changes, however, took place during the last decade of the past century when financial stringencies at the center led to the devolution of planning powers to local authorities. Most importantly, each municipality in Japan was mandated to develop a Master Plan as a guide for its future development. This plan and the policies that would give substance to the vision embodied in the plan were to be drawn up with the help of public consultation. For the first time in the country's history, a process of citizen participation in urban development was imposed. At the turn of the millennium, 608 local governments had complied with this central directive and produced their first-ever Master Plans that reflected long-term visions for change and the policies to accommodate them.

Prior to this explosion of master planning activities, local planners' responsibilities had been concentrated on zoning, the occasional preparation of district plans, and land readjustment on the urban fringe.[4] These activities, as Sorensen observes, were useful primarily for the improvement of small areas. Zoning, for instance, has always been the principal planning tool in Japan, but it was relatively inflexible in application and, in any case, a relatively "porous" instrument (Sorensen 2002: 303). In this context, the drafting and adoption of municipal master plans was regarded as a major innovation. For the first time, cities would be allowed to chart their own future without central guidance. Master plans, however, are in the nature of blueprints, and in practice, local governments have very limited powers to make them stick. Moreover, municipalities are far from being financially independent of the central government. And major projects in infrastructure and transportation are the responsibilities of other levels of government that are not required to conform their decisions to the municipal plan.

The nineties were also a decade during which civil society in Japan became reanimated, particularly around environmental issues. In planning, this new activism took the form of citizen participation in neighborhood development, or *machizukuri*. The focus here was on the quality of urban life, the widening of narrow roads, providing parks, playlots, and street trees, building community centers, and exercising development controls over urban sprawl. Municipalities could now pass *machizukuri* ordinances that would be binding, but for the most part, neighborhood councils could only lobby authorities and use moral suasion with property developers. Still and all, what some have referred to as Japan's "lost decade" in terms of reinvigorating the national economy, was quite the opposite in a city planning perspective, as cities and neighborhoods became empowered to gain a measure of control over their own futures.

Planning in China

Three features starred

China's current system of physical planning is, one might say, still "under construction."[5] Underpinned by national legislation that went into effect in 1987, it represents a significant departure from city planning during the Maoist era when, following the Soviet model, physical planning was narrowly defined and, in the end, suspended altogether, as planners were sent down to the countryside to be 're-educated' by peasant farmers. After a decade or so of rapid urban growth following the accession to power of the Communist Party in 1949, the government decided to halt the flow of city-bound migrants and even attempted, though with only limited success, to reverse it.

Since the onset of the reforms in 1978, and especially after 1989 when basic planning legislation was first promulgated by the State Council, planning has returned to favor and is now perceived as a prestigious profession. The development paths of every city are expected to conform to a long-term comprehensive physical plan. But under conditions of hyper-rapid economic growth, such planning tends to issue in plans whose capacity to guide developments is undermined by the very speed of double-digit economic growth. Still, a formidable planning bureaucracy has come into existence that employs more than 60,000 "planners" with varying degrees of competence to manage urban space for about 400 million people across the vast expanses of China's provinces. City planners – once trained in Moscow but now increasingly in American and European institutions as well as in China – work through their own institutions and are exclusively focused on the physical dimensions of planning. There is little coordination with economic, social and environmental planning bureaucracies, all three of which work through their own organizational channels and are accountable to different ministries in Beijing.

Although local government officials in China, including the mayor, are centrally appointed, they enjoy a good deal of discretion in practice, which becomes greater as one descends from city to district and especially to the so-called Street Committees that are responsible for a large variety of public services in their boroughs and neighborhoods. Street Committees, along with other government and quasi-government organizations, have been called "amphibious," because in order to fund the public work they do, they must also engage in business activities for profit. In short, they are largely self-financing rather than dependent on central budget allocations. And while amphibious organizations no doubt accomplish a great deal – the impressive physical appearance of new urban districts in major cities attests to that – they also give rise to corrupt practices of sometimes staggering proportion.[6]

Critical to successful planning in China is its articulation with the socio-economic development plans that follow the sequence of national five-year plans. Local versions of these plans are prepared for provinces and cities and, in the perspective of development planners, the job of physical planning is simply to make possible their realization. This expectation is rarely fulfilled, however, partly because the two forms of planning – developmental and land use – are institutionally separated. Another reason for this inability to successfully articulate socio-economic development and physical city plans stems from the system of land apportionment (Wong and Zhao 1999). Rural land in China is owned collectively by administrative villages, but urban land is held by the State, which retains title to it even after the transfer of land use rights to work units (*danwei*) and other developers (though sometimes they are one and the same) either through administrative means, as in the case of government offices, hospitals, schools, the military, etc. or through a process of negotiation, tenders, and auctions for residential, commercial, and industrial uses.

☆ Key feature: institutional separation b/wn domains of planning

Land apportionment is administered through the State Land Administration Bureau (SLAB) whose main responsibility is to formulate national policies and regulations with respect to land conservation, development, and use. In the case of large-scale projects, it draws up land use maps in coordination with the Planning Bureau in the Ministry of Construction. It is also charged with cadastral registration and the survey of land use boundaries (Wong and Zhao 1999: 115). Branch offices of the SLAB have been set up at all administrative levels, and by the early 1990s, nearly all major cities had established their own land administration bureaus that were vertically linked with SLAB.

The land apportionment system is supposed to follow a formal process of project approval, allowing for the possibility that, after their transfer to developers, land use rights could be bought and sold in secondary and tertiary markets. In the following, however, I want to focus on the informal and quasi-legal land transfers, which are the more common and socially embedded processes. Wong and Zhao provide a concise account:

> Evidently, local governments are intricately involved, often anonymously, in many land development projects. The common practice is that they fundamentally reverse the "bottom-up" approach of the formal process of land apportionment into a top-down approach. Local governments, particularly the mayor's office together with the LAB [Land Administration Bureau] and CPB [City Planning Bureau], will first set up new parcels of land that they consider have their greatest potential market value. To monitor land transactions closely, the authority will exercise care in the selection of reliable partners or argents in the undertaking. [The "agents" could be anyone with access to the decision-making authorities on land apportionment, and are often close relatives or associates of influential government officials.] The agents act as the middlemen between investors and local authorities. They will look for prospective land developers or investors who might be interested in developing the parcel of land set aside by the local authority. They will then carry out informal negotiations with the prospective developers on behalf of the officials about the terms of the venture. Because of their extremely intimate *guanxi* (or relationship) with the officials, they can assure developers that they can acquire all the government approvals needed to obtain the LUR (land use right) permit. Of course, implicit in their negotiations is that they have to pay certain amounts of *guanxi* fees or bribes to the agents and the government officials concerned. (Wong and Zhao, 1999: 118)

 Urban developments that follow a version of this informal process will frequently clash with the formal requirements of the current master plan for the city. The best that can be said about this situation is that, in a process that is becoming increasingly contentious, the final result will often be a mixture of the formal and informal.

If there is one city in China that for exemplifies "best planning practice," it is the municipality of Shenzhen just north of the border with Hong Kong. Shenzhen emerged in the 1980s as an "instant" city; 20 years later, it is aspiring to become a "world-class" metropolis that by the turn of the millennium already boasted a resident population of over 4 million.[7] (Shenzhen's actual population, established in the 2000 census, is about seven million. The resulting difference with respect to the smaller number of the resident population is accounted for by the "floating" (or temporary) population whose residence permits (*hukou*) are in rural townships to which they are supposed to return when their work permits expire. Their presence in the city is thus not acknowledged, and master plans typically exclude them from calculations; "floaters" have no "right to the city.") In 1997, Shenzhen was designated a National Environmental Protection City. Many areas were redeveloped and a major "greening" program was undertaken, partly to lure foreign investors from abroad. To further enhance the city's image, the government cleared over 300,000 m² of illegal construction. Cultural development was also going to be boosted.

Between the early 1980s and the end of the millennium, Shenzhen planners were frantically trying to catch up with actual developments on the ground, as master plans quickly succeeded each other and planners scrambled to adjust them to an ever-changing reality. Although the blue-print approach of master planning seemed to work so long as government was the sole development agent, it was useless to guide development when ever more actors emerged. In 1997, the Shenzhen Urban Planning Committee was set up, including both city officials and – for the very first time in China – stakeholders representing local business interests. The assigned role of the Committee was to conciliate district-level plans with the municipal master plan. Ordinary residents and the floating population, of course, continued to be virtually invisible and inaudible. Many Shenzhen planners considered the Urban Planning Committee a nuisance, calling this attempt at enlisting participation of even a limited number of private stakeholders in the planning process as "too advanced" for China. Even so, the planning process was slowly becoming more transparent. The draft Third Master Plan was scrutinized for a 30-day period by the general public. Cadres and scholars from neighboring cities were invited to comment on the draft. And finally, after seven years of hard work, the plan received State Council approval in 2000. Whether this plan will be any more successful than its predecessors in shaping Shenzhen's future remains to be seen.

Finally, a word needs to be said about China's "civil society" and its (potential) role in planning. As in virtually all countries, planning in China is considered to be a responsibility of government. Furthermore, China does not have a politically active civil society, and the public media are only timidly beginning to "monitor" the performance of local government which, in any case, represents the central government in the city.[8] Although aggrieved citizens have the right to sue local authorities in the courts, this tends to be an expensive and risky undertaking, since the courts often side with the authorities. In a growing number of cases, therefore, people choose to write lengthy petitions to the government or, as a last resort, take their complaints to the street. But it is not clear that they are any more successful in being acknowledged and heard than those exceptional individuals who press their charges through a legal system that is still evolving.[9] As a result, planners have a relatively free hand to exercise their skills, whether for good or ill, without having to render accounts to local citizens.

Planning in India

India today is the world's second most populated country (having just topped one billion) and is governed by a robust, if turbulent, democracy with an unfettered press and an independent judiciary.[10] In contrast to China, it is also a federal system where the several states have considerable autonomy from the central government. The Indian administrative model takes its inspiration from the British system and was designed to separate the political and administrative arms of government. Planning is thus regarded as the responsibility of a highly esteemed and competent civil service at both federal and state levels. Admission and promotion within the civil service are based on merit rather than patronage, and the administrator in Indian society is regarded as both an employee of the state and a servant of the public. To accommodate the diversity of Indian society within the civil service, an official policy is in place to attract women, ethnic and religious minorities, the disabled, individuals of certain castes and rural inhabitants.

At the federal level, economic planning through the creation of Five Year Plans beginning in 1951 has given the Indian civil service the primary role in development administration. Over the last half century, however, its strategy for stimulating development evolved from one of state-centered entrepreneurship through direct public sector investment to that of a facilitator for private sector growth.

Urban land use planning and other forms of spatial development are largely the domain of state and municipal governments but are required by law to be consistent with the current 5-year national economic development plan. Over the past 50 years, Indian cities, along with cities in many other parts of Asia, have experienced phenomenal growth. Urban population has more than quadrupled, and 28 per cent or some 285 million Indians now call cities home.

Since 1991, the number of urban agglomerations with more than 1 million inhabitants has increased from 23 to 35, and India now has three mega-cities of more than 10 million. In this context of rapid urbanization, planning for urban development has tried to ensure that the housing, transport, employment, safety and entertainment needs of the millions of new urban dwellers are at least minimally met.

Within the Indian planning establishment, there is considerable official optimism about the socially transformative change and betterment that is afoot in India. The cadre of administrators responsible for planning are presented as socially representative, civic minded, and politically independent, who work tirelessly to improve the living conditions of Indian citizens. Yet, in many ways, this official story belies the realities on the ground, both in terms of empirical evidence and as perceived by the public.

To begin with, both central and state civil services are far from representative of the actually existing diversity within Indian society. Women are grossly underrepresented, and the civil service is staffed primarily by members of the urban upper middle class. More problematic, perhaps, are structural issues that have limited the actions of the civil service in India. At both federal and state levels, the civil service is a highly regimented work environment, defined more by procedural accountability than pragmatic decision-making. Hierarchical in structure, there is little direct communication between individuals of different ranks. The civil service entrance exams favor general knowledge over specific skills, leading to criticisms that the civil service lacks the professional and technical proficiency in planning. Finally, the theoretical separation between political and administrative functions is often tangled and blurred. In the field of planning, this has led to large-scale improprieties and corruption related to land allocation and development rights. Writing about the situation in Delhi for India's national magazine *Frontline*, Gopalakrishnan (2003) writes:

> The Delhi Development Authority (DDA) finds itself in the thick of a controversy following a series of raids by the Central Bureau of Investigation, which have pointed to corruption being rampant at every level in the DDA. Media exposés have meanwhile revealed connections between senior DDA officials and the real estate mafia, as well as the political skullduggery in land allotment.

The inability to elevate the living standards of the common Indian citizen in combination with the news of corruption scandals has begun to erode public confidence in the civil service, and the country's planning establishment is increasingly seen as a career-oriented elite with an incentive to maintain the status quo while minimizing public participation in the decision-making process.

In recent years, planning organizations throughout India have attempted to increase their accountability and have begun to open themselves up to inputs and collaboration from civil society. In 1992, the 74th Constitutional Amendment Act gave constitutional status to Urban Local Bodies (chiefly municipal governments) and granted them certain powers to better fulfill their role as provider of urban infrastructure and services. It also institutionalized the practice of public participation within the structure of what today is called integrated urban development planning.[11]

Clearly, as with many modernist planning systems around the world, India is still struggling to position an active civil society in the planning framework and to give voice to the multiple publics that actually exist in Indian society. A positive example is the story of a pro-poor alliance in Mumbai which is part of a global network of community-based housing activists that has engaged the state bureaucracy at all levels in the pursuit of improved housing conditions for the 40 per cent or so of the city's population that are still living in slums, deprived of even the most basic common facilities and services, from water to toilets (Appadurai 2004). By raising the capacity of the poor, who are now more informed and have gained a public voice, this alliance has created new choices for planners. Still, some critics argue that organized civil society is largely comprised of groups that, even as they seek to empower the locally disenfranchised, are unsure of what to do once they are "empowered." More fundamentally, as G.D. Verma argues, there is a participatory paradox with regard to planning in India (Verma 2002). By moving towards a collaborative planning system where basic decisions are negotiated between a variety of stakeholders and the State, there is the potential for an erosion of hard-won social rights that have been legally embedded in planning documents. This is marked by a trend towards settling for inferior alternatives in place of existing statutory provisions for slums, small industries, informal trade, schools, etc. As such, social welfare is repositioned as an issue deserving of charity, not statutory rights.

This insistence on statutory rights has little purchase, however, in a country where the urban poor often live on land which does not even appear on official maps and consequently has no legal standing. As a Calcutta newspaper remarked in the wake of a case that had been taken all the way to the High Court and had brought to light the lack of land records, maps, and a master plan:

> Unbelievable but true: Calcutta is the only city in the country without a master plan. The absence of the master plan supposedly came to light during a court case filed by an NGO in the public interest. When the CMC [Calcutta Metropolitan Council] failed to present the court with a master plan, the Chief Justice of the Calcutta High Court directed all chief engineers of all major city agencies to appear before him. The only plan they could produce was the CMDA's [Calcutta Metropolitan Development

Authority] Land Use and Development Control Plan for the CMC. The CMDA had been unable to prepare a master plan because of the lack of reliable data. All that the agencies have in their possession is a 75-year old survey map prepared by a British expert. (Cited in Roy, 2004: 157)

Planning in Russia (Yaroslavl)

The transition from a centrally planned to a market economy occurred more abruptly in Russia than it did in the People's Republic of China where the Communist Party continues in power.[12] Under the Soviet regime and until the beginnings of *perestroika* in the late 1980s, city planning was rigidly bureaucratized and, as Blair Ruble describes it, "enigmatic." City general plans, and the process leading up to them, were classified documents. Physical planning was understood to be a problem of urban design and was handled by enormous planning institutes in Moscow, Leningrad, and the capital cities of union republics. Every city had to have such a plan: between 1945 and 1977, for example, the Russian SFSR completed 720 general plans. Typically, they projected a 30-year future for a city. But because they were drafted by planners who had little, if any, direct knowledge of the cities for which they were preparing them, these idealized futures had only limited practical application.

What kept Soviet cities functioning were informal bureaucratic processes. For example, in the medium-sized city of Yaroslavl, located some 150 miles northeast of Moscow, "the massive Avtodizel' Motor Works opened schools, hospitals, and rest homes while constructing some thirty-five thousand apartments for its workers, largely with ministerial funds from Moscow that never passed through city coffers – or city control" (Ruble 1995: 107). Nothing illustrates better the sea-change that happened with the collapse of the Soviet system than the attempt by Avtodizel' to build new workers' cottages in a popular wooded park on the banks of the Volga River. Now obliged to seek city council approval, and to almost everyone's astonishment, the Motor Works failed in this attempt at a "land grab" (Ruble 1995: 125).

During the Yeltsin post-Soviet regime in Russia, planning was radically decentralized, giving local communities a greater say over the directions of future growth ... or decline. In Yaroslavl's case, the city invited the Moscow-based Central Scientific Research and Design Institute for City Construction to prepare a new city-wide development plan based on alternative projections about future demographic change. In discussions with city council – a first – the idea that Yaroslavl might have to face a future population decline was rejected, however. Even as this planning effort was going on, the regional (*oblast*) administration appointed by President Yeltsin launched its own planning scheme, bypassing city authorities. The consulting firm brought in by the region was a private venture, located in Moscow and headed by a former Russian prime minister who had good political connections with central ministries. Their proposal was for a new international airport on the city's outskirts. Although nothing seems to have come of this "plan," it illustrates how, in the transition period, the "Soviet-era tradition of establishing large-scale economic goals continued, leaving the details of consequent physical and social patterns for architects and city planners to worry about later on" (Ruble 1995: 120). It also reveals something about the politics of local development where city and region might go in opposite directions (with or without mutual consultation).

At least during the early period of the "transition," much time was spent in developing the new structure of local institutions through which planning might become effective. "The absence of zoning regulations," writes Ruble, "posed an immediate concern to city officials … [C]ity officials did not know how to proceed with regulating privately owned property. New owners, for their part, firmly believed that title would transfer total authority over a particular building or site. Bitter fights erupted …" (Ruble 1995: 122). But even as the city struggled to establish a new planning order, it had to confront entirely unforeseen problems, ranging from the threatened bankruptcy of older Soviet enterprises like Avtodizel', the arrival of refugees from Russia's war-torn zone in Chechnya, mounting unemployment, serious soil pollution with heavy metals,[13] a change in the political regime with the ascent of President Putin, growing social inequalities, inter-ethnic tensions, and large-scale corruption. Planning may have been opened up to public debate. But the city of Yaroslavl, with its woefully inadequate financial means, inexperienced in self-development under a capitalist system of "primitive accumulation," and beset by a new politics of money – Ruble's account of Yaroslavl's travails is tellingly entitled *Money Sings* – faces an uncertain future where the ingenuity of its leaders to improvise solutions is probably more important than the future-gazing of planning experts based in Moscow.

Planning in Africa (Johannesburg)

When discussing urban planning in a continent with the dimensions of Africa, any general statement is likely to be contradicted by specific non-conforming instances.[14] Estimated levels of urbanization, for example, range from below 10 per cent in Burundi, to 66 per cent for the Republic of South Africa and tiny Djibouti on the Red Sea – a virtual city-state – with 84 per cent. Nevertheless, the rates of urban growth are uniformly high for nearly all countries, averaging 5.3 per cent for sub-Saharan countries during the decade of the 1990s and running even higher for some of the least developed countries (Rakodi 1997: Table 3.4). According to Abdu Maliq Simone, this massive movement of people to the city has been compelled by the "long-term inability of many rural environments to provide for even subsistence needs" (2004: 120). Despite the lack of formal work, the city offers at least an environment where opportunities for livelihood can be pursued. The result is an accumulation of rural poverty in the principal cities of the continent and an implosion of an informal economy that is geared to physical survival.[15] None of the major cities in Africa are, in fact, financially capable of adequately servicing their population. Kadmie H. Wekweto asserts that "the per capita levels of investment in infrastructure have declined to zero for most major cities" (Wekweto 1997: 534). No governmental level at present has the resources or, for that matter, the institutional capacity to meet even the most minimal common needs of most African cities (let alone the needs of the rural population), relying upon the donations of foreign donors which, for the most part, disperse contributions through national and foreign NGOs.[16] But these donations are equally inadequate to cope with a pattern of urban growth that leads to a doubling of population every 15 years.[17]

Insufficient resources are only part of the problem, however. To the extent that we can speak of planning in African cities at all, it addresses principally the districts inhabited by urban elites. The poor majority who live in informal urban settlements and squatter areas – settlements that the state often defines as illegal and that are certainly not up to code – remain outside the official purview of planners.[18] In his study of Egyptian cities, Soliman and his colleagues found that at the beginning of the new millennium, 62 per cent of Greater Cairo's population (or more than seven million) and 72 per cent of Alexandria's (about 2.5 million) lived in semi-informal and squatter areas (Soliman 2004: 201). Here is how Bayat describes the situation:

> ... in Cairo, millions of rural migrants, the urban poor, and even the middle-class poor have now quietly claimed cemeteries, rooftops, and state/public land on the outskirts of the city, creating more than one hundred spontaneous communities which house more than five million people. Once settled, such encroachments spread in many directions. Against formal terms and conditions, residents may add rooms, balconies, and extra space in and on buildings. And even those who have formally been given housing in public projects built by the state, illegally redesign and rearrange their space to suit their needs by erecting partitions and by adding and inventing new space. Often whole communities emerge as a result of intense struggles and negotiations between the poor and the authorities and elites in their daily lives. (Bayat 2004: 91)

As Bayat describes them, these millions of informally housed Egyptians, "operate largely outside institutional mechanisms through which they might express grievances and/or enforce demands. They also lack an organizational power of disruption – the possibility of going on strike, for example" (Bayat 2004: 93). They simply "encroach" on public and private space on an individual basis, household by household. Bayat calls this process the "quiet encroachment of the ordinary."

Returning now to planning for the monied classes, despite the fact that general plans exist for most major cities on the African continent, they are seriously in default of implementation. In his study of Nairobi, for example, R.A. Obduho observes:

> [T]he process of land allocation is fraught with corruption and disregard for regulations and planning standards. Both the general public and private agencies ignore the regulations and this has led to irregular developments. Developers, for instance, have put up high-rise blocks and extensions in areas where such developments are prohibited by law. Slums and squatter settlements have also developed, and subdivision is occurring outside the boundary. The NCC [Nairobi City Council] is endowed with extensive development control powers but these have not been effectively enforced. (Obduho 1997: 308)

An "action plan" adopted in 1993 was meant to address critical city issues; it also highlighted the need to restore and reinforce professionalism and ethics in City Hall. But according to Wekweto, "there has been no follow up in terms of implementation" (Wekweto 1997: 549). Salah El-Shaks extends this observation to other African cities:

> [P]lans are developed with little or no local input or consultation. Further, even if these models were in themselves adequate as planning exercises, their implementation is generally beyond the resources and delivery capacity of the existing planning structures. Governments' ability to enforce rules and regulations is generally very weak in Africa, particularly when they relate to unrealistic standards or activities that go against the grain of market forces. Plans are often not respected even by those government bureaucrats and politicians who approved them in the first place. In addition, projects are frequently abandoned before they are given a chance to mature. Much of the problem lies in the undemocratic nature of the state itself. This leads to favouritism, nepotism, biased allocation of resources, distorted priorities, and stifling of local initiative and innovation. (El-Shaks 1997: 505–6)

Given this dismal assessment, one is perhaps surprised to learn that advanced planning degrees continue to be conferred in a number of leading universities in Dakar, Nairobi, Ibadan, Cairo, Dar-es-Salaam, Johannesburg, Durban, Cape Town, and elsewhere. Whether the new generation of graduate planners will be able to turn things around in urban Africa remains to be seen.[19] As for now, the central state in most African countries is so debilitated, that urban planning has little opportunity to flourish. The anthropologist Abdu Maliq Simone goes so far as to suggest a failed modernity in much of Africa.[20] Ex: South Africa

A rather different story is the new planning regime in the Republic of South Africa. The Town and Regional Planners Act in 1984 gave statutory recognition to the profession. But over the years, the country's planning apparatus was deeply compromised by its complicity with the apartheid system as planning rationales were advanced to create urban apartheid. Despite this, a small but energetic dissident movement of planners forged alliances with civic movements in South Africa's turbulent townships. Calling themselves Planact, the movement was primarily active in the Johannesburg region. Similar dissident movements may have existed in other major cities.

As the profession tries to reinvent itself in the post-apartheid era since 1994, South Africa's planning culture has become more strategic, participatory, and integrated. Tanja Winkler, a South African planner, explains:

> The clearest manifestation of this culture has been in the adoption of statutory Integrated Development Plans (IDP) – the centerpiece of planning in post-apartheid South Africa – by every local authority in the country to provide strategic guidance to newly constructed municipalities. IDPs were introduced by legislation in 1996, and are currently being implemented through the White Paper on Local Government (1998) and the Municipal Systems Act of 2000 as amended in 2003. New municipal boundaries were delineated between 1998 and 2000, and in December 2000, local government elections were held.
>
> IDPs share a striking similarity with international planning practices, including the reintroduction of regional planning policies by the new Labour government in the United Kingdom (1997); New Zealand's integrated planning performance monitoring; Switzerland's integrated regional policy; integrated area planning in the European Union; and the multi-sectoral investment planning promoted by the United Nations Development Programme. But as one observer has noted, "progressive concerns over transformation and the role of the state in securing more equitable living environments are being meshed with neoliberal concerns associated with efficiency and competitive cities."

In June 2002, the IDP for the newly constituted metropolitan City of Johannesburg was launched simultaneously with *Jo'burg 2030 Vision*. Its overarching vision promotes a "World Class City with service deliverables and efficiencies that meet world best practice standards. Its economy and labour force will specialise in the service sector and will be strongly outward oriented such that the City economy operates on a global scale. The strong economic growth resultant from this competitive economic behaviour will drive up City tax revenues, private sector profits and individual disposable income levels such that the standard of living and quality of life of all the City's inhabitants will increase in a sustainable manner."

To achieve this vision, the document clearly states a need to address two main current investment obstacles: "crime and the lack of appropriate labour skills … [as] 61 per cent of decisions to invest in Johannesburg are influenced by perceptions of crime, and one in five jobs in potential investment companies cannot be filled [despite] the City's 30 per cent unemployment rate … In the process of implementing *Jo'burg 2030*, Council itself will shift from being merely an administrator and service provider to being an active agent of economic development and growth."

Disappointingly, this IDP embraces a neoliberal "trickle-down" agenda to address poverty alleviation via "increased private sector profits." The Inner City Community Forum, a civil society-based advocacy group, is scathing in its criticism of the Jo'burg "vision," noting that "there has not been a proper and informed process where ordinary people agreed to such a strategy."[21]

The government's desire to turn Johannesburg into a "world class city" leaves little scope for creating a city that also serves the needs of the ordinary people of South Africa (and the many migrants from elsewhere in Africa who have come to the City of Gold seeking their fortune). Those few who can afford it escape into the wealthy suburbs with their gated communities and shopping malls, leaving downtown Johannesburg to the burgeoning street economy geared to survival. The apartheid city thus continues, albeit without official sanction and in new spatial configurations, and so long as the economy fails to generate enough jobs for those who seek work, which may well be never, spatial separation by class and race will continue.

Planning in the European Union

Meeting in Potsdam (Germany) in May 1999, the Informal Council of Ministers responsible for Spatial Planning adopted a document that had been years in the making: the *European Spatial Development Perspective* (ESDP).[22] Subtitled *Towards a Balanced and Sustainable Development of the Territory of the European Union*, it looked towards the near future when the present territory of the Union comprising 15 member states would be expanded by the accession of 12 new states from eastern, central, and southern Europe. It was a bold attempt to forge a new geography for this enlarged political structure embodying a set of common planning principles and norms.

Spatial planning was the Euro-English equivalent of the French *aménagement du territoire* and the American regional planning. As the Commission of the European Communities (CEC) explains it:

> Spatial planning refers to the methods used largely by the public sector to influence the future distribution of activities in space. It is undertaken with the aims of creating a more rational territorial organization of land uses and the linkages between them, to balance demands for development with the need to protect the environment, and to achieve social and economic objectives. Spatial planning embraces measures to coordinate the spatial impacts of other sector policies, to achieve a more even distribution of economic development between regions than would otherwise be created through market forces, and to regulate the conversion of land and property uses. (Faludi and Waterhout 2002: x)

The *Perspective* proposes what would amount to a superordinate policy framework for Europe. As such, it is to be applied flexibly across the many regions of the continent. Although the competence for making spatial policy and planning decisions rests with the several states of the Union, in making these policies and plans, the ESDP framework should be taken into account. Three major policy guidelines are proposed:

- Development of a polycentric and balanced urban system and strengthening of the partnership between urban and rural areas. This involves overcoming the traditional dualism between city and countryside.
- Promotion of integrated transport and communication concepts, which support the polycentric development of the EU territory and are an important pre-condition for enabling European cities and regions to pursue their integration into EMU [European Monetary Union]. Parity of access to infrastructure and knowledge should be realized gradually. Regionally adapted solutions must be found for this.
- Development and conservation of the natural and cultural heritage through wise management. This contributes both to the preservation and deepening of identities and the maintenance of the natural and cultural diversity of the regions and cities of the EU in the age of globalization (Commission of The European Communities 1999: 19–20).

The *Perspective* broadens considerably the focus of physical planning as traditionally understood in continental Europe as a form of urban design. It advocates multi-sectoral spatial guidelines and forcefully pleads for a multiscalar planning approach. Importantly, it argues for a "partnership" between urban and rural areas, although the key role for this is assigned to cities as dynamic centers of economic growth. Its key terms are *balance, integration, sustainability, cooperation,* and *partnerships*. Networks, as in inter-city networks, are proposed as a means for implementing cooperative arrangements.[23] The authors worry a good deal about their lack of competence to impose this policy framework, invoking a frequently used European *principle of subsidiarity* that the power to make binding decisions should be devolved to the lowest possible level capable of contributing to the achievement of overall EU policy objectives. They worry, too, that their Europe-wide vision will be seen as threatening cultural diversity (the identity question alluded to in the third policy guideline) and thus resisted.

EU member countries have committed themselves to begin applying the spatial development framework. The text of the Potsdam document has been translated into the official languages of all member countries and is widely disseminated. The hope is that the European Commission will use the ESDP as a guide in the allocation of the so-called structural funds, which amount to hundreds of billions of euros each year. It is also hoped that geography manuals will be prepared for use in secondary schools throughout Europe. And the spatial impacts of Community policies will be monitored. Overall, the *Perspective* is beginning to filter down into academic discourse and in the future will undoubtedly be discussed with growing frequency in spatial planning circles both inside and outside the academy.[24]

Netherlands: the case of mega-projects in Rotterdam

Having reclaimed much of their country from the sea, the Dutch, it is said, have a "soft spot" in their heart for planning (Faludi and Van der Valk 1994). Rather than delve into the institutional setting of city and regional planning, however, the following brief account will focus on a dimension of planning in the Netherlands that has become increasingly popular over the past two decades: the management of so-called mega-projects.[25] In addition to incremental zoning and the persisting attempts to chart the future of cities through a general plan that covers the entire territory of a municipality or region and embodies the restraining hand of government, mega-projects are undertaken in an entrepreneurial spirit to break through the routines of the everyday to build spectacular urban spaces that will, it is hoped, enhance a city's competitiveness in global capital markets. Because mega-projects often exceed the fiscal capacity of municipalities, the local state is obliged to seek partners in the corporate sector and the central government. As a rule, a newly formed public-private partnership (PPP) of this sort will by-pass routine planning procedures, creating their own organizational framework with varying degrees of autonomy and, it might be added, transparency as well as accountability. Frequently, it will also bring on board world-class architects who are expected to give memorable visual form to the undertaking. Beyond the Netherlands, well-known mega-projects of recent memory include East Shanghai (Olds 2001), the Potsdamer Platz in Berlin (Lehrer 2004), and a series of infrastructure projects with Frank Gehry's Guggenheim Museum at its center, designed to reinvent Bilbao, the de-industrialized economic capital of the Basque Country in Spain (Siemiatycki 2003).

The Rotterdam Central Station project is one of these.[26] In the mid-1990s, it was identified as one of the six "strategic" projects that would give a heightened international profile to this major port city. It was envisioned that a large area surrounding the central railway station would be given over to commercial developments particularly in the service and leisure sectors that would revitalize the city center. The station itself would be converted into an inter-modal transport node. To get this project underway, a partnership was formed among the City of Rotterdam, the Dutch rail company (NS), and two private property developers who had a long-term relationship with both the site and the city. The British urban design firm, Alsop Architects, was selected to redesign the entire area. The projected redevelopment period would extend for up to 18 years with three goals in mind: (1) the improvement and enlargement of the railway station, (2) an improvement of the interface between the station and the rest of the city, and (3) a property development program covering an area of 650,000m^2. A plan was discussed to set up a joint Land Development Corporation that would amalgamate all of the plans, buildings, and rights in a common enterprise, but this idea was eventually abandoned. Instead, the original project was divided into two sub-projects, each with its own organization: the railway terminal and transport node (with the railway company NS in the driver's seat) and a profit-oriented real estate venture guided by Council.

After 4 years of work, a Master Plan was published in April 2001. And then the sky fell in. In March of the following year, a new political party, calling itself *Leefbar Rotterdam* (Livable Rotterdam) and led by the charismatic Pim Fortuyn (who was tragically murdered two months later), received 30 per cent of the vote in municipal elections and fundamentally changed the coalition of forces that had supported the project. Together with two smaller political parties, Livable Rotterdam had succeeded in dethroning the social democrats who had governed the city since the end of World War II. A new set of values and ideals was coming to the fore. The Rotterdam Central Station project had been part of a strategy that was to turn Rotterdam into a "world city." The basic idea was to market the city to global capital, based on the argument that competitive economic growth was essential if the social needs of the city were to be met. But in 2002, the newly formed city council could not be convinced of this logic. A document published in September of that year shows a change in the privileged position of strategic projects, and so also in the position of city marketing in the political domain. With more than half of the new budget devoted to it, the new emphasis was to be on safety in the streets. The exuberant "champagne glass" design of Alsop Architects had to be scrapped. The old railway station was declared a heritage building, and a "home-grown" architect would be enlisted for the project, replacing the "foreign" Alsop. Also, the budget for the project was downsized from 875 to 410 million euros. Kooijman and Wigmans comment on these shifts in priority:

> [A]n externally based approach to the economic rejuvenation potential of the city has made way for a local, internal approach to the palpable day-to-day problems within the city limits of Rotterdam. The bond between the existing population and their city is central in this. The policy is geared towards the local needs and requirements of the people of Rotterdam that are immediately obvious … such as safety, drug problems, dissatisfaction with the multicultural society, the lack of naturalization [on the part of immigrant workers] and so on. (Kooijman and Wigmans, 2003: 321)

In this dramatic turn-around, globalization did not eliminate the local; it strengthened it. The new Council majority represented the interests of small businesspeople and petty bourgeois in the city who were feeling disoriented, their livelihood threatened by the seemingly irreversible forces of globalization. It was this majority that the formerly hegemonic social democrats, in their eagerness to put Rotterdam on the global map, had failed to perceive.[27]

Planning in the United Kingdom

In 1997, the British Labour Party ended 18 years of Conservative rule.[28] Under the leadership of Tony Blair, it set out a program, the Third Way, that promised to recover a tradition of social solidarity – a sense of community – that had been lost under the preceding regime. Highlights of the program included the devolution of certain governmental powers to Scotland, Wales, and Northern Ireland; a democratically elected government for the 33 boroughs of Greater London; a new approach to regional planning in England; social inclusion and citizen participation; the incorporation of sustainability agendas into local/regional planning; and a new focus on developing so-called brownfield sites for the rustbelt cities of the Midlands and other parts of the British Isles that had lost much of their traditional manufacturing base.

Most significant in this agenda, especially during the first term of the Labour regime, was the differential devolution of governmental powers. In Northern

Ireland, beset by decades of often violent conflict, a regional strategic framework was to set a long-term agenda for action that had been drafted in close consultation with key stakeholders and communities across the province. The hope was that this strategy would allow a broad societal consensus to emerge around development issues while political divisions would gradually fade away. In Wales, a renewed effort was made to "jump-start" the regional economy that for too long had relied on resource extraction. The economic spatial development agenda, drawn up in consultation with regional "stakeholders," was intended to provide a context for the work of the newly elected Welsh Assembly. Of the three principal regions affected by devolution, and with the election of a Parliament and the formation of a Scottish Executive, Scotland had made the most use of its newly won autonomy. Spatial strategies in Scotland would no longer be imposed from above but would emerge from a process of decentralized planning in which local authorities would play the major role.[29] Even so, in 2004 a national spatial plan for Scotland was produced as a "guideline" for local authorities whose spatial strategies would then emerge from a process of negotiation with the national government.

Until the devolution reforms of the late 1990s, the UK (which, like Japan, is a unitary state) possessed a strong bi-polar system, with a weak local level and a strong central tier. The national government had the power to change territorial boundaries and install or remove organizations engaged with regional matters. Above all, it retained the purse strings. As Herrschel and Newman observe, "the institutionalized government system is … strongly biased in favour of top-down, centralized regional governance, leaving much less scope for locally defined policy making."[30] Devolution seems to have worked particularly well in the case of Scotland, where a serious attempt is being made to empower local communities. In England, on the other hand, it was the central government that continues to define new development regions and set up centrally scripted and financed Regional Development Agencies (RDAs). According to the Ministry of the Environment (DETR), RDAs were supposed to "build up the voice of the region" (Herrschel and Newman 2002: 123). Nevertheless,

> …there continues to a strong centralist undertone: the RDAs based on the 12 regions have centrally determined constitutions and budgets. Their executive boards are appointed by government primarily from the business sector to underline the focus on economic development, but include civic leaders and university and trade union representation as a reference to democratic (regional) legitimacy. The primary role of the RDAs is to promote competitiveness, innovation and investment, and develop comprehensive regional development strategies. But [they have] only limited control of resources, and thus … rather limited *actual* power. (ibid.)

To give local legitimacy to RDAs, another innovation has been the establishment of Regional Chambers made up of local authorities and business leaders. How well this new institutional structure will work remains to be seen. With the 2001 general election, enthusiasm for further regional devolution (the creation of Regional Assemblies, for example) seems to have waned, and there appears to be a swing back to greater centralization. Draft economic strategies now have to be vetted by central government. RDA-specific functions (and a large slice of their budgets) include administering the government's urban renewal programs. And instead of hoped-for inter-regional cooperation, competitive regional marketing has become a feature of the RDAs. Because of this, as well as difficulties in program coordination, the regional oversight function of the Department of the Environment, Transport and the Regions has actually been shifted still further up the bureaucratic ladder to Cabinet level (Herrschel and Newman 2002: 124).[31] It is not clear, however, that this will lead to greater overall coherence in the implementation of regional programs. As Herrschel and Newman observe, "the central government has a deep-seated distrust of sub-national governments' ability to handle their own affairs effectively," though "distrust" in this context may be no more than a rhetorical cover for what is more likely an unending tug-of-war in the relations of power between center, regions, and local authorities (Herrschel and Newman 2002: 145). Coordination and cooperation are not the same thing, however. The center worries chiefly about "coordination," or its own ability to properly manage governmental actions on the ground. Cooperation, on the other hand, is a voluntary activity, less oriented to vertical than to horizontal relations in pursuit of common objectives. Too great insistence on coordination is likely not only to be resisted but to impede voluntary coordination of regional strategies. This dilemma has not yet been resolved in England.[32] power struggles b/wn levels of governance

Planning in the United States

In a formal, legalistic sense, city planning in the United States is a local responsibility, which makes for a good deal of diversity across the country.[33] There is another way of looking at planning, however, which expands the meaning of "planning" to include all those collective actors who contribute to shaping the city. We may call them the city-builders. In addition to the local state and its particular institutions, they would include developers and other business interests, organized civil society, and the judicial system. How these several actors intersect in given circumstances is the story of planning in America. Since the rise of neo-liberalist ideology, with its insistence that less government intervention is better than more, planning in this expanded sense has been market-led, with planning by local government playing primarily a facilitating or acquiescent role. City planning, with its traditional emphasis on land use controls and its restraining hand on market forces now has become more entrepreneurial, as the fever of inter-city competition has spread across the land.

Over the past 20 or so years, during which many American cities re-built their core, attention was focused on large-scale building ensembles. Downtown malls, often combining offices, apartments, hotels, entertainment and other activities with retailing, and thus creating a virtual "downtown" under one roof – a city-for-profit – were only part of the story. Major convention centers, huge stadiums for professional team sports (football, baseball), the so-called festival market place built as part of major waterfront regeneration projects, aquariums designed to attract millions of tourists … all preferably located in close proximity to each other and a sheltered tract of water, became a distinctively American contribution to urban regeneration planning (Ward 2002: 346). Needless to say, these projects were planned and built by private enterprise with only marginal contributions from city planning departments.[34] The same might be said about the so-called Edge City phenomenon in suburban areas, the new "downtowns" built out-of-town. "Apart from fairly permissive zoning regimes," writes Stephen Ward, "planning (and especially strategic planning) nowhere played much part in the growth of these places" (Ward 2002: 347).[35]

But could Edge Cities become real places, comparable to traditional downtowns? A response came from a group of private architect-planners who proposed sub-division developments, or even entirely new towns, whose perceived virtues lay in their clear definition of space and compactness, in contrast with the relatively low densities and open layouts of American suburbia. Places built according to this "new urbanism," such as Seaside, Florida, created a sensation. The new urbanism movement spawned a formal organization, which called itself Congress for the New Urbanism, to propagate the idea. Some extrapolated its philosophy into a model for sustainable metropolitan development, linking the classic garden city density of 12 houses per acre to the development of public transit (Calthorp 1993). At Redmond in suburban Seattle, for example, the approach was used to convey the feel of a traditional downtown, with open public spaces that avoided the typical enclosed mall (Ward 2002: 348–9).

On the rising tide of concern over the "sustainability" of American cities, a concern that was largely a product of the environmental movement, a new term came into wide circulation: smart growth. In 1999, writes Stephen Ward, "the Federal Environmental Protection Agency sponsored the creation of the Smart Growth Network. An umbrella organization, this brought together a wide range of existing organizations, including the Congress for the New

Urbanism, the Growth Management Leadership Alliance and many other professional and pressure groups in the field of conservation and environmental protection" (Ward 2002: 350). The federal government had taken these ideas on board, but their origin was entirely within civil society and was linked to the profit motive: new urbanism and smart growth were workable concepts because developers and the architect planners who worked for them could make good money out of them. Official city planners could do little more than to accommodate them and many have leaped on the bandwagon, embracing the concept as the new Holy Grail of the city planning profession.

A rather different story from the 1990s comes out of Los Angeles and concerns the interests of poor minority sectors of the city's polyglot population. It is a rare success story of how civil society organized to fight for more equitable treatment in public transit development. And it illustrates with particular clarity how, in America, many planning issues are finally settled in the courts (Grengs 2002). Here, the story can only be told in highly compressed form.

The quintessential automobile city, Los Angeles was becoming ever more congested and steeped in smog, its famous freeways clogged with bumper-to-bumper traffic for most of the day. Public transport was provided through an efficient region-wide bus system that served primarily low-income people, many of them recent immigrants, who used buses to get to and from work. But transit enthusiasts kept the dream of a rail-based system alive. Defeated but unbowed in a series of public consultations about funding such a system, proponents of rail transit persisted in their efforts and, in the 1980 local election, were finally successful in persuading voters to tax themselves and underwrite public borrowing. Soon after, and despite continuing opposition, construction was begun. As Grengs describes it,

> The choice of rail as a solution to the transport mess was highly controversial. Critics from across the political spectrum insisted that rail was far too expensive and inappropriate for Los Angeles' geography of dispersed economic activity. They warned that rail would not attract enough riders, that it would do little for congestion and air pollution, and that it would siphon away subsidies from the more cost-effective bus system. (Grengs 2002: 167)

The Los Angeles County Metropolitan Transportation Authority (MTA), created in 1992 by an act of the State legislature by merging the agency that operated the bus system with another that controlled the transit funding, was plagued with controversy from the start. There were costly (and embarrassing) construction blunders, allegations of corruption, fraud, and cases of rigged bidding, property owners had filed a $3 billion law suit, and the agency found itself mired in debt. And then there was the Labor Community Strategy

Center (LCSC) which had emerged at the forefront of several community-based organizations to begin scrutinizing the distressed rail program. The LCSC's goal was to be a "multiracial 'think-tank/act-tank' to help build democratic, internationalist Left social movements at the intersection of ecology, civil rights, workers' and immigrants' rights and a direct challenge ... to transnational corporations."[36]

An opportunity for action arose in early 1994, when, as Grengs describes it, the high cost of the rail program forced the MTA to look for new revenues. A convenient source, they thought, was the pockets of bus passengers. Bus fares would rise from $1.10 to $1.35, monthly passes used by many poor bus riders would be eliminated, and service on several bus lines would be curtailed. The bus riders, quite naturally, protested, but the MTA board approved the proposal. Then, just seven days later, it voted to spend an additional $123 million on the next phase of the rail program. This decision broke the camel's back.

But how to build a mass-based opposition to what were perceived to be grossly discriminatory actions on the part of the MTA when there was no territorial community for which LCSC wanted to speak? The functional community of bus riders was their only chance, and recruiters soon started to board buses and pass out leaflets, explaining the purpose of what was to become the Bus Riders Union (BRU). With 1,500 dues-paying members, mostly low-income bus riders, BRU would organize opposition to the MTA. "To stop the fare hike," writes Grengs, "the BRU ... assembled a coalition to file a class action lawsuit against the MTA on behalf of 350,000 bus riders with the help of the NAACP (National Association of Colored Peoples) Legal Defense Fund."[37]

This was in 1994. Two years later, the case was settled by a consent decree. It was not a complete victory, but it included commitments to increase the bus fleet and established a joint Working Group of MTA representatives and bus riders to ensure implementation. The rail program was not stopped, however, and the MTA has still not fully complied with the decree, prompting intervention by the courts and protests by the BRU that continue to this day. On the other hand, newspapers and politicians today recognize the BRU as a legitimate representative of transit-dependent bus riders, and advocacy groups in other cities have invited the BRU to help with similar movements (Grengs 2002: 170).

With a weak state, planning in the US is largely driven by private interests. The Irvine Corporation, the Disney Corporation, and lesser corporate entities engaged in giving shape to America's cities are often more powerful than any local state in the areas in which they operate. The "new urbanism" was branded and marketed by architects; the very concept of Edge City was copyrighted by its inventor, Joel Garreau, a journalist; sprawling suburban malls are a law unto themselves. It is therefore not surprising that dis/empowered citizens, such as the bus riders of Los Angeles, resort to civic action and the courts in seeking redress of their grievances. The judicial system in the United States has probably more influence on planning outcomes than the official planning process centered in City Hall.

The Vancouver Story, British Columbia

Like the United States, Canada is a federal state, and urban policies are a prerogative of the provincial governments.[38] In the following account of Canada's planning cultures, I will focus on Vancouver which, with a population of 583 000, serves as the economic capital of British Columbia, the country's western-most province. It is also the center of a metropolitan region nearly four times its size which has its own unique form of regional government. In 1953, the Province adopted the so-called Vancouver Charter which granted the municipality of Vancouver substantial autonomy over its own affairs.

Municipal political parties are somewhat improvised affairs in Canada, and are generally independent of major political blocks that function as electoral machines at the federal level. In 1972, a reform party, The Electors Action Movement (TEAM) ousted the business-friendly Non-Partisan Association (NPA) that heretofore had dominated city politics. As reported by Leonie Sandercock, "TEAM had a more sensitive approach to development, a more inclusive vision for the future of the city, and [was committed to] a more participatory planning process" (Sandercock 2005: 37). A Toronto-based planner, Ray Spaxman, was hired as the new director of planning, and thus began a new era of urban development which over the next three decades completely transformed the city from a small provincial city at the far end of the transcontinental railway into a global metropolis where more than 50 per cent speak a language other than English.[39]

A major planning achievement during this period was the redevelopment of Vancouver's downtown district which not only turned the city towards the water that flowed around its edges but also brought about a dramatic change in the form of its built environment. Within the past 10 years, nearly 40,000 people have moved into more than 150 high-rise towers that sprouted within a one-mile radius of the central business district, raising its total population to 80,000. This new forest of glass and steel is also a city of neighborhoods, of green spaces, of mixed use, of schools, shops, and community centers, and of 20 km of continuous seawall for public recreational use encircling the downtown peninsula. Arguably, it is the highest quality urban public realm in North America.

How this transformation of Vancouver's central district came about reveals *which public?* a planning culture that is based on a consensual process initiated and led by the local state that involved, in addition to the City Council itself, city planners, architects, developers, and the general public. The current co-director of planning responsible for the central city, Larry Beasley, characterized this process in a simple but telling phrase: "What we finally determine to do is the result of thousands of conversations" (Sandercock 2005: 36).

One of the first steps undertaken by the newly elected TEAM Council under Mayor Art Phillips, a millionaire businessman, was the establishment of a three-person Development Permit Board, chaired by the Director of Planning ex officio. (Today, the chair is no longer the Director of Planning. But the Co-Director of Planning in charge of downtown development continues to serve as a voting member.) The Board was to meet in public and keep minutes of its proceedings, thus giving transparency to its decisions. To work with the Board, the Council also approved an Urban Design Advisory Panel, made up of two representatives each from the development industry, the design professions, and the general public. Thus was brought into being a design-sensitive permit system that has prompted one commentator to acclaim Vancouver as "distinguished by its sustained commitment to deploy civic powers and resources to reshape its urban space, form, and development trajectory" (Hutton 2004: 485).

A milestone in the city's effort to re-imagine itself was Expo 86, a major "world's fair" that was sited on a swathe of abandoned industrial land and railway yards on the south shore of the downtown peninsula. The Province had acquired the land in the late seventies from Canadian Pacific Railway and, shortly after Expo, decided to sell it. An international sale of this 76 ha site was organized, based on a financial bid and a specific design concept. Eager to extend his property portfolio to North America, Hong Kong's wealthiest developer, Li Ka-Shing, had long before sent his son Victor to Vancouver to acquire citizenship and establish himself as a residential developer. This was the beginning of Vancouver's "Asia connection," that would ultimately lead to a stream of Chinese immigrants from Hong Kong and the mainland, some of whom would come to reside in the residential towers of the new "Hong Kong on False Creek." As Sandercock observes, "unlike most waterfront mega-projects elsewhere, from London to Sydney, no special legislation was created to override local planning provisions and processes to give developers what they wanted. On the contrary, the long gestation process of the official development plan of False Creek North produced design principles that have shaped all subsequent residential mega-projects in Vancouver and that give the new vertical city its distinctive design, attractiveness of public realm, and attentiveness to social planning issues" (Sandercock 2005: 39). Among the social provisions was the planners' insistence that the new housing would have to set aside 25 per cent of all units for families and 20 per cent for social (affordable) housing. In addition, neighborhood facilities would have to be provided within each tower complex, such as community centers, primary schools, leisure facilities, and neighborhood shops and offices, as well as a seawall with a 35 ft wide promenade that would link a system of public parks along the entire extent of the project. These and other provisions would be paid for by the developer.[40]

All this was made possible by a collaborative planning process that is unique to Vancouver. Leonie Sandercock writes:

> The emphasis is on collaboration by teams comprised of developer and city staff to prepare master plans and convert them into official development plans, rezoning plans, and design guidelines rather than on planners preparing concept plans on their own. The developer pays for the creation of a dedicated planning team to work full-time on project preparation, while the city works corporately, linking the planning function with other departments (Engineering, Social Planning, Parks) as necessary. Over almost three decades, the evolution of this approach has socialized a new generation of talented designers into a civic-oriented design culture exceptional in North America, producing not only some excellent architecture and urban design ... but also an outstanding urban public realm, defined in particular by the public spaces of the seawall itself, the parks strung along and connected by the seawall, and the public art in this area. (op. cit.: 42)

It is important to note that the evolution of this planning culture was grounded in an extraordinary public consultation process. Between 1988 and 1993, over 200 public meetings on the False Creek North (or Concord Pacific) project were held, with 25,000 citizens in attendance.

Sandercock concludes her story of the remaking of downtown Vancouver with the following comment:

> ... as a planning model, Vancouver's shift to discretionary zoning for the Central Area proved crucial in allowing a flexible approach to development proposals. But this discretionary approach is only as good as the technical competence of planning staff and, even more important, of the values shaping the overall planning environment. Here is perhaps the heart of the Vancouver story: over three decades of public debate and slow gestation processes for official development plans, during which intensive design negotiations were undertaken, a unique local planning and design culture has evolved in which not only public sector planners but also designers working for private firms have been socialized into a vision for Vancouver livability and civility, safety

what about equity and inclusion?

and vitality, and have worked collectively to generate the design and planning tools to create such a city. (Sandercock 2005: 43)

A comparison with the adversarial planning culture in the United States is inevitable. Canadian culture generally can perhaps be characterized by a greater reliance on the state to defend the public interest and to resolve ensuing conflicts with a consensus-building approach involving lengthy negotiations among the contending parties – Larry Beasley's "thousands of conversations." It is also more seriously concerned with social issues of urban development and with listening to a multiplicity of voices. Organized civil society is perhaps no stronger in Canada than in the United States, but it is politically more active, in part because it is encouraged to occupy political space at the municipal level. This has shifted Canadian politics, and especially urban politics, to the "left" of the economically dominated planning that rules south of the border.

Planning cultures: a preliminary assessment

The foregoing thumbnail sketches of selected global planning cultures reveal an enormous variety of institutional and political settings. As a way of classifying planning cultures, the following distinctions may be a bit crude, but *political sys.* these institutional settings do exert a substantial influence over both the substance of what planners do and how they do it. As a start, planning takes place in *unitary* states (such as Japan, China, and the UK), in *federal* states (India, Russia, USA, Canada), and in states (some unitary, some federal) that belong to the European Union, a *multi-national* entity that has no direct counterpart anywhere else. Superimposed on these constitutional structures, *econ sys.* some countries (Russia, China) are *in transition* from a command to a market economy and are still grappling with the institutional foundations that enable a market economy to function effectively, while other countries, such as the United States, Canada, and the countries of the European Union are already *fully developed market societies.*

The achieved *level of economic development* is another criterion for *economic development* differentiating societies in ways that influence planning cultures, ranging from impoverished African nations to lower income countries such as India and China, to the high-income, post-industrial societies of which the USA is a prime example. In general, poorer countries are still *urbanizing rapidly* under the influence of rural-urban migration as well as natural increase, while other *degree of urbanizati* countries, such as the Netherlands and the UK which have *mature urban systems* are left with only residual rural areas that are themselves undergoing low-intensity urbanization and have a dwindling agricultural population.

Much of their urban growth is therefore the result of domestic inter-urban migration and immigration from abroad. In the case of mature systems, managing urban growth is less of an issue than it is in rapidly urbanizing societies whose urban systems are still evolving. In both cases, however, social problems must be addressed, as cities fill up with people from different cultural backgrounds, and income inequalities become more pronounced.

political culture

Finally, there are marked differences in *political culture*, a broad term that includes the extent to which organized civil society is an active participant in public decisions particularly at the local level, the degree to which the political process is dominated by a single party or subject to political competition, the degree of "openness" in the political process and the role of the media, the application of principles such as hierarchy and subsidiarity, legal traditions, the relative autonomy of local governments, and so forth.

always changing

institutions

Within this congeries of differences, however, there is at least one constant: all existing planning systems (and cultures) are *in movement* in the sense that they are continually being revamped to adapt to perceived changes both internal and external in origin. Notable are efforts at creating new institutions. The leading example, perhaps, is the Republic of South Africa. Consider the following: Integrated Development Plans were introduced by legislation in 1996 and are currently being implemented through the White Paper on Local Government (1998) and the Municipal Systems Act of 2000 as amended in 2003. Between 1998 and 2000, new municipal boundaries were delineated, and in December 2000, the first local government elections were held. In other words, the entire local government system, including planning, has been restructured over a period of only 4 years, and the process is still far from concluded! South Africa is reinventing itself and the country's planning culture will require a long period of adjustment to the post-apartheid society that is coming into being. Other countries are experiencing similar, if not quite so intensive pressures to restructure the institutional setting for planning, including China, Russia, and Japan.

Less dramatic but still important institutional innovations include the asymmetrical devolution under Britain's Labour government that was high on the list of national priorities in the late nineties. Greater London elected its first-ever mayor in 2000. Scotland and Wales elected local parliaments (Scotland added an executive branch as well, formerly simply called the Scottish Office), thus asserting their increased national autonomy. The see-saw struggle in England between central powers (Whitehall), local authorities, and the regions continued throughout this period and remains without resolution. In the Netherlands, as indeed happened elsewhere, the national legislature authorized public-private partnerships (PPP), in the hope that this would facilitate large-scale infrastructure projects, such as the Rotterdam central station redevelopment, a PPP venture that was projected to last for nearly two

jurisdiction

decades. The insertion of the European Union into local planning activities through its European Spatial Development Perspective (ESDP) is yet another example. In all these cases, the role of national governments in urban management is actually being weakened while that of regional and local governments is being strengthened. But the issues are far from settled. Lively discussion continues on what planning powers belong to each level of governance, and how they are to be employed.

But who controls the $?

Overall, one notes a trend away from planning conceived as a *restraint* on market forces (e.g. through zoning legislation) to a kind of *entrepreneurial planning* that seeks to facilitate economic development through the market. The extreme case of this is without question the United States. Here, both suburban and inner-city mega-malls have created virtual cities-for-profit; suburban Edge Cities across the country have sprung up without significant inputs from public planning (but with a great deal of ad hoc private planning); and the privately promoted, popular New Urbanism (which has been taken on board by the Federal government) has offered to tackle the problems of metropolitan regions primarily through neo-classical urban design.

get incorporated into policy

The *differential role of civil society* in city and regional planning is yet another dimension which differentiates among planning cultures. If civil society refers to autonomous social organizations that lie beyond the direct control of the state and, more specifically, refers to social organizations that actively participate in the debates over public issues, then countries such as China can be said to have no civil society at all. Other countries – Japan being a prime example – have only a weak civil society sector relative to centrally wielded power. A new era may be dawning in Japan, however, where social movements around environmental issues as well as the *machizukuri* movement that is focused on small, neighborhood-level projects are both gaining ground. It is true that Japanese municipalities can now pass *machizukuri* ordinances, but not being a part of the traditional hierarchy of government, empowered neighborhood groups (called councils), are principally engaged in lobbying local authorities or using moral suasion with property developers. In the Netherlands, by contrast, local civil society is playing a significant oppositional role. In municipal elections, movement coalitions, such as *Livable Rotterdam* or Vancouver's NPA, TEAM, and COPE, can present themselves as political parties and be elected to local Councils in order to further their respective agendas. But it is again the United States which is the country with possibly the greatest role for civil society in local affairs. A side-effect of this is the weakening of city government relative to both business interests and a civil society that often avails itself of the legal system to countermand public decisions. The example of how a coalition of the Labor Community Strategy Center, the National Association of Colored People, and the Bus Riders Union joined in a coalition to fight the Metropolitan Transportation Authority

We should not conflate a robust civil society w/an inclusive planning process

in the federal court of Los Angeles over an increase in bus fares, but with the wider objective of creating a more equitable public transit system, illustrates the options that are open to an engaged, activist civil society in America as well as the critical role of the judicial system in mediating conflicts over urban policy issues.

Notes

1. Mary Douglas, one of the great contemporary anthropologists, defines culture in a way that is useful in the present context. She writes: "At any point in time the culture of a community is engaged in the joint production of meaning ... In reality, the connected meanings that are the basis of any given culture are multiplex, precarious, complex, and fluid. They are continually contested and always in process of mutual accommodation" (Douglas 2004: 88). The term "community" can be applied here to the community of planners, national and local, but increasingly in touch with each others across boundaries.
2. Based on Sorensen (2002). For a specific case study, see Kitajima (2000).
3. Unlike in the West, where the "values and ideals of the international planning movement were largely generated from within the institutions of civil society, not within the central state, which tended to follow rather than lead" (Sorensen 2002: 336).
4. Land readjustment (LR) is one of the distinctive Japanese contributions to the planning sciences. Sorensen gives a brief account: "Organised either by local government or private associations of landowners, its most common use has been to develop land on the urban fringe for urban uses. In essence, LR is a method of pooling ownership of all land within a project area, building urban facilities such as roads and parks and dividing the land into urban plots. There are two aspects of the uses of the method in Japan. First is that all landowners involved must contribute a portion of their land – usually about 30 per cent – for public uses such as roads and parks and some to be sold as urban plots at the end of the project to help pay for projects design, management and construction. Second is that in the case of Association projects, which are the most common type, if at least two-thirds of the landowners owning at least two-thirds of the land in the designated project area agree, all landowners can be forced to participate in the project and contribute their share of land area. This prevents projects being blocked by a single uncooperative landowner, or by free riders who want to gain project benefits without contributing to project costs" (Sorensen 2002: 122–123).
5. Based on Friedmann (2005: Chapter 6) and the specialized literature cited therein.
6. In 2002, China ranked 59th among 102 countries in the Transparency International Corruption Perception Index, below Brazil (45th) but above Russia and India (jointly 71st), and Nigeria (101st). See http://www.transparency.org/cpi/2001/cpi2002.en. html, accessed September 29, 2003.
7. The following is based on Ng and Tang (2002).
8. This is not the case, however, either in Hong Kong or Taiwan where civil society is alive and well.
9. In a recent article, O'Brien and Li (2004) have this to say about what they call "suing the local state": "The promulgation of the Administrative Litigation Law (ALL) in 1989 was hailed in China as a 'milestone of democratic and legal construction.'

Hopeful observers anticipated that the law, by empowering citizens to dispute unlawful administrative acts, would curb official misconduct. However, more than a decade after the ALL came into force, the best evidence suggests that its deterrent effect has been modest. While the number of cases has grown [to about 100,000 a year], and about two-fifths of these reportedly result in some sort of relief, the law's implementation has been hounded by interference and feigned compliance. To this day, the law is widely regarded as a 'frail weapon' that has not greatly reduced administrative arbitrariness" (O'Brien and Li 2004: 75–6).

10. This section on India was contributed by Mattie Siemiatycki, a doctoral student in the School of Community and Regional Planning at the University of British Columbia, and is based on Mishra (1997).
11. Tiwari, D.P. 'Challenges in Urban Planning for Local Bodies in India.' Available online at http://www.gisdevelopment.net/application/urban/overview/urbano0037. htm. See also Mohanty (1996).
12. Based on Ruble (1995).
13. In 1989, Yaroslavl was listed among the 99 most polluted cities in the Russian Federation (Ruble 1995: 108).
14. Unless otherwise indicated, this account is based on essays in the compendium edited by C. Rakodi (1997). Rakodi's collection focuses on urban management of which traditional land use planning is only a small a part. For a more recent assessment of African cities and urban life, see Simone (2004).
15. Informality by itself tells us little of significance. It is a category of activity that results from the interweaving of the formal and informal and of the informal legal and the illegal and criminal. Because of these overlaps, which cut across social class, ethnic identity, and national citizenship, many are able to make a precarious living in the city and a few can actually amass some wealth, a wealth, however, that may quickly dissolve into thin air at the next turn of the wheel of fortune.
16. Simone (2004: 163) writes: "Cities across the continent, for the most part, still don't have appropriate forms of governance ... Thus a piecemeal approach to development has prevailed, which usually entails selective interventions that, above all, constitute a rationale for turning land into a commodity ... Where systematic planning was attempted, it often occurred only at the level of the master plans informed by Western assumptions that had little correspondence with reality."
17. Akin Mabogunje (1990) argues that post-colonial cities in Africa have been shaped by the particular assumptions and paradigms of development that focused on nation-building while ignoring urban realities.
18. Simone (2004: 196) reports: "In Kinshasa ... illegally developed plots [of urban land] outnumber legal ones by tenfold ... Also in Kinshasa, public officials working with cadastral maps have acquired substantial power by working a parallel land market for land expropriation. Here, land problems ... are reinforced by civil servants so that they can offer their services on a private basis to resolve the issue."
19. The first pan-African planning conference was held in Durban, S.A. from 17th to 20th September 2002. Four hundred delegates from many African countries as well as from the UK took part. But what strikes one from a perusal of the papers, is how much they sound as a though the conference might have been held somewhere in Europe or North America, and this despite the five themes in which the plenary and parallel sessions were based. There was no sense of imminent crisis. The topics chosen for presentations were fashionable in professional circles, such as transnational planning, identity formation, the integration of planning with development, sustainability, what

to do about peripheral settlements, and so forth. One did not get a sense from these papers that African cities could be pulled back from the brink of disaster only through extraordinary, unorthodox means. The conference was very much in tune with "business as usual." See http://saplanners.org.za/SAPC/pa-sum.htm.

20. Simone (2001). His case studies, however, suggest a less defeatist conclusion: the inherited modernity left behind by the colonial powers is gradually being replaced by a new, indigenous modernity in Africa's informal cities. See also Simone (2004).

21. Winkler (2002), as amended with personal communications; see also Harrison (2001a, b) as well as Harrison and Kahn (1999), three documents on which Winkler based her own analysis.

22. Based on Faludi and Waterhout (2002) and Commission of The European Communities (CEC) (1999).

23. For an example of the potential role of inter-city networks in regional development, see Friedmann 2001.

24. See, for example, Harris and Hooper (2004).

25. For good or ill, mega-projects are now increasingly popular not only in the Netherlands but in all parts of the world. See Altshuler and Luberoff (2003) and Flyvbjerg *et al* (2003).

26. The following account is based on Kooijman and Wigmans (2003).

27. Patsy Healey refers to this example as the "power of the local." It is by no means unique to Rotterdam. Based on her researches, Healey argues that the quality of urban life is a key issue around which citizens mobilize and exercise electoral power. Politicians, officials, and planners at national and regional levels feel this power but have difficulty grasping its political significance (personal communication).

28. Based on Herrschel and Newman (2002).

29. Community planning in Scotland involves local authorities working together with their principal public sector partners to plan for and deliver services that meet the needs of their local constituencies (Lloyd and McCarthy 2002: 111).

30. Herrschel and Newman (2002: 118).

31. Herrschel and Newman comment: "only two years into the RDA experiment, the two forces of devolution and centralization continue to pull in different directions, and traditional tensions in the structure of British government have reasserted themselves."

32. In a fascinating article by Marvin and May (2003), the authors report their research on the views of urban policy on the part of 26 senior civil servants responsible for urban affairs in the central government (Whitehall), including the Urban Policy Unit in the Office of the Deputy Prime Minister, Cabinet Office, Treasury, Department of Education and Science, Home Office, and Neighbourhood Renewal Unit. "From the point of view of the centre," they write, "the single problematic is how to effect real change in cities according to the expectations of central policy. The key challenge then becomes the manipulation of the external world via the shaping of intermediaries' actions outside Whitehall" (p. 215). Put more simply, the challenge is what they term the "implementation gap," which is a conflict between central control and local autonomy. In central perspective, the authors argue, cities are constructed according to three stylized models. In the first and dominant view, cities (understood here in the narrow sense of local authorities) are, for all practical purposes, "invisible," in the sense that relations with them are uniform and homogeneous. Cities here are simply a class of objects with respect to which the center formulates policies and prescribes programs that are applied unvaryingly across the nation. In the second, which is the emerging view, cities become "visible" in that particular cities are perceived as having potential

for development. These cities, particularly those of the so-called Core Cities Group (Birmingham, Bristol, Leeds, Liverpool, Manchester, Newcastle, Nottingham, and Sheffield) become individualized in some senior civil servants' minds and are regarded as suitable partners with the center. The basis of relations with them is, therefore, negotiation and dialogue. The third view (or "model") is that of "active" cities. According to the authors, it is the most marginal and ambiguous of the three groups. In this perspective, cities are perceived as spatially clustered local authorities, or city-regions, that can be treated as corporate entities and through which special programs can be launched via central urban "compacts" that will promote policies and agreed-upon visions of city futures. The significance of this research is that central government views of cities in the U.K. (and by implication in other highly centralized governments, such as Japan) are not singular but multiple and contested. In models two and three, cities are individualized and treated preferentially (or not) according to perceived opportunities for the implementation of central policies. By implication, some cities will become models of "best practice," while other cities remain "invisible," part of the normal routine practices of government and passive recipients of central government funding, except insofar as they are successful to press their own case with the center through lobbying or social network relations.

33. Based on Ward (2002: 341–54).

34. As Stephen Ward observes, "National policies which cut federal spending programmes and relied on market solutions encouraged a pragmatic and often reckless entrepreneurialism at city level" (Ward 2002: 346).

35. Speaking of the behemoth West Edmonton Mall in Alberta, Canada, an early incarnation of the Edge City phenomenon, Ward comments: "It goes without saying that the role of public planning in the creation of the WEM (and most of its off-spring) was essentially passive and did not impede the creative aspirations of the developers. This had always been, to some extent, the American way of planning, but the market-led model was in the 1980s achieving a wider international salience. Though it was a few years before Joel Garreau popularized the term "edge city" in 1991, West Edmonton, located in the affluent suburbs of Alberta's largest city, was an essential building block of his concept. It was, at once, a monument to the passive Anglo-American planning of the 1980s and a challenge to the new paradigm of sustainable planning in the 1990s" (Ward 2002: 347).

36. Quoted from an LCSC brochure in Ward (2002: 169).

37. Ward (2002: 169).

38. The following account is based on Sandercock (2005). For more details, see Olds (2001) and Punter (2003).

39. TEAM lasted only a few years in office. But its innovative approach to urban development was taken on board by a restructured Non-partisan Association (NPA) which, compelled by an active citizen movement on the left, moved towards the political center, remaining in power until 2002 when it was replaced by another "left-wing" movement, the Coalition of Progressive Electors (COPE). Spaxman served as planning director for 16 years, from 1973 to 1989.

40. One reason for Concord Pacific's acquiescence to assume development costs for social facilities was the very low price for which the company acquired the land on which it would build.

Bibliography

Altshuler, A. and Luberoff, D. (2003) *Mega-Projects: The changing politics of urban investments*, Washington, DC: Brookings Institute Press.

Appadurai, A. (2004) 'The capacity to aspire: culture and the terms of recognition', in V. Rao and M. Walton (eds) *Culture and Public Action*, Stanford, CA: Stanford University Press.

Bayat, A. (2004) 'Globalization and the policies of the informals in the global south', in A. Roy and N. Alsayad (eds) *Urban Informality: Transnational perspectives, from the Middle East, Latin America, and South Asia*, Lanham: Lexington Books.

Bourdieu, P. (2002) 'Habitus', in J. Hillier and E. Rooksby (eds) *Habitus: A sense of place*, Aldershot: Ashgate.

Calthorp, P. (1993) *The Next American Metropolis: Community and the American dream*, Princeton: Princeton Architectural Press.

Castells, M. (1996) *The Rise of the Network Society. The Information Age: Economy, society and culture*, vol. 1, Oxford: Blackwell Publishers.

Commission of The European Communities (1999) *European Spatial Development Perspective: Towards balanced and sustainable development of the territory of the EU*, Luxembourg: Office for Official Publications of the European Communities.

DISP 115 (1993) *Themenheft: Planungskulturen in Europa: Erkundungen in der Schweiz, in Deutschland, Frankreich, und Italien.*

Douglas, M. (2004) 'Traditional culture – let's hear no more about it', in V. Rao and M. Walton (eds) *Culture and Public Action*, Stanford, CA: Stanford University Press.

El-Shaks, S. (1997) 'Towards appropriate urban development policy in emerging megacities in Africa', in C. Rakodi (ed.) *The Urban Challenge in Africa*, Tokyo: United Nations University.

Faludi, A. and Van der Valk, A.J. (1994) *Rule and Order: Dutch planning doctrine in the twentieth century*, Dordrecht: Kluwer Academic Publishers.

Faludi, A. and Waterhout, B. (2002) *The Making of the European Spatial Development Perspective: No masterplan*, London: Routledge.

Flyvbjerg, B., Bruzelius, N. and Rothengatter, W. (2003) *Megaprojects and Risk: An anatomy of ambition*, New York: Cambridge University Press.

Friedmann, J. (1986) 'The world city hypothesis', *Development and Change*, 17(1): 69–83.

——(2001) 'Intercity networks in a globalizing era', in A.J. Scott (ed.) *Global City-Regions: Trends, theory, policy*, Oxford: Oxford University Press.

——(2002) *The Prospect of Cities*, Minneapolis, Vancouver: University of Minnesota Press.

——(2005) *China's Urban Transition*, Minneapolis: University of Minnesota Press.

Friedmann, J. and Wolff, G. (1982) 'World city formation: an agenda for research and action', *International Journal of Urban and Regional Research*, 6(3): 309–44.

Gopalakrishnan, A. (2003) 'A house in disorder', *Frontline*, 10: 20, available online at http://www.frontlineonnet.com.

Grengs, J. (2002) 'Community-based planning as a source of political change: the transit equity movement of Los Angeles' bus riders union', *Journal of the American Planning Association*, 68(2): 165–78.

Harris, N. and Hooper, A. (2004) 'Rediscovering the "Spatial" in public policy and planning: an examination of the spatial content of sectoral policy documents', *Planning Theory and Practice*, 5(2): 147–70.

Harrison, P. (2001a) 'Romance and tragedy in (post) modern planning: a pragmatist's perspective', *International Planning Studies*, 6(1): 69–88.

——(2001b) 'The genealogy of South Africa's integrated development plan', *Third World Planning Review*, 23(2): 175–93.

Harrison, P. and Kahn, M. (1999) 'Ambiguities of change: the case of the planning profession in the province of Kwa-Zulu, Natal, South Africa', in A. Thornley and Y. Rydin (eds) *Planning in a Global Era*, Aldershot: Ashgate.

Herrschel, T. and Newman, P. (2002) *Governance of Europe's City Regions: planning policy and politics*, London: Routledge.

Hutton, T. (2004) 'Review of John Punter, the Vancouver achievement', *Journal of the American Planning Association*, 70(4): 485.

Keller, D.A., Koch, M. and Selle, K. (1996) '"Either/or" and "and": first impressions of a journey into the planning cultures of four countries', *Planning Perspectives*, 11: 41–54.

Kitajima, S. (2000) 'Local restructuring processes and problems of governance: a case of an old industrial city in Northern Japan', *Asian Geographer (Hong Kong)*, 19(1/2): 89–106.

Knox, P. and Taylor, P.J. (1986) *World Cities in a World System*, Cambridge: Cambridge University Press.

Kooijman, D. and Wigmans, G. (2003) 'Managing the city: flows and places at Rotterdam central station', *City*, 7(3): 301–26.

Lehrer, U. (2004) 'Reality or image? Place selling at Potsdamer Platz, Berlin', in Inura and R. Paloscia (eds) *Metropolis: Seven cities at the beginning of the twenty-first century*, Birkhäuser, Berlin.

Lloyd, M.G. and McCarthy, J. (2002) 'Asymmetrical devolution, institutional capacity and spatial planning innovation', in Y. Rydin and A. Thornley (eds) *Planning in the UK: Agendas for the new millennium*, Aldershot: Ashgate.

Mabogunje, A. (1990) 'Urban planning and the post-colonial state in sub-Saharan Africa', *African Studies Review*, 33: 121–203.

Marvin, S. and May, T. (2003) 'City futures: views from the centre', *City*, 7(2): 213–26.

Mishra, R.K. (1997) 'National civil service system in India: a critical view', paper presented at the Civil Service Systems in Comparative Perspective Conference, School of Public and Environmental Affairs, Indiana University (Bloomington), April.

Mohanty, P.K. (1996) 'Urban development planning in India', in J. Stubbs and G. Clarke (eds) *Megacity Management in the Asian and Pacific Region*, Manila: Asian Development Bank.

Ng, M.K. and Tang, W.S. (2002) 'Building a modern socialist city in an age of globalization: the case of Shenzhen special economic zone, People's Republic of China', in conference proceedings: Theme 4: Globalization, Urban Transition and Governance in Asia. Forum on Urbanizing World and UN Urban Habitat II, New York: The International Research Foundation.

Obduho, R.A. (1997) 'Nairobi: national capital and regional hub', in Carol Rakodi (ed.) *The Urban Challenge in Africa*, Tokyo: United Nations University.

O'Brien, K.J. and Li, L. (2004) 'Suing the local state: administrative litigation in rural China', *The China Journal*, 51: 75–96.

Olds, K. (2001) *Globalization and Urban Change: Capital, culture, and Pacific Rim megaprojects*, Oxford: Oxford University Press.

Punter, J. (2003) *The Vancouver Achievement*, Vancouver: University of British Columbia Press.

Rakodi, C. (ed.) (1997) *The Urban Challenge in Africa: Growth and management of its large cities*, Tokyo: United Nations University.

Roy, A. (2004) 'The gentlemen's city: urban informality in the Calcutta of New Communism', in A. Roy and N. Alsayyad (eds) *Urban Informality*, Lanham: Lexington Books.

Ruble, B. A. (1995) *Money Sings: The changing politics of urban space in post-Soviet Yaroslavl,* Cambridge: Cambridge University Press.

Sandercock, L. (2005) 'An anatomy of civic ambition in Vancouver: toward humane density', *Harvard Design Review,* 22(Spring/Summer): 36–43.

Sanyal, B. (ed.) (2005) *Comparative Planning Cultures,* London: Routledge.

Sassen, S. (2001) *The Global City: New York, London, Tokyo,* 2nd edn, Princeton, NJ: Princeton University Press.

——(2002a) 'Locating cities on global circuits', in S. Sassen (ed.) *Global Networks, Linked Cities,* London: Routledge.

——(2002b) (ed.) *Global Networks, Linked Cities,* New York: Routledge

Siemiatycki, M. (2003) 'Beyond moving people: excavating the motivations for investing in urban public transit infrastructure in Bilbao, Spain', unpublished thesis, Oxford University.

Simone, A.M. (2001) 'Straddling the divides: remaking associational life in the informal African city', *International Journal of Urban and Regional Research,* 25(1): 102–17.

——(2004) *For the City Yet to Come: Changing African life in four cities,* Durham, NC: Duke University Press.

Smith, R.G. (2003) 'World city topologies', *Progress in Human Geography,* 27(5): 561–82.

Soliman, A.M. (2004) 'Tilting at the sphinxes: locating urban informality in Egyptian cities', in A. Roy and N. Alsayyad (eds) *Urban Informality,* Lanham: Lexington Books.

Sorensen, A. (2002) *The Making of Urban Japan: Cities and planning from Edo to the twenty-first century,* London: Routledge.

Stiftel, B. and Watson, V. (2004) *Dialogues in Urban and Regional Planning,* vol. 1, London: Routledge/Taylor and Francis Group in Conjunction with the Global Planning Education Association Network.

Taylor, P.J., Walker, D.R.F. and Beaverstock, J.V. (2002) 'Firms and their global service networks', in S. Sassen (ed.) *Global Networks, Linked Cities,* London: Routledge.

Verma, G.D. (2002) *Slumming India: a chronicle of slums and their saviours,* New Delhi: Penguin.

Ward, S.V. (2002) *Planning the Twentieth Century City: The advanced capitalist world,* Chichester: Wiley.

Wekweto, K.H. (1997) 'Urban management: the recent experience', in C. Rakodi (ed.) *The Urban Challenge in Africa,* Tokyo: United Nations University.

Winkler, T. (2002) 'South Africa's complex planning culture', unpublished manuscript.

Wong, K.K. and Zhao, X.B. (1999) 'The influence of bureaucratic behavior on land apportionment in China: the informal process', *Environment and Planning C: Government and Policy,* 17: 113–26.

Study questions

The essay you have just read had a very modest objective: to call attention to differences in the way that spatial planning is actually performed across the globe. I have not done so systematically but, to the extent possible, through a series of case studies that often belies one of our fondest fantasies that planning is somehow a rational, orderly, and universal process, like engineering, for example.

This dream is largely based on the discourse in planning; it is what we have learned at the university and what got many of us started in the planning field. Planning practice, however, turned out to be something altogether different, *Friedmann* and to be immersed in it was often a surprising, and even painful process, *generally again* something like jumping into an ice-cold stream on a hot day. Whether we will *argues that* ever be able to close the gap between discourse and practice remains an open *objectivity* question. But what we can do is to look at how planning is actually practiced *(disproves)* in different parts of the world and in different cities within the same country – in short, engage in the empirical and critical study of planning – so that we will be better prepared to deal with the differences when we find ourselves in situations where these differences must be addressed.

Here are 10 structural features that contribute to these differences in planning practice. They are not weighted, of course, nor do I show interrelations among them. That is a job for the empirical researcher who is trying to unravel the mysteries of actual practices. The order in which I have listed them is random:

> degree of local autonomy – role of politics – democratic traditions – level of economic development – prevalence of corruption – planning education curricula – political involvement of civil society – professional status of planners – institutional setting – official language of planning discourse.

Following are some exercises that may help you to understand what we mean by a planning culture:

1. Taking a planning situation with which you are familiar, perhaps in your home town or place of study, describe the features listed above in their complex relationship to planning and provide a thumbnail sketch of the local planning culture. You may also want to interview some planning practitioners or invite them to come to class to talk about their experiences.
2. Divide your class into two- or three-person groups and ask each group to report on a planning culture chosen from the additional bibliography shown below. Discuss these differences and attempt to understand why they exist.

3. The essay we are discussing claims that because of global interdependencies and a globalizing planning discourse, we may well observe a gradual convergence of planning cultures. Using your own experience as a guide, discuss this proposition.

Selected additional readings

Angotti, T. (2008) *New York for Sale: Community planning confronts real estate*, Cambridge, MA: MIT Press.

Faludi, A. and Van der Valk, A.J. (1994) *Rule and Order: Dutch planning doctrine in the twentieth century*, Dordrecht: Kluwer Academic Publishers.

Healey, P. (2007) *Urban Complexity and Spatial Strategies: Towards a relational planning for our times*, London: Routledge (includes three European case studies).

Healey, P. and Unger, R. (eds) (2010) *Crossing Borders: International exchanges and planning practices*, London: Routledge (includes a number of case studies pertinent to a discussion of planning cultures).

Newman, P. and Thornley, A. (2005) *Planning World Cities: Globalization and urban politics*, New York: Palgrave Macmillan.

Porter, L. (2010) *Unlearning the Colonial Cultures of Planning*, Farnham (UK): Ashgate.

Sanyal, B. (ed.) (2005) *Comparative Planning Cultures*, New York: Routledge (see especially the chapters by Leonie Sandercock on Australia, André Sorensen on Japan, and Michael Leaf on China).

10

The uses of planning theory

I wrote this essay partly in response to a frequent criticism that practicing planners don't need theory, that they learn primarily from practice. The implication is that planning theorists are pursuing little more than a personal hobby which, though they may find amusing, is without wider significance for the field. Whether I have succeeded in this volume to address this criticism is for others to say. Here I want to change tack and attempt to answer a related question: what do planning theorists do – or think they do – when they theorize?

This question sounds simple enough, but complications immediately arise, because the first thing we need to do is to identify the universe of planning theorists. From past efforts at arriving at a consensus about this, we can confidently assert that agreement on whom to put on a reading list of "must" contributions to planning theory is virtually impossible. I have already referred to this problem in Chapter 7. In the sciences, to say the least, this is an odd situation. An international journal with an eponymous title has been in existence for years, but limiting ourselves to only the authors who have published there would draw an unnecessarily restrictive boundary around the invisible college of planning theorists. The problem is not only that there are other outlets for those who address theoretical questions in our field but, more importantly, that salient contributions have been made by authors who are not even remotely connected to the planning profession. For instance, speaking of writers who had a major influence on my own approach to planning and the theories that inform it, I could mention Lewis Mumford (a philosopher), Karl Mannheim (a European sociologist), and John Dewey (an American educator and philosopher). The conclusion we can draw is that planning and its theories is an eclectic field par excellence, and trying bound it is to cut off its supply of fresh air.

Until his recent retirement, Andreas Faludi held the chair in planning theory at the University of Delft. In an early publication, he distinguished between theories *in* planning and theories *of* planning. The first category refers to theories planners use in their analyses, such as in solving a transportation problem. The second addresses questions that relate directly to the activity of planning itself. It is also the kind of theorizing that informs this volume, so that theories of regional planning, for example, about which I have also written extensively, have been rigorously excluded. But austerity is not essential for good theorizing. In fact, many of my colleagues prefer to work with models that are less than 100 per cent "pure," where planning is not carefully cleansed of its particular applications, whether in regions, cities, or otherwise. I say this, because how we theorize, how we identify a problem, and the approach we use to write about it, are ultimately matters of personal choice. And yet, for all the diversity of approaches, we seem to be moving forward in tandem with changing socio-economic and political conditions, paying close attention to how planning is actually done in a world that is continually in flux.

In making his or her choice of approach, what are the major options for a theorist? Here are three ways of doing planning theory. In *Planning in the Public Domain* (Friedmann 1987), I started by defining the object of planning as the linking of knowledge to action. I came to this definition through deep reflection on my own work as a development planner that eventually led me to questions about epistemology; about the actors whose knowledge was pertinent for planning interventions; and finally about the actual processes by which knowers and doers might be joined in practice. This broad inquiry also led me to identify civil society along with the state and the corporate world as one of a trio of collective actors in physical and societal change and thus to a new conceptualization of radical planning.

A second way is to closely observe actual planning practices at work in a particular place. A model for this was the early study of public housing in Chicago by Meyerson and Banfield (1955). In my own work, the lone example of an empirical study was my examination of national planning in Venezuela (Friedmann 1965). More thorough and historically grounded is Sorensen's excellent research on the evolution of Japanese planning (Sorensen 2005) or, to cite another example, Yiftachel's critical studies of planning apartheid in Israel (Yiftachel 2006; 2007).

A third approach is openly normative, that is, a study driven by value propositions such as Forester's work, initially inspired by the Habermasian theory of communicative action (Forester 1989; 1999). My own searches for, respectively, the "good society" and the "good city" (Chapters 3 and 8, this volume) may also serve here as an example. Perhaps, then, it is these three – reflective practice, empirical and/or critical inquiry, and normative explorations – that constitute the major methodological options facing a theorist.

In the essay below, I decided again, as I had done in 1987, on a reflective approach. In this instance, however, it was a theoretical practice that I contemplated, my own and others'. I had been an active participant in theoretical discourse about planning since my student days, and as I thought about this unbounded domain of work by dozens of scholars, three reasons for writing planning theory emerged: the search for a deeply considered humanist philosophy of interventions in the collective life of a community; the identification of constraints on planning with regard to scale, complexity, and time; and the translation of concepts and insights generated in other fields into the language of our own domain, thus rendering them useful for planning practice. I turned these reasons into the tasks or moral obligations of planning theorists as they go about their work.

An essay such as this is necessarily written in a style that is more or less impersonal. I will therefore interject more personal comments from time to time. The reader will recognize them by the italic script.

Bibliography

Forester, J. (1989) *Planning in the Face of Power*, Berkeley: University of California Press.

——(1999) *The Deliberative Practitioner: Encouraging participatory planning processes*, Cambridge, MA: MIT Press.

Friedmann, J. (1965) *Venezuela: from doctrine to dialogue*, with an introduction by B. Gross, National Planning Series vol. 1, Syracuse, NY: Syracuse University Press.

——(1987) *Planning in the Public Domain: From knowledge to action*, Princeton, NJ: Princeton University Press.

Meyerson, M. and Banfield, E.C. (1955) *Politics, Planning, and the Public Interest: The case of public housing in Chicago*. New York: Free Press.

Sorensen, A. (2005) 'The developmental state and the extreme narrowness of the public realm: the twentieth century evolution of Japanese planning culture', in B. Sanyal (ed.) *Comparative Planning Cultures*, New York: Routledge.

Yiftachel, O. (2006) *Ethnocracy: Land and identity politics in Israel/Palestine*, Philadelphia: Pennpress.

——(2007) 'Re-engaging planning theory', *Planning Theory*, 5(3): 211–22.

The Uses of Planning Theory

Originally published in 2008

Introduction

Planning theory is becoming an increasingly global discourse. The eponymous journal *Planning Theory* was founded by Luigi Mazza of the University of Milano in the 1990s. Several volumes of Anglo-American planning theorists (Forester, Friedmann, Healey, and Sandercock, among others) have been translated into Italian and published by Dedalo under the general editorship of Dino Borri of the Technical University of Bari. In the United Kingdom, Patsy Healey, with the strong support of the Royal Town Planning Institute, founded the journal *Planning Theory and Practice*, which in 2008 is celebrating its tenth anniversary. In Germany, Klaus Selle at the University of Aachen has been a major contributor to planning theoretical discourse. Individual contributions have come from Israel, Brazil, Norway, Denmark, Belgium, and Greece. And as recent issues of the *China City Planning Review* (published in English) demonstrate, there is now even a small number of Chinese planners who have joined the discourse.

What is less clear is how we should answer the question, "Planning theory for what?" or why those of us who engage in theoretical practice choose to do so. Skeptics sometimes argue that the coterie of self-identified theorists talk chiefly among themselves, that theory is an esoteric game of little or no practical import. A contrary position such as Klaus Selle's (2006) sees it as having a central role in renewing planning practices. Being of Selle's persuasion, my purpose in this essay is to suggest three ways that theorizing in and about planning contributes to our professional field, with a particular emphasis on North America. Undoubtedly, there exist other ways of contributing to planning theory, but I regard the three to be discussed here as central to our endeavor. I refer to them as "tasks," which is to say that they are major concerns, whether explicit or implicit, of those participating in the discourse.

The first task is to evolve a deeply considered humanist philosophy for planning and to trace its implications for practice. This is the *philosophical* task of planning theory. The second task is to help adapt planning practices to their real-world constraints with regard to scale, complexity, and time. What I have in mind here are the constraints on and opportunities for practice with which the constant flux of the world presents us, along with the growing complexity and scale of the urban and the importance that "difference" makes. I call this the task of *adaptation*. The third task is to translate concepts and knowledges generated in other fields into our own domain and to render them accessible and useful for planning and its practices. I call this the task of *translation*. In the remainder of this essay, I elaborate on each of these tasks by drawing on specific examples from the literature.

Evolving a humanist philosophy for planning and its practices

It doesn't seem so very long ago that planning was perceived to be a value-free activity guided by professional if not scientific standards. Planners, it was argued, are guardians of the public interest. Today, it would be difficult to maintain this position – or is it? In Japan, for instance, planning is still largely perceived as a technocratic activity exercised by Tokyo-based bureaucrats (Sorensen 2002), and versions of this attitude are widely held throughout East Asia. And although North American planners no longer embrace technocratic hubris, architects and some urban designers by and large still do, and economists of the neoclassical variety regard their pronouncements as scientifically based advice to policy makers who can then exercise their values in whatever way they choose. They believe in the maxim of speaking truth to power. In their understanding, facts and values don't mix; they are derived from different logics.

And yet, as planners, we don't have a well thought-out philosophical position beyond the usual platitudes of "participation." Some planners today think of their primary role as that of facilitating public discussion or mediating disputes. While they may favor a different outcome, their professional skill is primarily to assist in "getting to yes" among stakeholders, in arriving at an actionable consensus, whatever that may turn out to be. This facilitative approach is a considerable distance from an understanding of a planning practice embedded in politics.

So the question for us is this: can planners evolve a value-based philosophy as a foundation for their own practices in the world? My personal view is that this is perhaps the major challenge before us in a world that, despite protestations to the contrary, is increasingly materialist, individualist, and largely indifferent to humans' impacts on the natural environment. In the absence of a human-centered philosophy or some other defensible construct, we will merely drift with the mainstream, helping to build cities that are neither supportive of life nor ecologically sustainable.

That planning is not a value-free activity has been widely acknowledged for some time, at least in North America, where value-based planning is no longer a salient issue. The Canadian Institute of Planners, for example, has an eight-point "Statement of Values" that is meant to serve as a source of inspiration and guidance for professional planners (www.cipicu.ca/English/members/practice.htm). Moreover, for progressive planners in the United States and Canada, social justice concerns have been an important focus for decades, ever since Paul Davidoff (1965) made the case for planners' advocacy of the poor and Chester Hartman's *Planners Network Newsletter* in 1975, which has now evolved into the quarterly journal *Progressive Planning*. Equally notable is Susan Fainstein's (2000, 2006) tireless advocacy of social justice in the city. More recently, some planning schools (especially in Canada), such as the School of Community and Regional Planning at the University of British Columbia, have declared themselves to be committed to sustainability and the democratization of planning, thus making a specific value orientation central to their mission. And over the years, various value claims have been embraced by both the planning academy and many individual practitioners, such as advocacy of the poor and other marginalized people, citizen participation, inclusiveness, and the right to housing.

These commitments did not, however, simply "drop from the sky" but were the result of political struggles, debates, and dramatic changes in the *zeitgeist* of our societies. Underlying them, too, were new researches, new discourses, and new common understandings about the contemporary world. These writings, addressed to planners but occasionally to a more general readership as well, are part and parcel of what I call the central tasks of planning theory. If planning practice is now, as I would argue, both societal and political, and if we live, unavoidably, in an increasingly interconnected world, we have to think more and more deeply about the values that should inform our practices, *including how to move from values to action*. In the following paragraphs, I give the merest hints of the extensive work that lies ahead of us.

I begin with what I believe to be our birthright to human flourishing. In an essay on the "good city," I argued that "every human being has the right to the full development of their innate intellectual, physical, and spiritual capabilities in the context of wider communities." I called this the right to human flourishing and proposed it as the most fundamental of human rights (Friedmann 2002: 110).[1]

Philosophical anthropology teaches us that individual human beings cannot be meaningfully described as an abstract concept such as the utility-maximizing "economic man" of neoclassical thought, which, when seriously applied in policy discourse, can have vicious consequences (Clark 2002). Rather, from the moment of conception until we die, human beings can only be understood as multidimensional, socially related beings, or *persons* who, over the entire arc of their lives, develop biologically, psychologically, and in the social relations that constitute our collective existence. More recently, we have come to understand human interdependence not only societally but also with the natural environment: both are essential to our continued sustenance and flourishing (Daly and Farley 2004; Clark 2002). This anthro-ecological model is essentially one of *limits*: limited, that is, by the requirements of biological and psychological life, culturally mediated social obligations, the extensive production of use values without which we would not survive and which some refer to as the moral economy, and nature's capacity to sustain human life on earth at socially acceptable levels of living (Polanyi 1977).

Two crucial observations follow from working with a model of limits. The first is that it clashes with the belief in the possibility of unlimited cumulative growth in material consumption and thus, presumably, of human happiness as well (an ever increasing "happiness"?), a belief that has become the dominant ideology in policy planning worldwide. The second is that an implication of working with either or both models is bound to lead to contradictions that can only be resolved either peacefully through a political process or, failing that, by deploying the police powers of the state. An example is the off-loading of the rising economic and environmental costs of unlimited material growth onto the least powerful sectors of the population (using the full powers of the state to enforce this solution) and/or onto the weakest countries of the global community, many of them in Africa and the Middle East. In other words, increasing domestic and global inequalities are partly responsible for generating the present world *disorder* ranging from drugs, people smuggling, hunger, and random violence against civilian populations to desertification, global warming, and the "long emergency" of post-peak oil (Kunstler 2006). Since violent solutions may be the most probable but are also the least desirable, we are for all practical purposes left with only a range of political options.

At a theoretical level, these options confront us with the challenge to devise political systems and/or processes capable of overcoming the inherent contradictions in public policy work. This line of argument takes us directly to the question of democratic theory, most of which, at least in recent decades, has had the nation state as its primary focus. Planners have made few contributions to democratic theory as such, possibly because our attention is overwhelmingly focused on the local.[2]

Twenty years ago, in an attempt to write the history of planning thought, I suggested that John Dewey's experimental pragmatism, Karl Mannheim's "third way" of democratic planning, Karl Popper's advocacy of an "open society", and Robert Dahl and Charles Lindblom's political economy offered planners a bridge to political theory (Friedmann 1987).[3] But turning to contemporary political theory directly, perhaps the most influential work over the past half century has been Sheldon Wolin's ([1960] 2004) *Politics and Vision*. In a more radical vein and especially relevant for planners are the writings of Iris Marion Young (1990, 2000) on social justice and the city and Chantal Mouffe's (1992) edited collection, *Dimensions of Radical Democracy: Pluralism, citizenship, community*, which brings together some of the most eloquent political philosophers of our time.[4]

During the past decade, a stir has been made (mostly in North America) by advocates of deliberative democracy. Various attempts have been made to define the meaning of this deliberative turn in political theory. Two of the leading advocates of the approach define deliberative democracy "as a form of government in which free and equal citizens (and their representatives) justify decisions in a process in which they give one another reasons that are mutually acceptable and generally accessible, with the aim of reaching conclusions that are binding in the present on all citizens but open to challenge in the future" (Gutmann and Thompson 2004: 7).[5] Virtually all the debates that have swirled around this concept, however, have cast their arguments in terms of a national polity, and the relevance of public "deliberation," as this term is used by political scientists, has found little resonance among planners.

An exception is Archon Fung's recent work. Using a series of six case studies from Chicago, Fung has given us a detailed look at deliberative democracy at work (Fung 2004; also see Fung, Wright, and Abers 2003). He calls it *Empowered Participation* and sees it as a strategy of administrative reform. Among political theorists, his work is exceptional, but his focus on the local community is a familiar one to planners, especially to those working in mediation and negotiation, such as Judith Innes and David Booher (2003).

It is John Forester (1999), however, who has taken deliberative democracy's moral vision furthest by working it into the language and practice of community planning. His early writings focused on the art of listening, but in *The Deliberative Practitioner* he departed from the rationalist models of political scientists and philosophers such as Jürgen Habermas to confront the deep grievances and passionate commitments people often bring to public deliberations. If the parties to a conflict seek to reach agreement, their pains, passions, and grievances, he argues, must first be publicly acknowledged. Most important for planning theory, perhaps, is his emphasis on what he calls *transformative learning,* which occurs when people honestly confront their emotions and those of others in the course of talking with each other.

Central to Forester's work is the principle of dialogue, which the Jewish philosopher Martin Buber (1965) has called *das Zwischenmenschliche,* that which binds humans together and, in a wider circle of interdependencies, joins us in loving attentiveness to all living beings on Earth. In a book I called *The Good Society,* I explored this principle in its multiple forms and ambiguities and suggested that human bonds can be formed into social movements (or temporary sodalities) that, through personal engagement and political struggle, act as the living germ cell in the moral transformation of human societies (Friedmann 1979). Today, Forester continues this exploration by focusing on more stable, place-bound communities in the small spaces of the city that are its neighborhoods and other neglected, often invisible spaces. It is interesting to note how despite the gigantism of the modern urban, spreading as it does over thousands of square kilometers, these intimate spaces of urban life survive, forming a tapestry of social relations that is deeply meaningful for those weaving its patterns. Efforts such as Forester's and others' at constructing a moral foundation for planning are essential if we want to further the good and avoid evil, which is the dark side of planning in the service of a powerful, essentially immoral state (Yiftachel 1998). *☆Big statement*

Adapting planning practices to their real-world constraints: scale, complexity, and time

Theorists are forever watching the world as it goes through its transformations. For some, this is an exciting prospect, but planners are not journalists who can dispassionately observe the passing scene. Given the reality of what is happening now, they have to ask themselves whether planning powers should intervene to shift the balance of forces toward goals of social justice and inclusion in the ongoing processes of urban and regional restructuring, and with what tools at hand?

The 60-plus years since World War II have been momentous ones as the world population increased threefold, while the ratio of urban dwellers increased by nearly five times to reach 50 per cent of the total by 2008. This scale of demographic growth is without historical precedent, and planners have had to work with only smidgens of knowledge to guide them. Someone once called it "planning without facts." None of us could claim to understand what was actually happening, or where we were headed, if indeed there was a destination. As a rule, we spoke with far greater certainty than was warranted; some might even argue that we were "whistling in the dark." Still, one had a sense of being close to the ragged frontlines of history. That at least is what I felt when I worked successively in Brazil, Venezuela, Chile, Korea, Mozambique, Thailand, Japan, and latterly China. But I believe that even back home in North America, planning was often more a venturing forth into the unknown terrain of the future than the precise surgical procedure involved in, say, removing a ruptured appendix. *limits*

I return then to the question of limits, this time the limits of knowledge about a world that despite incredible scientific achievements in some realms leaves many of us perplexed. We can imagine something better than what we see around us, but such visions are fugitive, and our actions, imperfect as they are, often contribute to the general sense of turbulence rather than bringing us closer to imaginary futures. Under these circumstances, the best we can hope for is to make pragmatic responses to emergencies that are already upon us. Global warming is a telling example. *☆☆ midgley*

This then is the story of how planning theorists have tried to close the feedback loop between observed events on the ground and the teachings of our profession. And in this, at least, as I will try to show, their efforts have been partially successful.

Wisdom has it that to be a good planner is to be acutely aware not only of what our work can reasonably be expected to accomplish but also what it cannot: as professionals, we have to be aware of our cognitive limitations. The absolute limits of planning are given by what can be reliably known, and this is a function of scale, complexity, and time. Although the scales of the urban are, in principle, infinite, spatial planning is always territorially bounded, and both the scales of the urban and the authority to act on them vary from the global to the infinitesimally small spaces of neighborhood and city block. This being the case, there can be no single, unalterable global hierarchy of the urban, which is multiply scaled at all pertinent levels.

The preceding paragraph requires a reflective comment. It assumes that planning has something to do with linking knowledge to action (Friedmann 1987). This is a widely accepted view within the profession, but it fails to acknowledge the sort of visionary, bold, and ultimately ruthless spatial planning for which, to cite two notorious cases, Baron Haussmann's Paris and Robert Moses's New York are well-known instances (Harvey 2003; Ballon and Jackson 2003). And yet these visionary and politically astute bureaucrat-planners who had the power to make things happen have bequeathed us cities that in retrospect, and despite critiques from various quarters, are often greatly admired. In contrast to these impresarios of urban transformation, Lewis Mumford (1938), though never a planner himself, likened planning to a form of gardening – a bit of pruning here, a bit of mulching there – that, in rhythm with the cycles of nature, would help to bring about a biocentric urban region. Environmentalists today are rediscovering Mumford, while other observers, impatient with contemporary New York's snail-paced planning process, cast nostalgic backward glances at Moses and his decisiveness, political acumen, and ability to give substance to his vision. So the jury on what sort of planning we should have, and how much "knowledge" (and even what *sort* of knowledge) is necessary for good planning, is, I'm afraid, still out.

There is also the question of what is meant above by a "reliable" knowledge for planning decisions. Or do visions suffice? Speaking prospectively as planners often do, what, for instance, is the best route for a new transit line, and would building it be an economically sound decision? Unfortunately, questions of this sort are never plausibly answered. Engineering criteria can be invoked, but in the end we know that forecasts of future transit demand are unreliable, the more so the longer the time period in view (Flyvbjerg, Bruzelius, and Rothengatter 2003; Altshuler and Luberoff 2003). Such decisions are ultimately left to politicians, bureaucrats, business lobbies, urban social movements, and the media to resolve – that is, to the political process. Parenthetically, it might be noted that local politicians' tenure is rarely long enough to experience the consequences of their choice. Since public memory is similarly short, political decisions are frequently irresponsible, if not reckless.

I return then to the question of knowledge for planning. Throughout the world, planning education requires at least a first university degree and, in many countries, the equivalent of an American master's degree. So one would think that a high measure of formal knowledge is after all required as a point of entry into the profession. Where planning is taught in schools of architecture, which is the case for about half of North American planning schools, planning knowledge is often taken to mean internalizing urban design principles (e.g. Hester 2006). On the other hand, where planning is taught in schools of public policy, as at UCLA, the University of Minnesota, and Rutgers, design may be neglected in favor of some amalgam of knowledge in urban geography, demography, statistics, public finance, and sociology. Policy planners may pronounce on planning issues, basing their conclusions on quantitative research and mapping exercises, but more often than not their findings will be challenged whenever they run counter to powerful private or political interests. In the policy-making arena, planning expertise is not necessarily accepted as superior to other people's judgments.[6]

There are good reasons for this. Planners' professional knowledge is necessarily based on a very limited reading of the urban complex. Obliged to make "comprehensive" or "strategic" plans for a city or region, they face the almost impossible task of representing the city or region in two-dimensional space at a scale that can be visualized at a single glance. Every map is a model, and every model is a radical simplification – an abstraction – of reality. What planners choose to show then is a *selection* of variables, all of which are subject to change over time, though the respective directions and velocities of change will vary. The first difficulty planners face, then, is to decide what variables to incorporate into their plan-making exercise and which to ignore (i.e. rendering some potentially important ones invisible). The inevitable bias in this initial choice will be in favor of variables to which their professional education has predisposed them as well as such data as are readily at hand. Absent such data, new research would have to be done, but funds for this are always scarce, and plans have to be produced according to a set schedule. In the natural sciences (and in economics), powerful models (or theories) are rewarded with lush research grants and Nobel prizes. Many planning practitioners, however, have little patience with formal models of the urban. Nor do they have any way of making long-term forecasts of how the urban complex at any given scale is likely to evolve under alternative assumptions, such as political change, demographic dynamics, economic performance, and sudden shifts in global trends to name only four sets of variables over which city planners have little or no control. Prospective land use and circulation plans, then, are mostly demand-driven wish images projected onto two-dimensional maps, images that reflect the hidden biases of their social class and professional training.[7]

Given how these circumstances constrain their craft, is it surprising that municipal planners are continually revising their plans to bring them up to date, while any specific proposals come inevitably under fire from adversaries both inside and outside the government? Speaking generally, the influence of this type of planning on the shaping of urban complexes has been minimal. Perhaps it is for this reason that planning practice in North America has increasingly become more entrepreneurial, focusing on projects and partnership arrangements rather than comprehensive city plans, and why theorists such as Forester (1989) and Flyvbjerg (1998b) have strongly argued for a style of politically savvy planning.

For many planners, this was already clear during the turbulent sixties when social movements flourished. [Many American planning schools became hot spots of social activism that soon overshadowed more traditional planning concerns, such as land use (Soja 2010).] In 1959, Lindblom, a political economist at Yale, published what was to become his most popular journal article ever (reprinted more than 40 times!), provocatively titled "The Science of Muddling Through" (Lindblom 1959). In it, he argued against "synoptic" planning which he dismissed as a utopian endeavor, proposing instead a "disjointed incrementalism" in which a large number of relatively autonomous but networked actors would adjust their own short-term plans, each according to the continually changing conditions confronting them. This was the competitive market reinterpreted for the world of policy and planning. But few planners in the academy heeded his call; most were still in thrall to the ideal of comprehensiveness. Etzioni's (1968) attempt to combine broad visions with incremental steps to achieve them, which he called "mixed scanning," was similarly unpersuasive. Planning theorists were still in thrall to a model of how to make decisions more rational.

In *Retracking America: A theory of transactive planning* (Friedmann 1973), I attempted to realign the meaning of planning in a country that had passed through a decade of social turmoil. Conscious that a historical era was coming to an end, I outlined a new kind of "postindustrial" planning based on social learning. I saw planners engaged in seeking positive social change and proposed joining up what they knew as a result of their specialized education with the experiential knowledge of ordinary citizens who would be affected by their decisions. I called this a process of "mutual learning" that would take place through a series of face-to-face transactions. Three years later, Argyris and Schön (1978) published the results of their own extensive researches on organizational learning. Together, these influences, seeping out of the academy into everyday life, helped create a broad learning metaphor for a type of planning practice that, in the United States if not elsewhere, has become increasingly participatory on the scale of local communities and occasionally larger ensembles.

The surge of neoliberal ideology in the late seventies and continuing right up to the end of the millennium posed new challenges for planning. Private-public partnerships started to be formed that coined a new category of "stakeholders," most of whom came from concerned government agencies and

✫This is key.

the corporate sector, with a new "third sector" embracing civil society at some distance behind. Self-identified stakeholders now had a legitimate claim to sit at the table when decisions affecting their interests were being made.[8]

The seventies and eighties were indeed an era of historical transition whose profound effects would be felt around the globe. Marxists explained what was happening as a crisis of accumulation, and some authors even toyed with the ambiguous phrase *late capitalism* to characterize this period (Mandel 1975).

What they failed to grasp was the regenerative powers of a system engaged in an ambitious project of global restructuring. Neoliberalism served as its mantra.

As neoliberal national regimes began downloading usually unfunded responsibilities to states and cities, they left lower-order governments to fend for themselves. Local governments were thus forced to compete against each other as cities tried to ensure their fiscal viability by attracting inbound investments to shore up their ever-vulnerable economies (Porter 2001). This left neighborhood communities that had been particularly hard hit by the transition to a service-based economy to manage the shift from "Fordist" production on their own. Many were left stranded.

Analyses of what was happening were carried out chiefly by geographers, sociologists, and economists. From a Marxist perspective, David Harvey (1982, 1988) explored capital theory and, later, postmodernity. But it was Bluestone and Harrison's (1982) *Deindustrialization of America* and Harrison and Bluestone's (1988) *The Great U-Turn: Corporate restructuring and the polarizing of America* that became the most influential stories of the decade. *✫✫ key*

In a historical treatment of planning doctrines, I signaled the same perception of a sea change in American life: the last third of *Planning in the Public Domain* acknowledged a form of planning I called radical, which had its antecedents to the left of the political spectrum, sprouting in many directions over two centuries (Friedmann 1987). Radical planning today, I argued, was grounded in the myriad organizations of civil society: beyond the reach of the state, it would often be in opposition to the state and sometimes to corporate interests as well. Planning by mobilized communities (in softer language, planning "from below") was thus acknowledged as a new reality. Manuel Castells (1983) summed up a decade of field research into urban social movements in his masterful *The City and the Grassroots*, before turning to trace *Look up.* the lineaments of the emerging new network society (Castells 1996). Ten years later, Leonie Sandercock (1998a) would extend radical planning to the struggles of marginalized peoples for their "right to the city," including indigenous First Nations, women, gays and lesbians, and other "voices from the borderlands."

The 1990s and spilling over into the first few years of the new millennium gathered the harvest of decades of social change and experimentation.

Participatory planning had reached its apogee with the introduction of the participatory budget by Porto Alegre's new Labor government (Abers 2000), an experiment that has inspired similar endeavors throughout Brazil, Europe, and Canada, though none as attention-getting as the original experiment. As nongovernmental organizations proliferated throughout the world, community empowerment was being touted as a panacea for marginalized neighborhoods in the Global South (Friedmann 1993a). Civil society, a term with a long historical pedigree in political philosophy, had been reinvented by the liberation theology movement of the Catholic Church in Brazil and then in Latin America more generally (Lehmann 1990; Escobar and Alvarez 1992). Independent of its Latin American usage, it was also used to describe the source of political liberation as Eastern Europe shook off its decades-long yoke of communist rule (Cohen and Arato 1992). With these contemporary experiences as background, civil society was introduced into the vocabulary of planning in a book that included case studies from Porto Alegre, Frankfurt (Germany), Los Angeles, Santiago (Chile), and Pacific Rim cities (Douglass and Friedmann 1998; see also Friedmann, Abers, and Autler 1996).

[margin note: Deconstruct "who has the ownership of the situation?"]

In a major contribution to the literature at roughly the same time, Healey's (1997) *Collaborative Planning* argued persuasively that the challenges of urban development in the neoliberal era could no longer be handled effectively by government alone but required the participation of all sectors of society in a form of planning that involved dialogue and negotiations among stakeholders seeking an actionable consensus. Consensus building among people with conflicting interests, however, often required the intervention of mediators, and by the end of the century mediation had become an important new branch not only of planning but of legal studies as well (LeBaron 2002). Larry Susskind and John Forester made key contributions to this new specialization, the first in a series of publications culminating in *The Consensus Building Handbook: A comprehensive guide to reaching agreement* (Susskind, McKearnen, and Thomas-Lamar 1999), the second in *The Deliberative Practitioner: Encouraging participatory planning processes* (Forester 1999). Not all planning theorists, however, saw consensus building as the wave of the future. In *Rationality and Power*, Flyvbjerg (1998b) embraced a model of planning that was based explicitly on the writings of Machiavelli, Nietzsche, and Foucault. It was a trenchant critique of planning that acknowledged the inevitable presence in society of differences in power and the ability of different groups to use it. "In a Foucauldian interpretation," Flyvbjerg (1998a: 209) writes, "suppressing conflict is suppressing freedom, because the privilege to engage in conflict is part of freedom." Thus, he expressed skepticism about the non-politicized processes of mediation and building consensus.

Mediations notwithstanding, and with the appearance of an increasingly vocal and politically active civil society, politics and therefore conflict around

[margin note: whose civil society? (brought this up last week)]

values and priorities have become central to planning. James Holston ([1995] 1999), an urban anthropologist who has done extensive field work in Brazil, introduced the term *insurgent citizenship*, which was subsequently adopted by Sandercock, who made insurgent practices central to her path-breaking work on accommodating difference in the contemporary metropolis, though she was quick to point out that "conflict" around differences need not be violent. In an urban world, she wrote, insurgencies can result from "a thousand tiny *can they?* empowerments" rather than from revolutionary adventures (Sandercock 1998b: 129–59). Like Lindblom, she knew that big changes often come from an accumulation of many small ones. Although dialogue and mediation have their place in the political life of cities, where power differences are great, and *Agree.* fundamental worldviews or strongly held principles are at stake, such as the universal right to housing, mediation cannot be the default position. Political struggles are needed.[9]

In concluding this part of the essay, I want to mention a final planning invention that owes as much to theory as to practice. I have in mind the new interest in "visioning" that has emerged in response to the increasingly fragmentary character of planning practices that either are project focused or take place only in isolated local neighborhoods slated for redevelopment. In Europe, visioning exercises are often referred to as "spatial strategies" (Healey *et al* 1997; Albrechts 2004; Healey 2006, 2007). For Healey, who has been a leading voice expressing this approach in places such as Northern Ireland and the Amsterdam region, spatial strategies have transformative potential. They are meant to enlarge the thinking of policy communities, to explore new options in a coordinated way but without requiring a formal commitment to carry them out. In her latest book, she explains,

> Strategy-making, understood relationally, involves connecting knowledge resources and relational resources ... to generate mobilization force. Such resources form in institutional sites in governance landscapes from which a strategic framing discourse diffuses outwards ... Efforts in strategy-making may be initiated in many different institutional sites, but to have significant effects, the mobilization dynamic ... has to move towards arenas that are central to accessing the resources (over which a strategy needs) to gain influence. (Healey 2007: 198)

Summary:

When we look back over the past half-century, as I have done here, it is amazing to note the changes that have occurred in our thinking about planning and its practices. I have tried to track some of the relevant theoretical debates, and if I were to summarize I would say that three big shifts have occurred. The *first* has been toward making planning more of a *whole-society process* rather than primarily a technical one (e.g. Healey 2007: 280–2). As a corollary, the *second* shift has turned planning increasingly into a *political art,* with planners needing to be acutely aware of power and the difference that power makes (Flyvbjerg 1998b). Practicing planners now have a stake in certain outcomes and therefore need to be clever in devising ways that will allow them to insert their own values and perspectives into ongoing (societal) decision processes (Krumholz and Forester 1990). A *third* shift has been the direct engagement of planners with the art of getting things done and so with planning in "real time" (Pressman and Wildavsky 1984; Friedmann 1993b; Albrechts and Lievois 2004). Today's planners are no longer merely analysts advising politicians; they have (or can) become *political actors* in their own right. Forester (1999) has put the political in the context of mediation and conflict resolution in which, echoing Bent Flyvbjerg, he prioritizes "practical judgment."

Before proceeding to planning theory's third task, let me recall the major "adaptations" over the past fifty years or so to the continually changing if not turbulent context in which planning practice is embedded in North America: *dialogue, social learning, mutual learning, social participation, collaboration, mediation, social mobilization, social and political empowerment,* and *strategic planning or visioning.* Taken together, these terms and the theories to which they are linked have contributed to changing the face of our profession.

Planning theory as the work of translation

Planning theory, like planning practice, is an eclectic or, put more elegantly, an interdisciplinary, even transdisciplinary field. As planners, we have a growing literature of our own, of course, and our professoriate is increasingly homegrown rather than imported from allied disciplines. This was not always the case, however, and as a planning student at the University of Chicago, virtually all of my teachers were economists, geographers, sociologists, anthropologists, students of politics, communication specialists, various development types, and even the odd historian. Mel Branch, the first planning PhD out of Harvard's Graduate School of Design, was our physical planner, but his was a lone voice for the city as artifact among a faculty of social scientists. The University of Chicago did not teach architecture, and an early attempt to link up with the Illinois Institute of Technology, which did architecture and urban design, failed to materialize because of the deep cognitive division between the design tradition and the critical-analytic social science orientation we professed. Nevertheless, we prided ourselves in being "interdisciplinary," a pride that would ultimately come to fall when 10 years after its founding the Program for Education and Research in Planning was redlined during a major budget crisis. In its wisdom, the university decided that if anything needed preserving, it was the disciplines with their large undergraduate following; a small, relatively young, interdisciplinary graduate program such as ours was dispensable.

Planners' work has mostly to do with urban and sometimes regional issues and their dynamics that cannot be properly understood except in a way that cuts across disciplines. Most graduate planning students are enrolled in a two-year master's program and tend to take, I would guess, 90 per cent of their course work in their own department rather than go "shopping" in the disciplines let alone in other professional schools. They tend therefore to imbibe most of their knowledge about planning from professors many of whom have themselves graduated from planning schools. There is plenty of diversity within their own department, of course, since a range of specializations, including transportation, public health, housing, urban design, community development, and the like, have nested under the planning umbrella. But two years is a short time, especially when core requirements take up a considerable portion of their time, and most students graduate as generalists with only a vague grasp of what the university as a whole has on offer.

Yet without reaching beyond its own borders in the search for pertinent knowledge, it is easy for planning to become more and more inward oriented, a professional field that defines itself chiefly by its own technical competencies. In the longer term, building walls around our little turf will inevitably lead to intellectual stasis. It is for this reason I want to argue for a third task of planning theory I call translation, a task that raises our horizon to include the vast field of human knowledge or perhaps, to speak with Leonie Sandercock, of knowledges in the plural (Sandercock 1998b: appendix).

I see planning theorists actively engaged in mining expeditions into the universe of knowledge, on the lookout for concepts and ideas they believe to be of interest in planning education. Their specific contribution to theory is to return from these expeditions to home base and translate their discoveries into the language of planning where they will either take root or be unceremoniously forgotten.

As discussion in the preceding parts of this essay has shown, planning theorists typically venture beyond the boundaries of their profession. Here then I will not try to reprise the transdisciplinary generation of planning knowledge. Instead, I will highlight the work of a leading planning theorist to whom we are indebted for expanding our understanding of the domain of planning: Susan S. Fainstein. I might equally have chosen other prominent scholars, such as Flyvbjerg, Forester, Sandercock, or Healey, whose writings have inspired generations of students. But space limitations prevent me from citing more examples.

Fainstein works from within a political economy tradition whose origins can be traced in Marxist and neo-Marxist writings. Her contributions to planning theory are distinctive in two ways. First, she has consistently eschewed abstract theorizing in favor of grounding theory in the realities of specific cities such as New York, London, or Amsterdam. Much of her work has been critical of planning and was frequently regarded as having more to do with the urban than with planning as such. Over the past two decades, however, and this is her second mark of distinction, she has been developing a normative basis for planning the "just city" (Fainstein 2000, 2006). As distinct from process theorists, she insists on the importance of looking at planning outcomes. What this means is that planning and, more specifically, planning theory cannot be studied apart from the study of particular cities and their political dynamics (Fainstein 1994).[10]

In her quest for the "good city," Fainstein not only critically examines alternative visions of the city, such as the new urbanism, but also engages authors who, though remote from most planning reading lists, have had much to say on how to think about the quality of urban life. Among them are John Rawls, Amartya Sen, Martha Nussbaum, Jürgen Habermas, and, most important, Iris Marion Young. Drawing specifically on Young (1990, 2000), she argues for a politics of collective identities, of groupings according to gender, race, sexual orientation, and immigrant status beyond those of social class, which had been the tradition on the Marxist Left throughout most of the nineteenth and twentieth centuries. She also supersedes the customary equity argument of this tradition by arguing not merely for greater income equality but also for improvements in the total circumstances of life of both poor and middle-income groups in their particular living environments. She writes, "Failure to acknowledge the coherence of collectivities and their structural relationship to each other evades a fundamental social issue of redistribution – how to avoid imposing an unacceptable burden on the better-off. How much social conflict is an acceptable price to pay for greater justice? What circumstances allow the diminution of control (political and material) of those who have a disproportionate amount?" (Fainstein 2006). Increasingly, her writings emphasize society's stake in better services, amenities, and other collective goods for everyone.

Fainstein is painfully aware of the difficulties faced by a progressive politics in the United States. But, she says, it is important to remain optimistic. "By continuing to converse about justice, we can make it central to the activity of planning. The very act of naming has power" (Fainstein 2006).

Conclusion

I have argued that doing planning theory has three tasks that are central to its endeavors: the philosophical task of evolving a humanist philosophy to guide planners in their work, the task of adapting planning practices to the continually changing course of human events, and the task of translating knowledges and concepts from fields other than planning into our own language. I see these tasks as making a distinctive contribution to the planning literature and ultimately to professional practice as well.

★ what Friedmann sees as the main point of

I have also tried to show how pursuing these tasks gradually affects planning intervention practices, usually via professional education, when students are first introduced to academic discourses in the field. As an integrative, transdisciplinary field of studies, planning addresses life in all of its on-the-ground complexity. Such an understanding of its mission cannot dispense with a normative foundation such as human flourishing and the just city, which of course will be always contested, forever remaining "under construction." In a rapidly changing world, the planning profession needs also to continually adjust its orientation to what is happening, as these changes are interpreted by an array of disciplines supplemented by planners' own perceptions and experiences. Finally, these two tasks call for a third, a reaching out beyond one's own bit of turf to bring back to our workshops at home the insights gained from the knowledge pursuits of others. These three tasks are what I regard as central to the concerns of planning theorists and as essential to the vitality of our field.

Notes

1. A right is any claim, individual or collective, on organized society and its institutions, even though not all such claims are universally acknowledged (Sen 1999). Derived from the human right to flourishing are "human needs" that can serve as guideposts to planning work, such as Max-Neef's "matrix of human needs" that is based on the four existential categories of being, having, doing, and interacting (Daly and Farley 2004: 239–40).
2. Two exceptions to this generalization come to mind: Abers (2000) and Hajer and Waagenar (2003). Both have one foot in planning and another in political science.
3. A significant spin-off from Dewey is the pragmatic communicative action theory of Charles Hoch (2007), as well as Harper and Stein's (2006) "neo-pragmatic" planning theory.
4. Bent Flyvbjerg has brought to my attention the edited volume *Making Political Science Matter* (Schram and Caterino 2007), in which his theories of *phronesis* or practical judgment are taken up by a number of political scientists – a rare but significant instance where a planning academic has influenced political theory.
5. For another formulation by the originator of the deliberative democracy debate, see Cohen (1998); for critiques, the volume by Elster (1998) is probably the best starting point.
6. In principle, urban design could be faced with the same skepticism, but the language of design is foreign to most people who are prepared to leave designs to star architects or architectural juries adjudicating among alternative visions.
7. For a trenchant critique of what planners can know "reliably," see Lindblom and Cohen (1979).
8. Organized labor, never very interested in local planning issues, was further marginalized through antiunion legislation and the ongoing processes of deindustrialization.
9. For a brilliant analysis of the unresolved tension between consensus and power conflicts as directions of political practice, see Mouffe (2005).
10. Sandercock's (1977, 1990) political economy of land deals in Melbourne (Australia) is an early precursor to Fainstein's analysis.

Bibliography

Abers, R. (2000) *Inventing Local Democracy: Grassroots politics in Brazil*, Boulder, CO: Lynne Rienner.

Albrechts, L. (2004) 'Strategic (spatial) planning reexamined', *Environment and Planning B: Planning and Design*, 31: 743–58.

Albrechts, L. and Lievois, G. (2004) 'The Flemish diamond: urban network in the making?', *European Planning Studies*, 12: 351–70.

Altshuler, A. and Luberoff, D. (2003) *Mega-projects: The politics of urban public investment*, Washington DC: Brookings Institution.

Argyris, C. and Schön, D.A. (1978) *Organizational Learning: A theory of action perspective*, Reading, MA: Addison-Wesley.

Ballon, H. and Jackson, K.T. (eds) (2003) *Robert Moses and the Modern City: The transformation of New York*, New York: Norton.

Bluestone, B. and Harrison, B. (1982) *The Deindustrialization of America*, New York: Basic Books.

Buber, M. (1965) *The Knowledge of Man: Selected essays*, (ed.) M. Friedman, New York: HarperCollins.

Castells, M. (1983) *The City and the Grassroots: A cross-cultural theory of urban social movement*, Berkeley: University of California Press.

——(1996) *The Rise of the Network Society*, Cambridge, MA: Blackwell.

Clark, M.E. (2002) *In Search of Human Nature*, London: Routledge.

Cohen, J. (1998) 'Democracy and liberty', in J. Elster (ed.) *Deliberative Democracy*, Cambridge, UK: Cambridge University Press.

Cohen, J.L. and Arato, A. (1992) *Civil Society and Political Theory*, Cambridge, MA: MIT Press.

Daly, H.E. and Farley, J. (2004) *Ecological Economics*, Washington, DC: Island Press.

Davidoff, P. (1965) 'Advocacy and pluralism in planning', *Journal of the American Institute of Planning*, 31 (4): 331–8.

Douglass, M. and Friedmann, J. (eds) (1998) *Cities for Citizens: Planning and the rise of civil society in a global age*, New York: John Wiley.

Elster, J. (ed.) (1998) *Deliberative Democracy*, Cambridge, UK: Cambridge University Press.

Escobar, A. and Alvarez, S.E. (eds) (1992) *The Making of Social Movements in Latin America: Identity, strategy, democracy*, Boulder, CO: Westview.

Etzioni, A. (1968) *The Active Society: A theory of societal and political processes*, New York: Free Press.

Fainstein, S.S. (1994) *The City Builders: Property development in New York and London, 1980–2000*, Oxford, UK: Blackwell.

——(2000) 'New directions in planning theory', *Urban Affairs Review*, 35 (4): 451–78.

——(2006) 'Planning and the just city', paper presented at the Conference on Searching the Just City, Columbia University, New York.

Flyvbjerg, B. (1998a) Empowering civil society: Habermas, Foucault and the question of conflict, in M. Douglass and J. Friedmann (eds) *Cities for Citizens: Planning and the rise of civil society in a global age*, New York: John Wiley.

——(1998b) *Rationality and Power: Democracy in practice*, Chicago: University of Chicago Press.

Flyvbjerg, B., Bruzelius, N. and Rothengatter, W. (2003) *Megaprojects and Risks: An anatomy of ambition*, New York: Cambridge University Press.

Forester, J. (1989) *Planning in the Face of Power*, Berkeley: University of California Press.

——(1999) *The Deliberative Practitioner: Encouraging participatory planning processes*, Cambridge, MA: MIT Press.

Friedmann, J. (1973) *Retracking America: A theory of transactive planning*, Garden City, NY: Anchor/Doubleday.

——(1979) *The Good Society*, Cambridge, MA: MIT Press.

——(1987) *Planning in the Public Domain: From knowledge to action*, Princeton, NJ: Princeton University Press.

——(1993a) *Empowerment: The politics of alternative development*, Oxford, UK: Blackwell.

——(1993b) 'Toward a non-Euclidean mode of planning', *Journal of American Planning Association*, 59 (3): 482–5.

——(2002) *The Prospect of Cities*, Minneapolis: University of Minnesota Press.

Friedmann, J., Abers, R. and Autler, L. (eds) (1996) *Emergences: Women's struggles for livelihood in Latin America*, UCLA Latin American Studies Vol. 82, Los Angeles: University of California, Los Angeles, Latin American Center Publications.

Fung, A. (2004) *Empowered Participation: Reinventing urban democracy*, Princeton, NJ: Princeton University Press.

Fung, A., Wright, E.O. and Abers, R. (eds) (2003) *Deepening Democracy: Institutional innovations in empowered participatory governance*, London: Verso.

Gutmann, A. and Thompson, D. (2004) *Why Deliberative Democracy?* Princeton, NJ: Princeton University Press.

Hajer, M. and Waagenar, H. (2003) *Deliberative Policy Analysis: Understanding policy analysis in the network society*, Cambridge, UK: Cambridge University Press.

Harper, T.L. and Stein, S.M. (2006) *Dialogical Planning in a Fragmented Society*, New Brunswick, NJ: Center for Urban Policy Research Press.

Harrison, B. and Bluestone, B. (1988) *The Great U-turn: Corporate restructuring and the polarizing of America*, New York: Basic Books.

Hartman, C.W. (2002) *Between Eminence and Notoriety: Four decades of radical urban planning*, New Brunswick, NJ: Center for Policy Research.

Harvey, D. (1982) *The Limits of Capital*, Oxford, UK: Blackwell.

——(1988) *The Condition of Post-modernity*, Oxford, UK: Blackwell.

——(2003) *Paris: Capital of modernity*, London: Routledge.

Healey, P. (1997) *Collaborative Planning: Shaping places in fragmented societies*, London: Macmillan.

——(2006) 'Relational/complexity and the imaginative power of strategic spatial planning', *European Planning Studies*, 14: 525–46.

——(2007) *Urban Complexity and Spatial Strategies: Towards a relational planning for our times*, London: Routledge.

Healey, P., Khakee, A., Motte, A. and Needham, B. (eds) (1997) *Making Strategic Spatial Plans: Innovation in Europe*, London: UCL Press.

Hester, R.T. (2006) *Design for Ecological Democracy*, Cambridge, MA: MIT Press.

Hoch, C.J. (2007) 'Pragmatic communicative action theory', *Journal of Planning Education and Research*, 26 (3): 272–83.

Holston, J. ([1995] 1999) 'Spaces of insurgent citizenship', in J. Holston (ed.) *Cities and Citizenship*, Durham, NC: Duke University Press.

Innes, J.E. and Booher, D.E. (2003) 'Collaborative policy making: governance through dialogue', in M. Hajer and H. Wagenaar (eds) *Deliberative Policy Analysis: Understanding governance in the network society*, Cambridge, UK: Cambridge University Press.

Krumholz, N. and Forester, J. (1990) *Making Equity Planning Work: Leadership in the public sector*, Philadelphia: Temple University Press.

Kunstler, J.H. (2006) *The Long Emergency*, New York: Grove Press.

LeBaron, M. (2002) *Bridging Troubled Waters: Conflict resolution from the heart*, San Francisco: Jossey-Bass.

Lehmann, D. (1990) *Democracy and Development in Latin America: Economics, politics and religion in the post-war period*, Philadelphia: Temple University Press.

Lindblom, C.E. (1959) 'The science of muddling through', *Public Administration Review*, 19 (2): 79–99.

Lindblom, C.E. and Cohen, D.K. (1979) *Usable Knowledge: Social science and social problem solving*, New Haven, CT: Yale University Press.

Mandel, E. (1975) *Late Capitalism*, Atlantic Highlands, NJ: Humanities Press.

Mouffe, C. (1992) *Dimensions of Radical Democracy: pluralism, citizenship, community*, London: Verso.

——(2005) *On the Political*, London: Verso.

Mumford, L. (1938) *The Culture of Cities*, New York: Harcourt Brace.

Polanyi, K. (1977) *The Livelihood of Man*, (ed.) H.W. Pearson, London: Academic Press.

Porter, M.E. (2001) 'Regions and the new economics of competition', in A.J. Scott (ed.) *Global City-regions*, Oxford: Oxford University Press.

Pressman, J.L. and Wildavsky, A. (1984) *Implementation*, Berkeley: University of California Press.

Sandercock, L. (1977) *Cities for Sale*, Melbourne, Australia: Melbourne University Press.

——(1990) *Property, Politics, & Urban Planning: A history of Australian city planning 1890–1990*, 2nd edn, New Brunswick, NJ: Transaction Books.

——(1998a) (ed.) *Making the Invisible Visible: A multicultural history of planning*, Berkeley: University of California Press.

——(1998b) *Towards Cosmopolis: Planning for multicultural cities*, New York: John Wiley.

Schram, S.F. and Caterino, B. (2007) *Making Political Science Matter*, New York: New York University Press.

Selle, K. (ed.) (2006) *Zur räumlichen Entwicklung beitragen. Planung neu denken*, Vol. 1, Dortmund, Germany: Dorothea Rohn.

Sen, A. (1999) *Development as Freedom*, Oxford, UK: Oxford University Press.

Soja, E. W. (2010) *Seeking Spatial Justice*. Minneapolis: University of Minnesota Press.

Sorensen, A. (2002) *The Making of Urban Japan*, London: Routledge.

Susskind, L., McKearnen, S. and Thomas-Lamar, J. (1999) *The Consensus Building Handbook: A comprehensive guide to reaching agreement*, Thousand Oaks, CA: Sage.

Wolin, S. ([1960] 2004) *Politics and Vision: Continuity and innovation in Western political thought*, expanded edn, Princeton, NJ: Princeton University Press.

Yiftachel, O. (1998) 'Planning and social control: exploring the dark side', *Journal of Planning Literature*, 12: 396–406.

Young, I.M. (1990) *Justice and the Politics of Difference*, Princeton, NJ: Princeton University Press.

——(2000) *Inclusion and Democracy*, Oxford, UK: Oxford University Press.

Study questions

This essay argues for the practical relevance of planning theory. I identify three tasks that characterize the work of planning theorists: evolving a philosophical basis for planning, adapting planning thought and practices to ever changing world conditions, and traveling across the boundaries of the planning field to other academic disciplines in search of concepts and empirical generalizations that might be fruitfully applied in our own practices. This last is perhaps the reason why planning is considered to be a multidisciplinary and even, as some would say, transdisciplinary field. The task of translation involved in these forays into other disciplines is important for keeping planning aligned with the best current thinking across the human, social, and natural sciences.

Leaving this last task aside, let us turn to the question of an appropriate philosophical basis for planning. One way to begin to think about this is to ask the very broad, very basic question of what it means to be human. One answer, or rather set of answers is given by the anthro-ecological model of limits presented in the work of Mary E. Clark (see additional readings below). Here are some related questions.

What sort of limits are identified by this model? And in what ways does the model constrain human flourishing, which I propose as a fundamental value for planning? Can planners take it for granted that human flourishing is a universal human right? What do we do when it is contested, for example, in societies in which human flourishing is not granted to women? Or when it is denied to people born into poverty? Other scholars, such as Susan Fainstein, have given pride of place to the fundamental value of social justice. What, then, is the connection between human flourishing and social justice as fundamental values for planners? Are they complementary or opposed to each other? Do they suggest different priorities for practice, or different strategies? Would social justice have wider applicability than human flourishing?

This chapter assumes that planning must be a value-based practice. This is an axiomatic principle adopted by some planning theorists, such as Bent Flyvbjerg and Leonie Sandercock who are working with the Aristotelian principle of *phronesis* or practical wisdom (see additional readings below). Others, however, would seriously contest this principle, arguing for the essential value neutrality of planning or, as Aron Wildavsky has claimed, that policy analysts should "speak truth to power."

Do you agree with Wildavsky? Or, alternatively, given the long tradition of pragmatist thinking in planning (see Patsy Healey, below), do you believe that planners should abandon values altogether for whatever may be expedient? Do planners have primary responsibility towards, alternatively: their client, employer, the public at large? Or should they put – as many have argued – the least privileged first? And finally, do planners deal with "truths" at all? In value-based planning, can there even be such a thing as "truth"? And if not, why not? In what ways are truth and value relevance linked to each other?

The second major task of planning theory is to keep planning practice pertinent in a world that is in constant movement. I call this the task of adaptation. Towards the end of the chapter, a set of planning innovations is named that includes dialogue, social learning, social participation, collaboration, mediation, social mobilization, social empowerment and strategic planning. All these innovations occurred over the course of the past 50 years, primarily in the Western world of Europe and North America.

Choosing one or two of these terms, to what specific conditions in the real world were these planning innovations a response? And what pressing challenges are there today as we begin the second decade of the 21st century, such as climate change, the prospect of so-called peak-oil, and overshoot of the ecological footprint? What are some possible planning responses to these urgent questions that affect us all, and what planning concepts are likely to be applied, as we face these challenges (see the Epilogue to this book for some hints on how you might want to answer this question)?

Selected additional readings

Castells, M. (1983) *The City and the Grassroots: A cross-cultural theory of urban social movements*, Berkeley: University of California Press.

——(1996) *The Rise of the Network Society*, Cambridge, MA: MIT Press.

Clark, M.E. (1989) *Ariadne's Thread: The search for new modes of thinking*, New York: Palgrave Macmillan.

——(2002) *In Search of Human Nature*, London: Routledge.

Healey, P. (2009) 'The pragmatist tradition in planning thought', *Journal of Planning Education and Research*, 28: 277–92.

——(2010) 'In search of the "strategic" in spatial strategy making', *Planning Theory & Practice*, 10: 439–57.

Sandercock, L. and Attili, G. (forthcoming) 'Unsettling a settler society: film, phronesis and collaborative planning in small-town Canada', in B. Flyvbjerg *et al* (eds) *Real Social Science*, Cambridge: University Press.

Epilogue: citizen planners in an era of limits

In relatively developed countries, much of today's planning discourse is about what we call the sustainable city, about cities becoming "smart" or "green." This discourse has spilled over into other fields as well. For example, the *Financial Post* of my hometown newspaper, the *Vancouver Sun*, recently published an article, "It's not just about being green," by Tima Bansal, director of the Centre for Building Sustainable Value at the Richard Ivey School of Business at the University of Western Ontario (September 23, 2009, p. D6). What she means to say is this: "Sustainability is often assumed to be just about being green or being good. But, it's more than that – it's also about being profitable."

That may be appropriate advice to business people, but it is not my meaning for this chapter. Sustainability is not only about the triple bottom line of physical environment, social justice, and economic viability. Sustainability may be a good political slogan, but it doesn't tell us what to do. To bring a fairer, more livable city into being, we have to go beyond mouthing slogans.

What we should think about is how to reshape the city and its region in ways that are not simply a linear projection of present trends, but actions that will eventually lead to an historic break with both past and present arrangements. It is scarcely news to say that we are living in an interdependent world, and if we care for ourselves at home, we must equally care for those who are distant from us but whose predicament is as much our responsibility as theirs. We all have a stake in planet Earth. We have a shared responsibility.

My view, then, is as much global as it is particular and local. We don't necessarily have to agree on the actions I will detail below. But we have to start somewhere, and here are some thoughts about what strategies are necessary so that we don't end up destroying the very things we love the most.

I will propose six strategies for the good city. They are strategies for individuals, groups, and networks dedicated to positive change. Having listed them, I will then try to clarify and, to some degree, justify them, one by one:

1. Learn to live with the reality of a finite material world, a *world of limits*.
2. Work towards an *ecologically sustainable, resilient city*.
3. Work towards a local economy that, as a matter of priority, is oriented to the *satisfaction of basic human needs*.
4. Devise systems of accounting in which the *production of both use values and market-valued goods and services* are acknowledged as equally important, and where the production of the former is strategically promoted to create more livable cities.
5. Work towards *a convivial city that nourishes the spirit*, cherishes the diversity of its citizens, engages in fashioning a mosaic of distinctive neighborhoods, and harbors inclusive democratic institutions.
6. Restore a sense of *civic virtues* as a mark of local citizenship, a commitment to and pride in creating convivial, livable, urban places through deliberative practices.

1. Learn to live with the reality of a finite material world, a world of limits

The material world on which human life depends for sustenance and survival is a finite world. Only our spiritual life in all its multiple forms – mathematics, mysticism, creative imagination – is unlimited.

Capitalist ideology has assumed otherwise. Believers argue that economic growth, and its correlates, is unconstrained by any limits, that the material world harbors inexhaustible riches that are ours, by right, to appropriate and enjoy. Human ingenuity, they assert, will somehow discover technical solutions to any problems that might arise from presumptive limits such as "peak-oil." We can fool ourselves for a while into believing this by shifting the negative consequences of cumulative growth to weaker countries whose own struggles for survival often take self-destructive, atavistic forms, or by displacing them into a far-off dystopia that may or may not come to pass.

Belief in the reality of unlimited growth is actually quite new, no more than 50 or 60 years old, and was given the appearance of a natural fact only by the invention of national economic accounts and of universal indicators of progress such as the gross domestic product. This measure, widely used now as a guide to economic policy, was critiqued from the beginning. Attempts to introduce alternative indicators, such as the United Nations' Human Development Index and the ecological footprint, have to date had little practical impact. The latest critical assault is a report prepared for French President Sarkozy by co-chairs Joseph Stiglitz and Amartya Sen which was released in September 2009.[1] The authors argue that measures of sustainability and human well-being (including data on the distribution of income and wealth) be added as proper guides to public policy.

Measures of economic growth are usually constructed at the national level. At sub-national levels, however, policy makers and planners rely on these same faulty indicators, even though they have the opportunity to devise rich data profiles for their respective areas – neighborhoods, towns, cities, and regions – and use these data in a balanced way to ensure a healthy environment and a good quality of life for local citizens. To create livable cities and regions, we need more complex policy guides.

2. Work towards an ecologically sustainable, resilient city

A great deal has been written about the sustainable city, now sometimes referred to also as a resilient city.[2] But the evidence for what is actually sustainable, or will move us closer to a dynamic long-term equilibrium, is scattered, with some cities doing a great deal better than others. And indeed, *every* city has work to do if it wants to move closer to the desired end state.

What needs doing is, first of all, acquiring a new mindset, a deeper philosophical understanding that cities are embedded in a natural environment that stands in symbiotic relationship with them. Some would call it a bio-regional philosophy. At the beginning of the 20th century, Patrick Geddes and Lewis Mumford were among the first to trace its lineaments. Today there are many variants of bio-regionalism. For example, one of my students, Sarah Church, argues that bioregionalism "promotes active participation and collaboration in creating place and a politics of place. This is done through connecting people to their place within nature and ecology, through changing the urban form to respond to nature and ecology, by restoring and maintaining the ecology of the city's place, and through committing ... to the local environment and the community as a whole" (unpublished paper 2009). In her view, bio-regionalism is both a specific process and a set of desired outcomes.

Once an appropriate philosophy is embraced, the second step is to carry it forward into practice. There are many ways this can be done, not only by changing personal behavior, such as eating locally grown food, but also by devising and implementing public policies such as investing in public transit rather than highway construction. Efforts are now being made to change building codes that will lead to energy conservation, lay out a net of bicycle paths for leisure and commuting, promote the adoption of solar energy, encourage urban agriculture and tree planting, take energetic measures to reduce air and water pollution, encourage recycling, and so forth, all of which are designed to reduce the city's ecological footprint while encouraging a healthier, convivial life.

3. Work towards a local economy that, as a matter of priority, is oriented to the satisfaction of basic human needs

Robert Chambers of the Sussex Institute of Development Studies once used a biblical phrase to make an emphatic point: *the last shall be first.* That is the matter of priority to which a basic needs strategy makes reference. For countries that have already achieved a certain level of material affluence and which the World Bank calls "upper middle-level income" countries, its priorities should ensure the social integration of all citizens, especially the poorest among them, by honoring their claims for basic human needs of food, water, housing, access to good health, and an education appropriate for a full, productive life. For other countries, where the majority are poor, priorities must be different, and international income transfers from rich to poor should become mandatory.

Once born into this world, we all claim certain rights by virtue of being human. Among these are non-material rights, such as the claim to life itself and human dignity, as well as material rights, such as to decent housing and good health. It is the lack of access to material rights such as these in countries where the majority of the population lives well in excess of what are basic levels of satisfaction that leads to my third strategy for a resilient city, which could also be called a strategy for eliminating mass poverty.

In British Columbia, Canada's western-most province, which has been my home for the last nine years, at least one out of five persons lives at or below the poverty line. By some estimates, the proportion is higher. Mass poverty is thus an unacknowledged fact of Canadian life. There are welfare provisions, and there is universal health insurance for everyone. But, one by one, welfare provisions are being eliminated from public budgets, and homelessness is increasing. Anti-poverty legislation is not high on either provincial or federal legislative agendas.

4. *Devise systems of accounting in which the production of both use values and market-valued goods and services are acknowledged as equally important, and where the production of the former is strategically promoted to create more livable cities*

When we talk about "the economy," no one thinks of the immense volume of necessary work performed outside the monetary economy and which is generally referred to as the direct production of use values. A significant proportion of this work is devoted to "social reproduction" and takes place in people's homes: the preparation of food, the nurturing of the sick, the birthing and rearing of children, the caring for the frail elderly. Traditionally, this has been largely but not exclusively women's work, and it is typically unpaid. But there is more to the production of use values and which we refer to as voluntary work. Many not-for-profit organizations, such as music festivals or neighborhood centers, engage hundreds of volunteers who, without getting paid, devote their time, skills, and energy in support of one or another cause. The contributions of volunteers are often acknowledged "in-house," but to the larger public, their work remains invisible. And yet, adding up the numbers, voluntary contributions to society are immense, whether through non-profit organizations, churches, or community-based agencies, among many others. Volunteers are often retired folks who discover new meaning in their lives by becoming engaged in schools, hospitals, and other institutions, using a lifetime of experience to make these institutions more effective.[3]

And yet, wherever performed, unpaid work is left out of the official bookkeeping of cities and regions. The fourth strategy is therefore intended to make unpaid work a fully legitimate part of cities' economic life and a measure of its societal well-being. When viewed against prevalent trends in many countries, such as prolonged life spans, aging populations, rising educational thresholds for employment, and the adoption of technologies that increase production but do not add significant numbers of full-time jobs, a regime that has come to be known as "job-less growth," the importance of such a strategy acquires even greater urgency.

In a society where "success" is typically measured by how much money one makes, people who earn nothing are seen as parasites on the social body, a view that diminishes their sense of self-worth. What I have in mind here is therefore more than an annual honors roll for mothers and volunteers, but an active promotion of unpaid work through capacity building, volunteer exchanges, and other forms of channeling unpaid human energy into socially useful work. Single mothers could be paid the equivalent of what they would earn in the economy to nurture their young children. Youths for whom paid jobs may not exist might be guided into voluntary work such as environmental reclamation, and perhaps paid stipends to do such work. Old folks and youngsters could be partnered in various creative ways. In a society that is no longer single-mindedly devoted to unlimited cumulative expansion (see strategy 1), new ways must be found to make people feel wanted and useful even when they are not competing in the labor market. This is especially important for rapidly aging societies, where the expected lifespan is steadily rising.

5. Work towards a convivial city that nourishes the spirit, cherishes the diversity of its citizens, engages in fashioning a mosaic of its distinctive neighborhoods, and harbors inclusive democratic institutions

The fifth strategy is designed to accomplish a gradual shift from a materialist present to an increasingly dematerialized city in which the social and cultural dimensions of collective life trump consumerism, and creativity in all its forms is celebrated. By the fact of their (relative) non-materiality, it is the one dimension of our world that is not absolutely limited. I call this the transition from the city of consumption to the ludic city.[4]

Diversity is the lifeblood of creativity; encounters with different world views and ways of being in the world stimulate creative activity. While the creative act itself remains mysterious, urban diversity and the conviviality associated with it forms the essential context. Urban diversity is not a random but highly structured phenomenon, and much of it is spatially deployed. One of the crucial elements for the dematerialization of urban life is therefore the revitalization of urban neighborhoods, by which I mean small, centered, and walkable urban spaces whose character is a result, though never fully intended and always in flux, of human activity. It is the city of small spaces – its squares, tea rooms, coffee houses, libraries, skateboard parks, abandoned warehouses, and other tucked-away public and semi-public spaces – that generate the convivial life as a context for creative practice.

Creative life embraces diversity; it also claims a democratic disposition in which all voices, including those contrary to one's own, can be heard. Institutions of a certain kind are needed to ensure that this happens, and that all views, not only those of hierarchical authority, are granted a fair hearing. Creativity, I would argue, flourishes when authoritative voices can be fearlessly challenged. Certain institutions are necessary for this to happen. Creative ideas inevitably challenge the status quo and the authoritative structures that maintain it. Non-violent conflict lies at the core of the creative, ludic city.

6. *Restore a sense of civic virtues as a mark of local citizenship, a commitment to and pride in creating convivial, livable, urban places through deliberative practices*

In a world still dominated by neo-liberal cant, with hedonistic individualism running rampant, the idea of civic virtue sounds out of sync with the times. Along with the idea of the Athenian *polis* to which, as Aristotle argued, we owe the very meaning of our life, it has vanished from contemporary discourse. In classical Greece, to be expelled from the *polis* was to suffer a fate worse than death. This is why Socrates chose to take poison rather than to flee into exile abroad. Today, when all the talk is about rights, hardly anyone still talks of civic obligations. From time to time, the President of the United States will admonish Americans to be better consumers, to open their purses and go shopping. Other than this, the only civic obligation we apparently still have is to pay taxes. In most democracies even voting has become optional.

The sixth and final strategy, then, which is a call to civic virtue, seems faintly ridiculous to most people, as though our liberties had no more transcendent meaning than "free trade" which, as ideologues would have it, is the condition of our freedom, thus leaving us to shop ourselves all the way into bankruptcy.

What do I mean by civic virtue? One answer is to acknowledge the reality of something that we seem to have forgotten: *the public good.* In a fragmented political community that barely holds together, this may be a difficult pill to swallow. And yet, pure Hobbesian anarchy is loosed upon the world if political community is denied – the case of so-called failed states, from Somalia to Afghanistan. Except as meaning emerges from a political discourse this side of violence, the public good has no specific connotation. And this is the reason, indeed, it is the only reason, why a deliberative democracy is an essential part of our project: to give each and every one of us a chance to help to give shape to a specific and shared vision of ourselves as a political community. And that means we have to keep talking. It is a never-ending conversation. It is also a daily practice.

These conversations take place at different scales. For local citizens, they come together in the public spaces of urban neighborhoods, small towns, and villages. It is in these places of encounter, where something like a *polis* can perhaps be recreated, as we inform each other about our thoughts and questions of what we understand by the good life. And then take the appropriate actions to make it happen. This was the vision articulated over half a century ago by Hanna Arendt (1958). Perhaps the time for it has come.

My argument has been that the sustainable city as conventionally understood is not enough. I have proposed six interconnected strategies for the transition from where we are today to a time some decades from now when capitalism will have to be reined in and economics subordinated as a means to more transcendent ends than profits and consumption. In a finite material world, the only unconstrained frontier is cultural creativity in all its forms.

This argument is valid, I maintain, for countries that have already attained a certain level of affluence, say, of approximately PPP\$10,000 per capita.[5] Countries that fall below this measure, such as Haiti, have an obligation that is shared with wealthier countries to further their own economic future as a matter of priority. Above this threshold, however, they should direct their collective imagination to a higher, more spiritual form of civilization in which the realm of necessity can finally yield pride of place to human freedom.[6]

Notes

1. "The Measurement of Economic Performance and Social Progress Revisited," as reported in the *New York Times*, September 15, 2009.
2. Resilience is a relatively new facet or dimension of urban sustainability. It refers to the capacity of cities and regions to respond creatively to "serious threats and disruptive events, including economic crisis, dangerous climate change, extreme weather events, rapid demographic flows, terror campaigns, utility network disruption, and social and political unrest" (Association of American Geographers, 2010 annual meeting, special series organized by the Regional Studies Association, call for papers). For a concise exposition of *ecological* resilience thinking, see B. Walker and D. Salt (2006).
3. In a comprehensive study, C.C. Williams (2007) presents a typology of work which distinguishes between formal and informal work, and where the latter is further divided into self-provisioning, unpaid community work, and paid informal exchange (p. 15). Citing data for the year 2000, based on time-budget studies, *unpaid* work in the United States absorbed 58.5 per cent of total working time. The corresponding proportion of *formal (paid)* work was only 41.6 per cent.

4. In thinking of the ludic city, you may want to consider the role of rituals and festivals in everyday life.
5. PPP = purchasing price parity, an adjustment of GDP based on cost of living indices and prepared by the World Bank. Several Latin American countries, including Argentina, Brazil, Chile, Costa Rica, Mexico, Panama, and Venezuela fall within the suggested range. I cite these countries by way of examples. Obviously, other criteria, especially income distribution and non-monetary indicators of human well-being are additionally needed to suggest a middle-range of economic affluence and human well-being beyond which further economic growth as currently calculated is unlikely to lead to further increases in happiness.
6. Space limitations prevent me from addressing the question of how these strategies might be enacted. Let me merely mention that fruitful explorations might be conducted along the lines of J. Huizinga, a Dutch historian, who coined the term *homo ludens*. His book has become a classic (Huizinga 1970). Williams (2007) also contains many fascinating examples of post-capitalist experiments and imaginings. Finally, a seminal study by A. Gorz (1999), as well as several of his other writings, is worth reflection.

Bibliography

Arendt, H. (1958) *The Human Condition*, University of Chicago Press.

Gorz, A. (1999) *Reclaiming Work: Beyond the wage-based society*, Cambridge: Polity.

Huizinga, J. (1970) *Homo Ludens: A study of the play element in culture*, London: Maurice Temple Smith. (Orig. 1938)

Walker, B. and Salt, D. (2006) *Resilience Thinking: Sustaining ecosystems and people in a changing world*. Washington: Island Press.

Williams, C.C. (2007) *Rethinking the Future of Work*, London: Palgrave.

Name Index

Subject Index

References to Notes are followed by the letter 'n'

oikos, 87

open inquiry, 74–5

opposites, unity of *see* unity of opposites

organic social order metaphor, 36

Organization of American States, 12n

organizational forms, 35

paradigm shift, planning, 3–4, 12n, 46n, 134–5

Paris, Saint-Simonian *politechniciens* in, 6

parochialism, 69

participatory planning/budgeting, 70, 136, 220

person-centered relationships, 23, 24

Peru, 98, 122

philosophy: anthropology, philosophical, 212–13, 229; humanistic, 211–15; philosophical task, planning theory, 210, 229

Philosophy of Right (Hegel), 113

phronesis theories (Flyvbjerg), 225n

physical sciences, and objective knowledge, 34

physical states/historical events, world of (W I) (Popper), 30, 32, 35, 36, 37, 39, 43n, 49

place, politics of, 78

Planners Network Newsletter, 212

planning, defined, 1–2, 60, 133–4

Planning Bureau, Ministry of Construction (China), 172

planning cultures *see* cultures, planning

Planning in the Public Domain (Friedmann), 6, 60, 62–81, 129, 134, 138, 139, 148, 208, 219

planning practices, adapting to constraints, 215–22

planning schools, 212, 217

planning theory, 129–43; Euro-American collaboration, 135–6, 142; four modes, 129, 142; tasks, 210–11; theories in planning vs. theories of planning, 207–8; uses, 9, 207–30; as work of translation, 222–4

Planning Theory and Practice (UK journal), 166, 210

Planning Theory Revisited (Friedmann), 131–41

plant closures, 62, 63

pockets of poverty, 92, 93

Poland, Solidarity movement, 113–14

polis, 236

political claims, 94–5, 104n

political culture, 196

political justice, 119

political strategy (PS), 40, 41

Politics and Vision (Wolin), 213

populism, new, 83n

Porto Alegre, participatory planning, 220

positive-sum game, 68

posits, 32, 34, 43n, 45n

postindustrial planning, 218

poverty, 7, 12n, 87–108, 176, 179, 179–80; absolute and relative, 91, 92, 96; anti-poverty measures, 98–9, 116, 117–18; basic needs approach to, 87, 88, 93–9, 104n; bureaucratic, 90–3; dis/empowerment model, 99–103; pockets of, 92, 93

poverty line, 91, 104n, 234

power: coercive/enabling, 141; and planning theory, 137, 140–1; power to/power over, 143; social *see* social power bases, access to

Power of Place, The (Hayden), 122

power of the local, 200n

PPP (public-private partnership), 184–5, 196–7, 218